SOUTH AMERICAN FREE TRADE AREA OR FREE TRADE AREA OF THE AMERICAS?

To my mother,
To the memory of my father, and
To my wife, Olga, who made this book possible

South American Free Trade Area or Free Trade Area of the Americas?

Open regionalism and the future of regional economic integration in South America

MARIO ESTEBAN CARRANZA
Texas A & M University, Kingsville, USA

LONDON AND NEW YORK

First published 2000 by Ashgate Publishing

Reissued 2018 by Routledge
2 Park Square, Milton Park, Abingdon, Oxon OX14 4RN
711 Third Avenue, New York, NY 10017, USA

Routledge is an imprint of the Taylor & Francis Group, an informa business

Copyright © Mario Esteban Carranza 2000

All rights reserved. No part of this book may be reprinted or reproduced or utilised in any form or by any electronic, mechanical, or other means, now known or hereafter invented, including photocopying and recording, or in any information storage or retrieval system, without permission in writing from the publishers.

Notice:
Product or corporate names may be trademarks or registered trademarks, and are used only for identification and explanation without intent to infringe.

Publisher's Note
The publisher has gone to great lengths to ensure the quality of this reprint but points out that some imperfections in the original copies may be apparent.

Disclaimer
The publisher has made every effort to trace copyright holders and welcomes correspondence from those they have been unable to contact.

A Library of Congress record exists under LC control number: 00036349

ISBN 13: 978-1-138-72547-8 (hbk)
ISBN 13: 978-1-138-72545-4 (pbk)
ISBN 13: 978-1-315-19187-4 (ebk)

Table 5.2, p. 169, is reprinted by permission of Westview Press, a member of Perseus Books, LLC. Copyright © 1996 by Westview Press, Inc.

Contents

List of Figures vi
List of Tables vii
Preface and Acknowledgements viii
List of Acronyms and Abbreviations xii
About the Author xiv

1. Regional Integration Theory, Globalization, and Open Regionalism in South America — 1

2. From Old Style Integration to the New Regionalism in the 1990s: A Future Unlike the Past? — 41

3. Mercosur: Building Block or Stumbling Block towards a Free Trade Area of the Americas? — 73

4. Between Two Summits: From a NAFTA-Centred FTAA to SAFTA — 105

5. United States-South American Relations After the Miami Summit: Hegemony by Default or Lack of Hegemony? — 139

6. Beyond Open Regionalism: Mercosur, SAFTA, and the Future of Regional Integration in South America — 187

Bibliography 213

List of Figures

3.1	Two Views of the New Regionalism	74
4.1	Mercosur: Imports and Exports by Region	115
6.1	Globalization and South American Strategic Regionalism	190
6.2	Intra-Mercosur Trade Growth, 1990-1996	203

List of Tables

2.1	Intra-regional Exports of LAFTA/LAIA Countries	52
3.1	Mercosur and Latin America: Basic Data	80
3.2	Mercosur: Exceptions to the Common Trade Policy	86
3.3	Mercosur: Intra-zonal Exports in US$ Million	89
3.4	Estimates of Trade Diversion in Mercosur	91
5.1	Perspectives on the End of the Cold War and US Hegemony in Latin America	156
5.2	Gross Domestic Product and Population Size in Latin America and the United States, 1950-1995	169
6.1	US-South American Relations After the Santiago Summit: Three Alternative Scenarios	192

Preface and Acknowledgements

In the Summer of 1997 I taught a course on Latin American Foreign Policies at *Universidad de las Americas* (UDLA) in Puebla, Mexico, as part of our faculty exchange program. It was a very valuable experience, which gave me the opportunity to teach in Spanish (for the first time in 23 years!) while learning a lot about the North American Free Trade Agreement (NAFTA) and how it is perceived by the Mexican academic community. My Mexican students challenged my own image of hemispheric regionalism and for the first time, the idea of writing a book on the subject crossed my mind.

In March 1998 I was a discussant at the panel on *Regionalism II: Africa, Latin America and South Asia*, during the annual meeting of the International Studies Association (ISA) in Minneapolis, Minnesota. Back in Kingsville I was contacted by Kirstin Howgate, from Ashgate, who had attended the panel and expressed an interest in my research on South American regionalism. I had presented the paper "SAFTA or FTAA? 'Open Regionalism' and the Future of Regional Economic Integration in South America" at the same conference and Ashgate was willing to consider a book project on the same subject. I had done research on the new regionalism for some time (see Carranza, 1993a, 1993b, 1993c and 1995) and the book project was an excellent opportunity to "put all the pieces together" while pursuing my research interest in the Southern Cone Common Market (Mercosur).

The book is organised in six chapters. Chapter 1 examines the relationship between globalization and regionalism and challenges the idea that the new regionalism is just an aspect of globalization. The chapter questions the widespread belief that there is no alternative to globalization and examines the inability of the different strands of international relations theory to come to grips with the new regionalism. Chapter 2 overviews the history of Latin American integration and argues that the Latin American countries embraced the neoliberal model of economic development not because of the "failures" of import-substitution industrialisation, but because they were compelled by the US and the International Monetary Fund to adopt economic adjustment programs to obtain new loans and a rescheduling of their debts during the "lost decade" of the 1980s. Chapter 3 examines Mercosur's achievements in the 1990s and the alternative directions Mercosur might take, focusing on the prospects for Mercosur to become an autonomous trading bloc, or the hub of a potential SAFTA. The chapter addresses the "trade creation" versus "trade diversion" debate, and Mercosur's foreign relations with other Latin American countries, NAFTA, and the European Union.

Chapter 4 examines the Hemispheric diplomacy after the Summits of the Americas in Miami (December 1994) and Santiago (April 1998) focusing on the strengthening of the South American position in the FTAA negotiations and the Brazilian proposal for a South American Free Trade Area (SAFTA). Chapter 5 places the prior discussion within the broader framework of US-Latin American relations, asking the question: what kind of hegemony, if any, is the US still exercising over South America? The concluding chapter revisits the issue of globalization and the new regionalism and considers three alternative scenarios of US-South American relations at the beginning of the millennium.

It is always difficult to write on evolving current events. The politics of free trade (both globally and regionally) presents an ever-changing picture. For example, in the Summer of 1999 the conventional wisdom was that the future of regional trading blocs would be significantly determined by the World Trade Organization's proposed Millennium Round of global trade negotiations, due to start in November 1999. Yet the WTO's conference in Seattle collapsed in bitterness and discord. The trade ministers were unable to agree on a common agenda to rewrite the rules of world trade for a new millennium, amid street demonstrations organised by a variety of NGOs challenging the WTO's "supranationality" and its right to modify the domestic legislation of members states in the name of "free trade."

In this book I have attempted to go beyond current events, by looking at the structural trends behind the evolution of the new regionalism in South America and the Western Hemisphere. Although the Brazilian proposal for SAFTA has been temporarily shelved, my argument is that SAFTA *could become* an alternative to the Free Trade Area of the Americas (FTAA) considering the structural obstacles to achieve the latter and the structural *achievements* of Mercosur: establishment of a customs union on schedule, resolution of collective action problems between Argentina and Brazil; unified diplomacy during the FTAA negotiations (from Miami to Santiago); ability to attract new associate members (Chile and Bolivia) and the Mercosur-Andean Community negotiations to establish a free trade area that could be the "hub" for a SAFTA. Structural trends open up the possibility for the South American countries to define an independent role in the global economy, taking their destiny "in their own hands." Whether or not they do it will depend on a number of factors, including domestic politics (especially in Argentina and Brazil) and whether the neoliberal model can survive the ups and down of the global economy. A world slump at the beginning of the millennium would create strong incentives for Mercosur and its South American neighbours to cling together. A central argument of this book is that in a world of competing trading blocs South America is not necessarily condemned to greater integration with the US and could create its own autonomous trading bloc to maximise the subcontinent's relative gains and security vis-à-vis other trading blocs, including NAFTA.

This book has not been written "against" the US, even though it criticises the traditional US policy of "benign neglect" toward Latin America. There is an enormous potential for co-operation between the US and Latin America based on perceptions of convergent interests if the US can definitely abandon the "hegemonic presumption" in its relations with its Latin American neighbours and the image of Latin American elites as essentially "dependent."

The question of economic co-operation in the Western Hemisphere is inextricably linked with the issue of US hegemony in Latin America. Whether US hegemony in the global economy is declining is a controversial issue in the international relations literature. Chapter 5 presents an overview of the problem and a critique of some theoretical interpretations that portray economic integration in the Americas as reflecting mainly a renewal of US hegemonic influence—either by "recharge" or "default." The reasoning in chapter 5 is essential to my argument that Mercosur (and eventually SAFTA) may strengthen the position of the South American countries in their trade negotiations with the US and that SAFTA *is* a meaningful alternative to the "deep integration" agenda embedded in the US conception of the FTAA.

A critic might argue that the spread of the Asian financial crisis to South America in the Fall of 1998 (culminating in the Brazilian devaluation of the *real* in January 1999) shows that the SAFTA proposal has been overtaken by recent developments. Yet Brazil has begun to recover from its economic crisis; Mercosur has managed to survive recent Argentine-Brazilian trade disputes, and the neoliberal model of globalization and free trade has been challenged by NGOs in the streets of Seattle during the failed WTO's trade talks in December 1999. The structural basis for a greater South American autonomy vis-à-vis the US is already there: Mercosur. Moreover, the obstacles for a successful conclusion of the FTAA negotiations (overviewed in chapters 4 and 6) make the SAFTA option attractive.

This book was made possible by a number of people. First of all, I owe special thanks to my wife, Olga, who spent endless hours preparing the camera-ready copy and sacrificed many weekends to make this book possible.

My colleagues at the Political Science Department provided a collegial atmosphere and moral support through the different stages of this project. Dr. Mary Mattingly, a member of the department, and Dean of the College of Arts and Sciences at Texas A & M University Kingsville, supported this project from the very beginning and approved two travel grants from the Dean's Sharing Fund for library research at the Benson Latin American Collection, University of Texas at Austin.

Chapter 3 is a revised and updated version of a paper presented at the 40th Annual Meeting of the International Studies Association, Washington, DC, 16-21 February 1999. I am indebted to Clarence Zuvekas, Jr. (consulting economist, Annandale, Virginia) for thoughtful written comments. I also benefited from comments by Guy Poitras (Trinity University), chair of the panel "Free Trade and Regionalism in the Americas," and from comments from the audience. I am grateful to Claudia Sánchez-Bajo (who was working on her dissertation on Mercosur while I was working on my book) for interesting suggestions sent by e-mail from the Netherlands.

The staff at the inter-library loan office, Jernigan Library, Texas A & M University-Kingsville did a superb job at making available research materials in a timely fashion. I am particularly indebted to Maria Schueneman, Aggie Gonzales, Michelle Mendietta, and Robert Saenz.

I am especially grateful to Iris Carballido, the librarian at INTAL's *Centro de Documentación* in Buenos Aires for help during my visit in July 1998 and for bringing to my attention the most recent materials on Mercosur, some of them in Spanish and Portuguese.

Dr. George Philip (London School of Economics), Director of Ashgate's *Political Economy of Latin America* series provided extremely useful comments on my original book proposal. At Ashgate, I am indebted to Kirstin Howgate, Anne Keirby, and Jacqui Cornish for superb editorial assistance.

Finally, I owe special thanks to my Mexican students at *Universidad de las Americas*, Puebla, for unforgettable class discussions in the Summer of 1997 and for stimulating and challenging my thinking on Mexico and US-Latin American relations.

Mario E. Carranza
Kingsville, Texas, December 1999

List of Acronyms and Abbreviations

AC	Andean Community
ACS	Association of Caribbean States
ALADI/LAIA	Latin American Integration Association
APEC	Asian Pacific Economic Co-operation Forum
ASEAN	Association of Southeast Asian Nations
CACM	Central American Common Market
CARICOM	Caribbean Community and Common Market
CET	Common External Tariff
CUSFTA	Canada-US Free Trade Agreement
EAI	Enterprise for the Americas Initiative
EC	European Community
ECLAC	United Nations Economic Commission for Latin America and the Caribbean
EU	European Union
FREPASO	Frente País Solidario
FTAA	Free Trade Area of the Americas
FTAs	Free Trade Areas
GATT	General Agreement on Tariffs and Trade
GDP	Gross Domestic Product
IDB	Inter-American Development Bank
IMF	International Monetary Fund
INTAL	Instituto para la Integración de América Latina y el Caribe
IPE	International Political Economy
ISI	Import-substitution industrialisation
LAFTA	Latin American Free Trade Association
LDCs	Less Developed Countries
Mercosur	Mercado Común del Sur (Southern Cone Common Market)
MFN	Most Favoured Nation clause
NAFTA	North American Free Trade Agreement
NATO	North Atlantic Treaty Organisation

NGOs	Non-governmental Organizations
OAS	Organization of American States
OECD	Organization of Economic Co-operation and Development
PD	Prisoner's Dilemma game
PEIC/PICAB	Program for Economic Integration and Cooperation between Argentina and Brazil (1986)
SADC	Southern African Development Community
SAFTA	South American Free Trade Area
SELA	Latin American Economic System
SOA	Summit of the Americas process
TICD	Treaty for Integration, Co-operation, and Development between Argentina and Brazil (1988)
TNC	Trade Negotiations Committee during the FTAA negotiations
UN	United Nations
USIA	US Information Agency
USTR	US Trade Representative
WHFTA	Western Hemisphere Free Trade Area
WTO	World Trade Organization

About the Author

Dr. Mario E. Carranza is an Associate Professor of Political Science at Texas A & M University, Kingsville. He was born in Argentina and has lived in the United States since 1982. He earned a Ph.D. in Political Science from the University of Chicago in 1987 and is a specialist on Mercosur and regional integration in the Western Hemisphere. He has published articles in *Latin American Perspectives*, *Asian Survey*, *The Journal of Peace Research*, *International Politics*, and *The Nonproliferation Review*, as well as a book (in Spanish) on the armed forces in Latin America. He has been Visiting Professor at Universidad de las Américas, Puebla, Mexico; a MacArthur postdoctoral fellow at the University of Wisconsin-Madison; and Visiting Scholar at the International Peace Research Institute (PRIO), Oslo, Norway and at the Institute of Development Studies (IDS), University of Sussex, United Kingdom.

1 Regional Integration Theory, Globalization, and Open Regionalism in South America

Introduction

There are a number of case studies of subregional integration in South America, such as Mercosur (Common Market of the Southern Cone) and the Andean Community (AC) and of Western Hemisphere economic integration. Yet there is a dearth of critical analyses of the Latin American "new regionalism." Most of the literature focuses on the economic, rather than political and ideological dimensions of subregional integration. There is also a dearth of critical analyses of the neoliberal model underpinning the new regional integration efforts in South America, which are often depicted as part of the "inevitable" process of globalization of production, finance and markets. The purpose of this book is to challenge the dominant approach to the new regionalism, i.e., the idea that globalization has an inexorable logic to which "there is no alternative," and that the new regionalism is merely an aspect of globalization.

The book will unpack the contradictions of "open regionalism" as defined by mainstream economic theory and the rhetoric of neoliberal policy-makers and their "think tanks" who rationalise "free trade" and the "Washington Consensus" as the only alternative for the South America countries. Even if a South American Free Trade Area (SAFTA) does not come into existence in the immediate future, it is important to analyse the theoretical and policy implications of the SAFTA proposal, made by the Brazilian government in 1993. Mainstream theories of US/South American relations take for granted what Abraham Lowenthal two decades ago called the "hegemonic presumption."[1] I will argue that US hegemony in South America is declining, even if for the moment Mercosur and its associates do not directly challenge American leadership. The apparently irresistible tide of globalization seems to be contradicted by the emergence of regionalist projects. The central research question is whether these projects are a temporary phenomenon and will be overtaken by the pressures towards globalization or whether they will become an alternative to globalization. Is Mercosur an instrument of internationalisation and globalization? Alternatively, is it a last defensive ditch against globalization? Can Mercosur liberate itself from the "pull" of the NAFTA core? Is it condemned to extinction once an NAFTA-centred Free Trade Area of the Americas is formed? Will it survive as an autonomous trading and politico-military bloc?

The conventional wisdom is that the move toward regionalism in the post-Cold War era is a step (a "building block") towards globalization rather than an alternative to it. The purpose of this book is to challenge the conventional wisdom by examining Mercosur as a unique experience of subregional economic integration and the SAFTA project as a potential alternative to globalization as the inevitable final destination of contemporary regional integration efforts.

The Brazilian economic and financial crisis of January 1999 (following the Russian crisis of August 1998 and the Asian crisis that began in the summer of 1997) has caused considerable strains in Argentine-Brazilian relations thus raising the issue of Mercosur's survival in the complex dynamics between globalization and regionalization. Moreover, the Brazilian crisis gives the US more leverage in the negotiations to create a Free Trade Area of the Americas (FTAA) and might speed up their conclusion on schedule, by 2005. Yet, if President Clinton fails to obtain fast-track authority and Mercosur survives its present crisis it may be difficult for the next US administration to "lock in" the concessions made by the South American countries in the first stage of the negotiations, which ended on 31 October 1999.

The New Regionalism and International Relations Theory

Contemporary debates in international relations theory have neglected the new regionalism. For example, none of the available theories satisfactorily explains North/South co-operation in the Americas in the 1990s.[2] Although constructivism has recognised the importance of regions as units of analysis in the post-Cold War Era, a new paradigm to explain the new regionalism has not yet emerged. Neither the old theories of regionalism, such as functionalism and neo-functionalism, nor post-Cold War theories such as constructivism can satisfactorily explain the complexities of NAFTA or Mercosur, or predict whether they will "deepen," "widen" or just "disappear," absorbed by mega-trading blocs or the pull of globalization. In short, the new regionalism remains largely under-theorised and its relationship with globalization remains unclear, even if as yet it has not proved incompatible with globalization. Moreover, it is not clear whether and to what extent "territorially bounded" geo-economic regionalism will eventually prevail over "unbundled territoriality" and "open" regionalism and the real meaning of the latter in the post-Cold War era.[3]

During the Cold War, realist writers argued that common threat perceptions were indispensable for the emergence of regional economic integration efforts such as the European Community (EC) or the Association of Southeast Asian Nations (ASEAN).[4] From this perspective, these organisations were created for political and military-security reasons, rather than for economic considerations. For example, many scholars share Karl Kaiser's statement that "the three European Communities owe a great deal to direct American help at their inception and to the existence of the Soviet threat."[5]

Yet the end of the Cold War and the emergence of new (unforeseen) forms of regional and supra-regional economic integration challenge the realist interpretation of regionalism. Security frameworks have changed and the primacy of economics redefines military issues and the meaning of "threat." With global economic interdependence, economic issues are as "external" as security issues. The new international environment created by the end of the Cold War is redefining the meaning of "region" and "regionalism." Although the new strategic environment is still characterised by uncertainty, fluidity, and experimentation, there is a certain tendency toward co-operation among the great powers, which did not exist during the Cold War era of rigid ("bipolar") alliance systems.

There is general agreement on the trend toward multipolarity (because of a decisive shift in the balance of economic power) in the emerging post-Cold War international system. There is no agreement, however, on the significance and direction of the new regionalism, although the process of regionalization of world politics is being increasingly recognised. The main disagreement has to do with the distinction between "territorially bounded" vs. "open" or "unbundled" regionalism.

Optimists see the new regionalism as basically a new phenomenon, good for world order, and not representing a challenge to the globalizing tendencies of the world economy.[6] From this perspective, the old regionalism epitomised by the European Economic Community and LAFTA (Latin American Free Trade Area) exhausted itself in the 1960s and 1970s. Even one of the intellectual fathers of regional integration theory, Ernst Haas, proclaimed its "obsolescence" in 1975.[7]

On the other hand, pessimists argue that there are both internal and external limits to the new regionalism. Internal limits, as shown by domestic political opposition to opening up the market to new privileged trading partners. For example: domestic opposition to NAFTA in the US, opposition to the widening of the European Union in some EU countries, or domestic political opposition in Argentina to "Brazil-dependency" on the wake of the Brazilian economic crisis of January 1999. External limits: pessimists argue that in the long run the global economy will dominate, and tend to replace, the international economy, on which regional trading blocs are based.[8] From this perspective, regional trading blocs will become increasingly irrelevant, as inter-state agreements and practices become less important than global markets and global production.

A third approach is that globalization and regionalization are not incompatible: the latter may lead to the former, or become absorbed by it, if subregional economic integration is outward looking and supplements, rather than contradicts, a globally oriented system. "Openness" is generally presented as an essential characteristic of the new regionalism. Yet by the mid-1990s it was not clear whether the new regionalism would actually become a "building block" toward globalization. It all depended on whether the industrialised democracies would cooperate to sustain an open, market-oriented world trade and financial system, and whether the post-Cold War "emergent" market economies could be integrated into the global economy without suffering major crises or dislocations. Even before the Asian crisis of 1997 some critics wondered whether globalization had gone "too far."[9]

The absence of a theoretical framework to analyse the new regionalism has led some post-modern scholars to fall into a form of eclecticism that does not solve the problem. For example, Ruggie claims that each of three approaches to the European Union (neorealism, "microeconomic institutionalism" and neofunctionalism) "contains a partial truth" if one looks at post-Cold War regionalizing tendencies from the (presumably) vantage point of post-modern "unbundled territoriality."[10] While such an attempt to explain the emergence of "post-modern" (neither national nor supranational) international political forms is commendable, it would have to be tested across regions to become a plausible "theory" of the new regionalism. For even if the globalizing tendencies in the world economy are indisputable, the state (as realists always claim) is still alive and well. The real issues are the new forms of articulation of nation states with an increasingly internationalised world economy and a post-Cold War international security environment in which great power conflicts are no longer solved through military force. Arguably, despite the persistence of purely regional or subregional conflicts (such as the ethnic conflicts in the former Yugoslavia) the importance of military power has diminished on the global stage. As Edward Luttwak points out, in such a situation, states are compelled "by the bureaucratic urges of role preservation and role enhancement, to acquire a 'geo-economic' substitute for their decaying geopolitical role."[11] As Poulantzas noted some time ago, "the current internationalisation of capital neither suppresses nor by-passes the nation states."[12] This is still true, as recognised by leading analysts of the European Union.[13] Poulantzas, however, did not envisage the new forms of "open" supra-regionalism adopted by the internationalisation of capital in the 1990s, of which APEC (Asia Pacific Economic Co-operation) and ongoing negotiations to establish a Free Trade Area of the Americas (FTAA) are the more recent manifestations.

The uncertainties surrounding the post-cold war geo-strategic and economic environment make predictions hazardous. It will take many years, probably decades, until a full-fledged new international system emerges. It is not clear at all whether the rearticulation of international relations will result in Ruggie's "unbundled territoriality" (overlapping layers of "regional" economic and political "spaces") in a highly fragmented international system, or in relatively closed regional (or supra-regional) trading blocs. In the aftermath of the 1991 Gulf War, it was optimistically argued that a "New World Order" based on collective security, and a strengthening of the United Nations would arrive soon. The inability of the United Nations and the European Union to solve the Bosnian tragedy (1992-1995) and the Kosovo question, which resulted in NATO's declaration of all-out war on Yugoslavia in March 1999, have shattered that excessive optimism.

Is the regional integration theory of the 1950s and 1960s (Haas, 1968; Haas and Schmitter, 1966; Schmitter, 1970; Lindberg, 1963; Lindberg and Scheingold, 1970) useful to explain the new regionalism and predict its possible evolution? The new regionalism is an autonomous response to the post-Cold War/Gulf War international environment. Unlike the old regionalism it is (at least in its inception) independent from great power influence. And it has a strong economic component. Therefore, the old concepts of regional integration, particularly the distinction between free trade areas, customs unions, and common markets, are still useful to analyse the new regionalism. On the other hand, the globalization of production, finance, and markets was only incipient in the 1950s and 1960s. The articulation of the economic and the political under the new regionalism is different from the one under the old regionalism. What pessimists see as the limits of regionalism, are instead, a source of strength. In a "globalized" economy, "regional blocs would cut across the emergence of the complex cross-regional production arrangements that have developed within and between companies, and also across the rapidly expanding volume of foreign trade based on transnational production."[14] That helps to explain the increasing relevance of supra-regional blocs, such as APEC and the "open" nature of geo-economics after the Cold War.

Globalization and Regionalization

Globalization is not a "countervailing trend" vis-à-vis regionalization. Both can be seen as part of the same process; globalization can take place at the same time as regionalization. Yet both globalization and regionalization can only be understood in dialectical terms.[15] As Manfred Bienefeld points out, "globalization is no destination" and it will sooner or later generate a political and social backlash of which the reactions to the Asian economic crisis of 1997 and the threat of a world-wide economic slump in 1998 are just the first manifestations.[16] From this perspective, globalization is simply another phase of exploitative capitalism and will necessarily provoke counter-globalist political movements and reactions. Therefore it is misleading to attempt to overcome the "building blocks/stumbling blocks" dilemma (see chapter 3) by looking at the new regionalism as "just an aspect" of globalization.[17] Although for the moment the new regionalism seems to be "open" and fully accepting the globalization project, the proliferation of subregional blocks such as Mercosur in South America cannot be explained as part of the "inexorable logic" of globalization. The real issue is whether regional and subregional groupings such as Mercosur will survive globalizing trends toward wider regionalism, such as the Free Trade Area of the Americas. For the purposes of this book, the central research question is whether regionalism is simply a temporary product of the decline of US hegemony in the 1970s and 1980s. Will regionalism be overtaken by the pressures toward globalization, or, as Mittelman and others argue, is it an essential part of globalization? In the following chapters, a third possibility will be considered: regionalism as an *alternative* to globalization.

The post-Cold War international environment challenges the simplicity of old theories of "regionalization" of world politics. Three large regional trading blocs appear to be emerging: Asia-Pacific, the European Union (EU) and North America. Several scholars argue that they will become semi-closed trading blocs.[18] Other argue that the idea that the world is moving inexorably into regionalization and exclusive trading blocs is a myth, and that globalization will prevail over regionalization.[19] Yet scholars generally agree that the international system is becoming increasingly regional in structure, although the notion of "region" has undergone a fundamental transformation with the end of the Cold War and the globalization of the international capitalist economy. For example, the concept of "regional economies" or the emergence of "region states" is seen as part of the broader process of globalization, hence the concept of "open regionalism" defined as involving regional economic integration without discrimination against economies outside the region.[20]

The concept of "region" is highly ambiguous. In the early 1970s William Thompson listed at least 21 attributes often used to identify regional subsystems. Among them: geographic proximity, internal recognition, external recognition, subordination to a dominant system, some degree of shared ethnic, linguistic, cultural, social and historical bonds, and "some evidence of integration or a professed policy of achieving further economic, political, and social integration."[21] Arguably, geographical proximity and contiguity are essential elements of a definition of "region." Otherwise, as Oran Young points out, "any entities related to each other with respect to one or more attributes will meet the requirements for consideration as a region. This leads to a situation in which the term "region" is apt to become so inclusive that it is useless."[22]

After the Cold War, the "subordination to a dominant system" attribute has significantly changed. The bipolar distribution of power is gone; although the distinction between great powers and smaller powers is still valid, as is the question of who benefits from certain definitional delimitation of a region, as seen in current debates on the "widening" of the European Union. Yet, because of the excessive focus on the relationship between the dominant bipolar system and regions as subordinated systems, the role of middle powers (Brazil, India, South Africa) in post-Cold War regional integration efforts remains under-theorised.[23] In the case of South America, the neglect of middle powers has led to an excessive emphasis on South American dependence on the United States.[24] Thus, the role of Brazil as the regional hegemon around which regional co-operation can materialise and grow is often disregarded.

Manfred Mols makes a useful threefold distinction between different forms of regional integration. Type I forms of integration "contribute in their own right to the constitution of the international system" and have the capability to act as a counterweight vis-à-vis the big powers. The EC of the treaty of Rome (1957) is the typical example.[25]

Type II schemes of regional integration operate "as components within a pre-existent international division of labor and power." This form of defensive, or "benign" regionalism,[26] is aimed at avoiding "complete submission to hegemonic or superpower interests, to achieve a better representation of its own interests vis-à-vis international powers, and to strengthen capacities for international negotiation."[27] ASEAN's conception of national and regional resilience fits into this category, as well as the rationale for the creation of Mercosur in March 1991.

Type III regionalism does not easily fit into the traditional regional subsystem labels summarised by Thompson. This form of "soft," "informal," and outward-oriented regionalism, without integration as one of its key components, is epitomised by the beginnings of Asia-Pacific Economic Co-operation (APEC) and current attempts to create a free trade area in the Americas. According to Mols, type III regionalism deals with "visions and necessities of structuring and restructuring the international system, without putting much emphasis on formal and judicial constructions of regional entities."[28]

Types I and II are useful starting points to explain the new regionalism and envision alternative scenarios for its future.

The concept of "strategic regionalism" is closely related to the new trade theory of "strategic trade" and Edward Luttwak's "logic of geo-economics."[29] As Van R. Whiting points out, post-Cold War regionalization can be seen "as a partial product of interregional conflict and co-operation in which the concern with relative gains shifts from the national to the regional level."[30] As Luttwak notes, "while the methods of [traditional] mercantilism could always be dominated by the methods of war, in the new 'geo-economic' era not only the causes but also the instruments of conflict must be economic."[31] If "mercantilist regionalism" were to prevail over "benign regionalism" in the twenty-first century, "closed" regional trading blocs would become the instruments of geo-economic struggles among the major powers (the US, Japan, France, Germany) and eventually middle powers such as Argentina, Brazil, India, Indonesia or South Africa, as they proceed to compete to enhance their economic security in a world of globalized production, finance and markets.[32]

A key issue is whether globalization is an autonomous force, driven by free-market capitalism and the revolution in communications and computer technologies, or whether it is politically driven and reflects a particular distribution of power in the international system (unipolarity) that will not last forever. Arguably, sooner or later new great powers will rise challenging American unipolarity.[33]

Will globalization win out?[34] Whether globalization is irresistible and unstoppable has important implications for the future of the new regionalism. Will the new regionalism be "dissolved" by globalization? If not, what forms will it take? Is South America condemned to be subordinated to the United States in a world of "mega" trading blocs, or will it become a trading bloc on its own right, led by Brazil? Although a South American Free Trade Area (SAFTA) has not yet come into existence, exploring the SAFTA concept will help us to understand the new regionalism as a new phenomenon that goes beyond the false dilemma between globalization and regionalization.

The post-Cold War debate in international relations theory has been dominated by two schools of thought:

(1) *Neorealism*, with its basic assumptions about anarchy, states-as-actors, the balance of power, and the resort to war as the inevitable outcome of a "self-help" system. As Ian Clark notes, neorealism reinforces the notion of a "Great Divide" between international relations and domestic politics; thus amounting to "a formidable reassertion of the autonomy of the international as a domain with its own political structure."[35]

(2) At the other extreme, there is a burgeoning literature in the field of International Political Economy which tends to dissolve the international level of analysis into the domestic level; i.e., into national "coalitions" whose "grand strategy" would explain the dynamics of "regional orders."[36]

Both schools of thought neglect regions and the regional level of analysis as independent explanatory variables: neorealism, by exclusively focusing on state actors; coalitions theory by reducing regional politics to domestic politics and ignoring or neglecting the emergence of regional blocs such as Mercosur or NAFTA as independent actors in the global arena.

The purpose of this book is to correct the inadequacies of current international relations theory by looking at the new regionalism as a new (post-Cold War) phenomenon with a logic of its own, which is irreducible to domestic politics or states-as-actors; and by looking at regions as independent units of analysis and explanation. Whether individual states will behave geo-economically and whether the trend toward mercantilist regionalism will prevail are open questions. Clearly traditional military instruments and strategies are not suitable for dealing with post-Cold War economic security issues such as the challenges of industrial competitiveness in high-technology industries (e.g., semiconductors and electronics). As Luttwak graphically argues,

> Geo-economics is emerging in a world where there is no superior modality. Import-restricted supercomputers cannot be forcibly delivered by airborne assault

to banks or universities in need of them, nor can the sinking of export car ferries on the high seas assist competition in the world automobile market.[37]

The degree of geo-economic activism of individual nation-states will depend on their place in the world capitalist economy, i.e., on whether their economic security is affected by the "changing game" in the international political economy; and on the outcome of domestic political debates on trade and industrial policy in each country. In spite of the inevitability claims of globalization fundamentalists, "policy convergence" is not a foregone conclusion; international and domestic factors will determine whether and to what extent it will take place. Moreover, policy convergence at the regional level (e.g., a monetary union among the Mercosur countries) may not necessarily meet the requirements of international capital and/or external actors, such as the United States.

Because globalization generates its own contradictions, it is necessary to dispel the myth of globalization.[38] As Manfred Bienefeld and others have shown, there are serious reasons to believe that a "global future" is not inevitable and that national economies will reconstitute themselves, if for no other reason because unrelenting globalization may cause international instabilities and economic crises (even a global slump) that would endanger the success and prosperity of those currently enjoying the benefits of globalization.[39] On the other hand, the triumphalist view of globalization de-legitimises resistance and contending options, (such as autonomous regionalism) while presenting state elites with an "adjust or perish" dilemma. For example, Thomas Friedman celebrates globalization as the (US) victory of capitalism over communism and identifies protective tariffs or capital controls as "bad things that belong to the (Cold War) past." From this perspective, "the Berlin wall didn't just fall in Berlin. It fell East and West, and North and South, and it hit both countries and companies, and hit them all at roughly the same time." Regionalism is incompatible with this view of globalization, according to which countries will either adjust to the pace and demands of the "Electronic Herd" or fall far behind because of lack of foreign investment.[40]

Although the leading industrial countries have significant incentives to play the strategic trade game through regional trading blocs,[41] the "new regionalism" could be an intermediate step toward "managed multilateralism" while the internationalisation of production, trade and finance continues. There is a tension between the economic imperatives compelling states to behave geo-economically while engaging in territorially bounded regionalism (of which the European Union is the typical example) and post-Cold War pressures toward "open" regionalism. But it is also true that "open" regionalism has been difficult to implement, because as Bhalla and Bhalla point out, "any regional arrangements for trading purposes are bound to give preferences to members as against non-members."[42] In the case of South America, the achievement of genuinely "open" regionalism has proved to be a daunting task. For example, against the tenets of the neoliberal model, Mercosur has been accused of being "trade diverting" instead of "trade creating" (see chapter 3).

The SAFTA Proposal: Negotiating Tool or Strategic Alliance?

There are two possible ways of analysing the Brazilian project for a South American Free Trade Area (SAFTA): (1) as just a means to extract concessions from the United States during the Free Trade Area of the Americas (FTAA) negotiations or (2) as an end in itself. (1) Assumes that globalization is our final destination and that the FTAA will inevitably come into existence, in accordance with the main assumptions of globalization fundamentalism. (2) Looks at Mercosur and SAFTA as strategic alliances that will continue playing a role in world politics even if a Free Trade Area of the Americas comes into existence. From this perspective, regionalization in the Americas does not necessarily lead to inter-American co-operation. Mercosur could become SAFTA, if the South American countries are able to achieve a consensus among themselves on trade issues.

On the other hand, if protectionist tendencies in the United States take hold, in the absence of US leadership in the FTAA negotiations a return to the historical neglect of Latin America could result in a new "ball game" in inter-American relations at the beginning of the millennium. In this scenario, the US may no longer be able to act unilaterally and may have to seriously negotiate with South America, e.g., in the event of a European Union/Mercosur alliance that would strengthen Brazil's and Argentina's bargaining power vis-à-vis the United States.

One should not assume that the signing of NAFTA and the FTAA negotiations mark the beginning of a new era of unrelenting co-operation in US-South American relations. Although Mexico seems to have crossed a point of no return and the Mexican economy is becoming fully integrated to the US economy one should not extrapolate the Mexican experience to the rest of South America. It is premature to assume that hemispheric co-operation will last in the Americas. The fundamentalist view of US-Latin American relations assumes that globalization has gone so far that the South American countries have no alternative but to seek protection from the division of the global capitalist system into competing blocs by agreeing to an FTAA with the historical hegemon in the Western hemisphere: the USA. The FTAA negotiations were formally launched in April 1998 at the Second Summit of the Americas in Santiago, Chile. However, as we will see in chapter 4, the history of the preparatory works for the FTAA negotiations *before* Santiago is full of conflicts. Therefore, instead of focusing on "co-operation in the Americas" (a poorly specified dependent variable) this book will discuss two puzzles: (1) the contradictions of US policy toward South America, which have strengthened Mercosur and weakened NAFTA as the pole of attraction for a future FTAA; and (2) how does one explain the shift from the "extension of NAFTA" and "NAFTA plus" scenarios (1993, 1994) to SAFTA (1997, 1998), "the most ambitious conceivable model for regional integration without the United States"?[43]

The emergence of SAFTA as a possible alternative to the FTAA raises interesting questions for international relations theory. Is the concept of "open regionalism" the best way of characterising regional trading blocs in the post-Cold War era? Are we witnessing the emergence of post-sovereign forms of "unbundled territoriality"?[44] Is a new "post-modern" political form emerging in different parts of the world, different from the traditional nation-state?

The desire to avoid domestic protests against the loss of sovereignty to US influence has played a role, at least in the case of Brazil, in the strengthening of Mercosur and the slowing down of the FTAA negotiations (see chapter 4). Is a geopolitically based defensive regionalism (such as Mercosur/SAFTA) just a fall-back option, a tactical move aimed at consolidating domestic economic reforms and "buying time" until there is enough domestic political support for further liberalisation and integration in the global economy through "open regionalism"? Or does it mark a fundamental turning point in the evolution of post-Cold War regional integration schemes in Latin America, leading to the formation of "type II" defensive regional arrangements,[45] aimed at enlarging collective self-reliance while redefining state sovereignty as "regional sovereignty"? From this perspective the new regionalism is a response to changes in the global economy (the second industrial revolution, especially the communications revolution and the globalization of finance) which undermine national-level responses and press individual states toward regional economic integration, "both for economic efficiency and to ensure the political power necessary to bargain effectively over the rules and institutions that govern the world economy."[46]

Yet the concept of "regional sovereignty" is fuzzy and needs elaboration. A major shortcoming of regional integration theories is the unilinearity assumption, i.e., the idea that the new regionalism will follow the path of European integration. Unilinearity comes under different guises. The old literature on regionalism, focusing on the European Community, conceived the process of regional integration in several stages, eventually leading to political union. For example, Karl Deutsch considered regional integration as a process leading to an amalgamated or a pluralistic security community, depending on the main goals.[47] The functionalist and neo-functionalist models of European integration heavily influenced much of the early literature on regional integration in other parts of the world, including Central and Latin America. The functionalist model claimed that once initial integrative processes had started, they would more or less automatically expand through processes of spill over. As Caporaso and Keeler point out,

> Spill over referred to two different but related processes. The first, sector spill over, involved the expansion of integrative activities from one sector to another, e.g., from coal and steel to agriculture or from customs union to monetary policy. A second type of spill over involved increasing politicisation of sector activity as, for example, when the co-ordination of monetary policies was replaced by a more centralised system of governance.[48]

However, functionalism underestimated the role of politics in regional integration and could not foresee the resilience of state sovereignty, epitomised by Charles De Gaulle's resistance to European integration in the mid-1960s. The period from the early 1970s to the early 1980s proved to be the "Dark Ages" for the European Community; economic co-operation did not lead to "political federation by instalments," as envisaged by functionalist theory.

Neofunctionalism was an attempt to overcome the technological determinism of functionalist theory. Spill over was not a foregone conclusion; politics was involved in regional integration, which was not a one-way street and could suffer reversals. Ernest Haas had thus to recognise that regional integration and disintegration are two rival social processes simultaneously at work. Governments would not necessarily adjust to habits of co-operation developed by technocratic and scientific elites. Even if there were an ever-increasing amount of economic and social co-operation it would not necessarily "spill over" into the political arena.

Regional Integration Theories, European Integration, and South American Regionalism

The major shortcoming of regional integration theories was their neglect of the impact of international factors on regional integration, and the idea that regional integration had a "beginning" (intergovernmentalism) and an "end" (supranationality) in which political actors would shift "their loyalties, expectations and political activities toward a new centre, whose institutions [would] possess or demand jurisdiction over the pre-existing national states."[49] They did not envisage political co-operation and a growing sense of regional togetherness (such as that cultivated by the Association of Southeast Asian Nations, ASEAN, over the last quarter century) without economic co-operation also along the continuum "free trade area-customs union-common market." ASEAN's failure to make progress along these lines during the Cold War (it was then often portrayed as being "long on words and short on performance") is inexplicable using a functionalist framework. The ASEAN success story at *political* co-operation and regional resilience challenges the assumptions of functionalism and neofunctionalism, while the story of the Single European Act (1986) and the Maastricht Treaty (1991) challenges the functionalist "spill over" hypothesis. As Keohane and Hoffmann point out, "The 1992 program was much more strongly affected by events in the world political economy outside of Europe–especially by concern about international competitiveness–than it was driven by the internal logic of spill over."[50]

Recognising the importance of the external environment was one of the significant contributions of neofunctionalism. In the words of a senior executive of Fiat, "The final goal of the European 'dream' is to transform Europe into an integrated economic continent with its specific role, weight and ability on the international scenario vis-à-vis the US and Japan." Second, neofunctionalism contributed to a better understanding of spill over by showing that it had a mixed record across different sectors in the European Community. Arguably, a similar process has been at work in Mercosur (see chapter 3). Third, neofunctionalism showed that social and economic sectors would not automatically deepen regional integration; supranational institutions were critically important to achieve that goal.

After the resurgence of academic interest in European integration there was a lively debate between "supranationalists" and "intergovernmentalists." As globalization came to dominate the political and academic discourse in the 1990s the European Union was still the model of "successful" regional integration conceived as a unilinear process leading to a nebulous "terminal state."[51]

Yet, is regionalism in Europe model or exception?[52] The cultural dependence on Europe of the largest South American countries, Brazil and Argentina, is well known. Brazil has a strong "German connection" and Argentina has a history of looking at Europe as a "cultural model" to follow. Has this pro-European bias been affected by globalization? Is Europe still *the* model of regional integration? In the case of Argentina, the strengthening of ties with the US in the Menem era (1989-1999) and the strong interest in joining NAFTA in the mid-1990s seem to suggest that the United States, rather than Europe, is now the model. On the other hand, Brazil had from the beginning a different perception of South American regionalism, as an *alternative* to the NAFTA-centred hub-and-spoke model promoted by the United States.

Regional integration in Europe was the product of a unique international environment: the emergence of a bipolar international system and the Cold War. The United States promoted Western European integration as an effective strategy to counter the Soviet threat. As William Wallace points out, the EC was successful *Western European* economic integration; it was not Europe as a whole but Western Europe, and "the central reality was that West European integration was rooted in a wider security framework, and constructed in large part around the security dilemmas which faced France, the Low Countries, and a divided Germany."[53]

Contemporary South American economic integration does not have a protective "external" security framework, even if individual countries have external allies, for example, Argentina's recently acquired status as an "extra-area" associate of NATO.

The concept of "subordinate state system" was an important contribution of regional studies during the Cold War. As early as 1958, Leonard Binder argued that "we are confronted not with a single global international system, but with several in a variety of relationships," and that regional patterns of behaviour were relatively independent of the "rules" regulating the dominant bipolar system. However, regional subsystems were only relatively independent of US-USSR relations. Subordinate system theorists claimed that the Soviet-American bipolar system was the dominant international system and that "the relationship of other systems to it [was] that of subordination–in the sense that changes in the major system [would] have a greater effect on a minor system than the reverse."[54]

Yet with the end of the Cold War regional sub-systems are no longer subordinate international systems. Some scholars claim that the post-Cold War era is characterised by the emergence of a variety of new (independent) regional orders, rather than a single world order.[55] In the case of South America the end of the Cold War opened up the opportunity of creating a truly autonomous regional order, but because of the historical legacy of US hegemony over the area, the end of bipolarity could also lead to a US attempt to consolidate its "informal empire" over South America.[56] Which of the two scenarios will come into existence depends on a number of domestic and international factors.[57]

The subordination of the South American regional system to US hegemony in the post-Cold War era is not, as globalization fundamentalists would make us believe, "inevitable." As Jorge Castañeda points out, Latin America could get "the worst of both worlds" from the end of the Cold War: "the prospect of 'Africanization,' condemnation to the margins of world financial and trade flows," *and* "new forms of US intervention in domestic Latin American policies."[58] However, the end of the Cold War created a unique opportunity for Latin America. The South American countries, particularly, could now take charge of their future, defining their foreign policies in their own terms and not as a "dependent variable" of US foreign policy.[59]

Explaining the New Regionalism in Latin America

In the early 1990s, a "new regionalism" emerged in Latin America. Between 1990 and 1992 trade negotiations among Latin American and Caribbean countries produced sixteen new trade agreements related to the creation of free trade areas, customs unions, or common markets. All of these agreements adopted ambitious schedules. Examples: the Southern Cone Common Market (Mercosur) to create a common market among Argentina, Brazil, Uruguay and Paraguay by the end of 1994; the Argentina-Chile agreement to establish a free trade area in 1995; the Venezuelan-Chilean agreement to form a free trade area with full mobility of goods and factors in 1994; the Colombia-Venezuela-Mexico agreement to create a common market in 1995; the free trade agreement between Chile and Mexico; the treaty between Mexico and the Central American Common Market (CACM) to set up a free trade area in 1997. The North American Free Trade Agreement (NAFTA) among the US, Canada and Mexico entered into force on January 1, 1994. As of this writing (August 1999) Western Hemisphere countries have either signed or are negotiating over 50 sub-regional trade agreements.[60]

In Latin America, Mercosur and the Andean Community (Ecuador, Peru,

Bolivia, Colombia, and Venezuela) are the most important subregional agreements, by grouping nine South American countries with a volume of international trade that is expected to approach US$ 250 billion per year by the year 2000. These countries would be the bulk of a potential South American Free Trade Area (SAFTA).

The "new regionalism" in the Americas is generally presented as outward looking, much more ready than the old regionalism to eliminate both tariff and non-tariff barriers to trade and designed to achieve integration with the world economy rather than protection from it. Because of its outward orientation, it has been supported by the Clinton administration as an element of economic and political stability.

The proliferation of integration initiatives since 1989 and the revival of old initiatives (such as the Andean Community) raise the issue of the meaning of the new regionalism in Latin America in the era of globalization. How does one explain the new regionalism? What are the prospects for success of regional integration efforts in the new century? The scholarly debate on this issue is closely related to contemporary debates in international relations theory, which turn around the meaning and impact of two phenomena: the end of the Cold war and "globalization."

1. Systemic Theories

a. Realism and Neorealism

Latin American integration is an important aspect of the foreign policies of individual Latin American countries, which have been historically heavily influenced by their relations with the "colossus of the North." The immediate consequence of the end of the Cold War for Latin America was, in the words of Jorge Castañeda, the "fear of being left out" by the United States.[61] With the end of the Cold War, the US could pay more attention to Eastern Europe and the former Soviet Union than to Latin America, considering the traditional neglect on the part of the US for the countries South of the Rio Grande, with the possible exception of Mexico. "In this context, Latin American countries seem almost obsessed by the fear of 'falling off' the map of the world economy. Regionalism... is viewed as a precondition for securing effective competitiveness, better positions in global markets, and increased negotiating capacity."[62]

From this perspective, the new regionalism was a reaction to the new realities of the post-Cold War era, i.e., a political response to the trend toward regionalization of the global economy. In neorealist terms, the impact of outside pressures was crucial in determining the emergence of a geo-economic regionalism whose contours are still hazy but go beyond trade to include technological modernisation and industrial restructuring. The neorealist concept of relative gains comes into play here although the units of analysis are now regions, not nation-states. From this perspective, the end of the Cold War redefines relative gains concerns. First, because it redefines alliances while regionalizing world politics. Second, because it exacerbates the North/South divide, given the inadequacies of the international trade and monetary regimes for dealing with post-Cold War economic problems. Hence, states may forgo some relative gains in inter-regional relations to enhance their bargaining power at the South/North inter-regional level. If this interpretation is correct, Mercosur was basically aimed at strengthening the bargaining power of Argentina and Brazil vis-à-vis NAFTA. Post-Cold War regionalization can be seen "as a partial product of interregional conflict and co-operation in which the concern with relative gains shifts from the national to the regional level."[63]

The problem with the realist/neorealist interpretation of the new regionalism is that it unjustifiably ignores the impact of economic globalization on the nation-state and the question of the erosion of sovereignty in the post-Cold War era. Relative gains concerns within regional blocs still matter, as shown by the dispute over the automobile industry between Argentina and Brazil in 1995. However, the experience of Mercosur and the recent evolution of ASEAN show that after the Cold War states are more concerned with global trends and their negative impact on their welfare than with the relative gains problem inside regional blocs. This is not to deny the problems mentioned by Manzetti, such as the bickering over Mercosur's common external tariff because of Brazilian objections, or the Argentine-Brazilian mini-"trade war" following the Mexican peso crash of 1994.[64] The point is that Mercosur survived these crises, in spite of relative gains concerns on the part of Argentina, Paraguay, and Uruguay vis-à-vis Brazil. The neorealist explanation is that relative gains problems shifted to the regional level. Yet it would be erroneous to interpret such a shift as a "regionalization of sovereignty." The weakness of supra-national institutions makes the South American case very different from European integration and still Mercosur fits nicely in the neorealist logic of geo-economics: economic regionalism as a defensive strategy in an increasingly competitive post-Cold War neo-mercantilist environment. Also the fact that Mercosur has made progress because of presidential political will, despite real policy divergence between Argentina and Brazil, lends credibility to the idea of "territorially bounded" regionalism in South America to maximise relative gains vis-à-vis regional competitors.[65]

b. Dependency Theory

Dependency theory originated in Latin America in the 1950s and 1960s. The gist of the dependency approach is that Latin America has fulfilled certain definite functions in the world economy or world market, and that Latin American development has been limited or conditioned by the needs of the dominant economies within that world market. The most cited definition of dependence is by Theotonio Dos Santos:

> By dependence we mean a situation in which the economy of certain countries is conditioned by the development and expansion of another economy to which the former is subjected. The relation of interdependence between two or more economies, and between these and world trade, assumes the form of dependence when some countries (the dominant ones) can expand and can be self-sustaining, while other countries (the dependent ones) can do this only as a reflection of that expansion, which can have either a positive or a negative effect on their immediate development.[66]

As a systemic theory, dependency theory can be seen as a critique of neorealism, which provides an oversimplified account of the nature of the international system, without taking into consideration North/South cleavages. Two strands of dependency theory are relevant for the analysis of the new regionalism in Latin America. For the *orthodox version*, the historical development of the capitalist system generates underdevelopment in the periphery. According to Andre Gunder Frank, the "development of underdevelopment" is an essential component of the international capitalist system. Therefore, Latin American capitalism cannot be "improved" within the parameters of capitalism; dependency and development are incompatible. The centre exists at the expense of the periphery and the only way to achieve economic development is to break the dependency link with the centre through a socialist revolution.[67] The strategy of "delinking" or "self-reliance" favoured by this approach was represented by the Chinese and Cuban revolutions in the 1960s and 1970s. Yet with the end of the Cold War the very idea of a socialist revolution has lost clout. Marxism, the underpinning for orthodox dependency analysis is out of fashion and the main examples of non-capitalist development have disappeared. The Soviet Union has collapsed; China and Vietnam are adapting their development strategies to globalization rather than challenging it, while Cuba is no longer seen as the "alternative" path to economic development in Latin America. Short of a socialist revolution, orthodox dependency theory precludes the possibility of autonomous Latin American development, either by individual countries or via regional integration efforts.

The second strand of dependency theory is *unorthodox dependency*, best represented by Cardoso's concept of "associated dependent development." Cardoso challenged the assumption that dependency and development are incompatible, arguing that in the case of Brazil dependent development was possible, even if it entailed a number of serious economic, political, and social costs.[68]

Unorthodox dependency theory leaves room for the "new regionalism" (Mercosur, or even SAFTA) within the framework of US "benign hegemony." According to Helio Jaguaribe, US policy toward Latin America is "internally co-opted by several domestic groups" and "not externally unified, except in moments of crisis or over issues concerning very relevant strategic interests."[69] This leaves room for a "moderately autonomous" foreign policy on the part of the Latin American "middle states" (Brazil, Mexico, Argentina, Chile, Venezuela) and the recent wave of "open regionalism" in Latin America fits comfortably in the "associated dependent" model of development. Like neoliberal institutionalism (see below) unorthodox dependency theory leaves the door open for an FTAA (Free Trade Area of the Americas) agreement between Mercosur (or SAFTA) and NAFTA, led by the US, a "tolerant" hemispheric hegemon.[70] However, while neoliberal institutionalism would optimistically predict a successful conclusion of the FTAA negotiations by 2005; unorthodox dependency theory would be more cautious, considering both the possibility of *success* (because the US would be ready to make "some" concessions and tolerate "some" autonomy for the Latin American countries) and *failure* due to the internal contradictions of US foreign policy-making, including the US president's lack of "fast-track" authority and domestic political opposition to free trade agreements with Latin America in the US Congress.

2. The Domestic Politics/IPE Approach. Coalition Politics and the "Internationalist Revolution"

At the opposite extreme of systemic theories, the domestic politics/IPE coalitional approach emphasises the victory of pro-globalization "internationalist" *domestic* coalitions with an "internationalist" agenda as the main reasons for the emergence of Mercosur and other subregional integration agreements in the Third World in the early 1990s. From this perspective, *domestic* pressures for regional co-operation explain the new regionalism.

This approach is based on a sophisticated challenge to the realist assumptions of anarchy and states-as-unitary-actors in international relations.[71] As Helen Milner puts it,

> Relaxing [the unitary actor assumption] means bringing domestic politics back in. It implies moving away from using the state as the basic unit of analysis; instead, other domestic actors–such as the executive, the legislature, bureaucracies, political parties, and interest groups–become the primary unit of analysis.[72]

However, states *do* behave as unitary actors in regional integration efforts; domestic actors may be represented in regional institutions, but they don't have much power, even in the European Union, where all-important decisions are made by the Council of Ministers.[73] In the case of Mercosur, the adoption of a loose intergovernmental structure in 1991 meant that the four Mercosur partners would behave as unitary actors; decision making is concentrated in the presidency of each country and all important decisions have been made at the presidential summits (see chapter 3).

The political economy approach looks at states as polyarchies, not as unitary actors, challenging the validity of the concept of "national interest." Milner rightly points out the ambiguities of this concept. Yet in times of crisis, as during the Brazilian economic crisis of January/February 1999, the "national interest" becomes important. The Brazilian devaluation of the real affected Argentina as a whole, because Argentina sends roughly a third of its exports to Brazil. The Argentine state *had to* behave as a unitary actor to cut tariffs on capital goods from outside Mercosur from 14 percent to 6 percent to protect its automobile industry. Also, it had to consider a plan for subsidised job creation to stall the possibility of higher unemployment because of an impending recession.[74] If Argentina's, Uruguay's or Paraguay's rates of economic growth drastically decline because of the Brazilian crisis these countries' national interest is affected because everybody's standard of living suffers.[75]

Most of the literature considers "the link with globalization" as the fundamental assumption underlying the new regionalism of the 1990s.[76] Domestic level theories are an attempt to disentangle the link with globalization by looking at internationalist "winning coalitions" in individual countries. According to Etel Solingen,

> Mercosur was designed to strengthen the internationalist model at home, weakening groups and institutions opposed to reform, and increasing the costs of reversing tacks for potential domestic challengers. Private entrepreneurial associations played a leading role in shaping

Mercosur, in contrast to all preceding integrative efforts in the region. Brazilian business and investments in Argentina created a new lobby—Grupo Brasil—dedicated to defending Mercosur against protectionist attacks. Mercosur was also a means of lubricating external ties to the global political economy and of persuading global investors of the credibility of the internationalist shift, at home and in the region.[77]

Yet Solingen fails to address the real issue, i.e., what type of link with globalization do these countries establish? Full subordination, because it is the only way of successfully competing in a world now ruled by the global marketplace (Friedman's "Electronic Herd")? Or defensive linkages preserving regional autonomy (the Brazilian approach to regional integration)? The triumphalist, "end of history" approach to globalization had a certain basis in the first half of the 1990s. Yet in the second half, particularly after the Asian crisis of 1997, the global logic of liberalisation has been increasingly challenged, not only from the left, but also by people such as George Soros, who have enormously benefited from the unfettered free movement of capital and investment since the end of the Cold War.[78]

Like Thomas Friedman, Etel Solingen does not leave room for the possibility of autonomous regional economic blocs. Even if Mercosur and the Andean Community were to succeed in creating a South American Free Trade Area (SAFTA) it would be just "a building block and an accessory to the global logic of liberalisation."[79]

The domestic politics/IPE explanation of the new regionalism opens up the "black box" of the state to look at interest groups and political coalitions affecting state behaviour. The problem with this perspective is that it reduces regional politics to domestic politics, while neglecting the impact of the global international environment on regional politics. For example, domestic business organisations were *not* the driving force behind the formation of Mercosur in March 1991. Although business organisations managed to influence the timetable for trade liberalisation during Mercosur first stage (1991-95), government leaders and ministerial technocrats were the real decision-makers.[80] Mercosur was essentially "*a political initiative of the governments of Brazil and Argentina made in part to consolidate their economic direction as well as to respond to the trend toward regionalization of the global economy.*"[81]

Second, by lumping together the majority of the business community in Argentina and Brazil under the heading: "internationalist coalitions" Solingen neglects the important differences between the selective approach to trade liberalisation of the Brazilian industrialists and the self-destructive acceptance of the neo-liberal model by their Argentinean counterparts.[82] In fact, because of regional asymmetries, Brazil had a greater weight in setting the pace of Mercosur's negotiations and evolution than its minor partners. Argentina paid the heavy price of "Brazil-dependency" by committing itself fully to the neoliberal model at the cost of deindustrialization, the "destructive restructuring" of its economy and the weakening of the Argentine state.[83]

Third, the coalitional approach fails to explain the timing for the revival of regional integration efforts in the late 1980s and early 1990s. Relative gains calculations had been major impediments to economic co-operation in Latin America in the 1960s and 1970s. Why did they cease to play a role in the late 1980s and early 1990? The conventional explanation is that the new regionalism arose in a completely different political (end of the Cold War) and economic ("globalization") international environment. Solingen's answer is that "regional economic integration and broad-based regional co-operation were both an expression of grand internationalist strategies and also helped reinforce them domestically."[84] Yet her approach oversimplifies the problem since not all the cases of "new regionalism" have adopted open regionalism, or "internationalist" grand strategies. Again, relative gains concerns, this time among regions, come into play, showing the need of a "macro" or systemic approach to the new regionalism.

By blurring the boundaries between comparative and international politics the domestic politics/IPE approach makes the mistake of reducing the new regionalism to coalitional games and is unable to grasp the specific weight of regional economic organisations, such as Mercosur, in the global political arena. The implicit assumption is that the "big game" of globalization is untouchable–globalization has already won.

The emphasis on domestic political actors and coalitions is a healthy antidote to neorealism's reification of the state as a unit of analysis; international and domestic politics cannot be isolated from each other. However, the domestic politics/IPE approach overestimates the importance of domestic political actors and coalitions to the detriment of regional and international factors, and wrongly assumes that the state is merely an instrument of a dominant political coalition. Yet state preferences do not merely result from the preferences of a dominant elite coalition, even when strong internationalist coalitions are in power (as in Argentina under Menem, 1989-1999), for the simple reason that the state is relatively autonomous from the dominant classes of society.[85]

On the other hand, the domestic politics/IPE approach is not totally incompatible with neorealism. As Sandholtz and Zysman point out,

> Structural situations create the context of choice and cast up problems to be resolved, but they do not dictate the decisions and strategies. In other words, the global setting can be understood in neorealist terms, but the political processes triggered by changes in the system must be analysed in other than structural terms. The choices result from political processes and have political explanations. In this case, the process is one of bargains among nations and elites within the region [Western Europe].[86]

The structural explanation has arguably more weight in South America because of the historical dependence of the region on the US, the "colossus of the North" (see chapter 5).

3. Constructivism and the New Regionalism

Constructivism is closely related to the domestic politics/IPE approach. Constructivist scholars argue that the new regionalism in Latin America is strongly associated with transitions to democracy in the 1980s and 1990s. For example, Solingen claims that "regional democratisation may also provide a stronger guarantee against nondemocratic challenges to incumbent internationalists."[87] Alberto Van Klaveren argues that "political affinities have played an important role in the establishment of Mercosur and the renewal of the Central American Common Market."[88]

The claim that "democracies do not go to war against each other" is an important component of the constructivist approach to international relations. Constructivism is part of a broader critical international relations theory. Its basic claim is that world politics is "socially constructed," summarised in the title of Alexander Wendt's article, "Anarchy is What States Make of It."[89] The constructivist approach to regionalism is through the concept of "security communities" borrowed from Karl Deutsch, one of the fathers of regional integration theory.[90] As Andrew Hurrell points out,

> Constructivist theories focus on regional awareness and regional identity, on the shared sense of belonging to a particular regional community, and on what has been called "cognitive regionalism" (...) Instead of focusing solely on material incentives, constructivists emphasise the importance of shared knowledge, learning, ideational forces, and normative and institutional structures.[91]

Constructivists argue that states "are not structurally or exogenously given [neorealism's anarchy assumption] but constructed by historically contingent interactions."[92] This is an important insight. The concept of "structurally constituted identities" helps to analyse regional integration after the Cold War. Friendship, like enmity, is a *social* relation. As Hurrell notes, Wendt's brand of constructivism can be seen as a systemic theory, although his neorealist critics can argue that it overestimates the importance of regional identities and the discourse of regions and region building; and that it underestimates intra-regional contradictions and conflicts. For example, Mercosur illustrates the existence of different national conceptions of the South American region. For Brazil, regional autonomy and self-reliance is a paramount concern; for Argentina, sacrificing regional autonomy may be the price one has to pay to be in good terms with the US, the "only superpower left."

The problem with the constructivist approach is that it mechanically extrapolates Deutsch's concept of "security community" (which may be useful to understand European integration) to other regions of the world. It is difficult to apply the concept of "security community" to Argentine-Brazilian co-operation, and even more difficult to apply it to South American co-operation. Although a dramatic shift has taken place in Argentine-Brazilian relations (from enduring rivalry to bilateral co-operation) whether it is the same kind of stable co-operation that characterises French-German relations is an open question. Brazil's devaluation of the *real* in January 1999 has had a negative impact on Mercosur and Argentine-Brazilian relations (see chapter 3). Despite Andrew Hurrell's efforts to "fit" Argentine-Brazilian co-operation in the constructivist model, he can only conclude that Mercosur is a "loosely coupled" and "still imperfect," security community.[93] Whether the changes that have taken place in the core relationship between Brazil and Argentina are permanent is an open question, particularly considering a history of failed attempts at bilateral and South American co-operation (LAFTA and ALADI; see chapter 2). Although economic co-operation has led to increasingly strong security ties between the two countries, their new security relationship could easily unravel if Mercosur breaks down and/or Argentine/Brazilian trade disputes become more acrimonious leading to a diplomatic crisis between the two countries. Although shared democratic values have played an important role in the process of Argentine-Brazilian co-operation and Argentina does not seem to perceive Brazil as a threatening hegemon it is premature to describe Mercosur as a security community for at least two reasons. First, Argentina's and Brazil's foreign policies significantly diverge on a number of issues. Second, as we will see in chapter 3, Mercosur remains institutionally weak, because of Brazil's reluctance to accept the creation of supranational institutions.

Neorealism is better equipped than constructivism to explain the Brazilian proposal to create a South American Free Trade Area (SAFTA). As Hurrell points out, the process of increased co-operation among the Mercosur countries has been a strongly statist project, and a reaction to the uncertainties of the post-Cold War era and the prospective creation of NAFTA. Deutsch's transnational social networks have not played an important role in this case; although there has been increasing institutionalised interactions among bureaucracies.[94] Even Hurrell, who sympathises with constructivism, has to recognise that power considerations have played a role in the formation of Mercosur and are an important component of the SAFTA project: "the notion that a strong regional grouping will be better able to negotiate with the USA–a belief which explains the Brazilian emphasis on turning Mercosur into a South American grouping."[95]

On the other hand, constructivists have gone beyond the concept of states as agents, suggesting that a *new form of state* is emerging. The "international state", defined by Alexander Wendt as "the emergence of state powers at the international level that are not concentrated in a single actor but distributed across transnational structures of political authority and constitute a structural transformation of the Westphalian system."[96] James Caporaso has applied the concept to the European Union, arguing that it is "already" an international state.[97] Yet this concept remains fuzzy. Does it mean decentralisation of political authority? Or does it mean the emergence of a new form of truly international political authority? The big puzzle for theorists of European integration in the early 1990s is the resilience of the nation-state.[98]

The strong version of the thesis of economic globalization arguably exaggerates the limits placed by globalization on domestic politics and state authority.[99] The impact of globalization and regional integration on the transformation of the state in Latin America has not been considered in the literature. Even if as Caporaso and others argue a new form of "international" state is emerging in Western Europe one cannot assume that the same phenomenon is also happening in South America, a region with a different history, national ideologies and state institutions. As early as 1967 Ernst Haas warned against the danger of extrapolating the Western European experience to Latin American integration.[100] For example, European integration did not suffer from the "fear of the outsider" problem and was not perceived as conflicting with intensified economic ties with the United States. By contrast, Latin American integration efforts in the 1960s and 1970s were a response to

US attempts to dominate the region by opening the Latin American markets to "free trade" with the US (see chapter 2). As John Odell puts it,

> Most Latin American leaders were suspicious of free trade theories emanating from the United States after World War II... To many Latin Americans it seemed likely then (and still does today) that such free-trade advice was offered not honestly but as a device of US business for undermining potential new foreign competitors and thereby promoting its own interests.[101]

Is the internationalisation of the state a global process? Are there differences across regions? Wendt does not provide an answer to these questions, which are critically important considering the above mentioned ambiguities of the concept of "globalization." There is a lively debate within neomarxism on this topic. Is the internationalisation of the state, as Robert Cox argues a "top-down" process increasingly depriving the state of *any* autonomy while converting it "into an agency for adjusting national economic practices and policies to the perceived exigencies of the global economy"? According to Cox, in the era of globalization, the state has become "a transmission belt from the global to the national economy, where heretofore it had acted as the bulwark defending domestic welfare from external disturbances."[102] Or does the state still have, as Leo Panitch argues, a considerable amount of power, even though the "nature" of state intervention has changed?[103] Even if one settles this issue (one way or the other) for the European Union one cannot mechanically assume (unless one adopts a Eurocentric approach to world politics) that the answer applies to the South American countries.

4. Neoliberal Institutionalism

Neoliberal institutionalism is probably the most influential approach to the analysis of international co-operation and has been used to explain the revival of old regional integration schemes and the emergence of new ones in the 1990s. In essence, neoliberal institutionalism challenges the realist claim that state behaviour is driven by relative gains concerns, arguing that states will often prefer to co-operate in order to realise absolute gains rather than maximising individual short-term gains.

This approach combines the neorealist assumption of states as unitary actors rationally pursuing their self-interests, with the optimistic idea that international and regional co-operation are possible in spite of the relative gains problem. Neoliberals argue that states can work together to achieve mutual gains relying on rules and norms of co-operation and creating international (and regional) institutions and regimes. An international regime is a set of rules, norms, and decision-making procedures around which actors' expectations converge in a certain issue area, such as trade.[104] Neoliberals claim that states can overcome the Prisoner's Dilemma (PD) game by using a strategy of reciprocity (*tit for tat*) after an initial co-operative move in a repeated PD game, which accurately reflects the reality of international interactions, in which there is always a "shadow of the future."[105]

Neoliberal institutionalism helps to explain both conflict and co-operation at the regional level. Thus, for example, the "statist" side of neoliberal institutionalism helps to explain the recurrence of conflict between Argentina and Brazil in Mercosur. At the same time, its claim that states can overcome collective action problems helps to explain the resilience of Mercosur, and its survival despite serious relative gains problems between Argentina and Brazil and the asymmetric imbalance between Argentina/Brazil and Paraguay/Uruguay. The intensity of Argentine-Brazilian co-operation since the formation of Mercosur in 1991 cannot be explained using purely realist (or neorealist) premises. As Hurrell notes,

> Although there were certainly many difficulties in the 1990-1994 period caused most obviously by the divergence of economic policies between the two countries and the differential speed of economic liberalisation and tariff reductions, the two countries were able to agree on the implementation of a common external tariff that came into effect on January 1, 1995.[106]

Neoliberal institutionalism combines the strengths of neorealism with a recognition that institutions matter because they can reduce (or even eliminate), interstate conflict by changing actors' expectations and behaviour. If institutionalists are right, the region as a social structure is ontologically primary, thus challenging the realist claim that states are the basic units of analysis in international relations, constantly struggling for survival in an anarchic environment. As Goldgeier and McFaul note, "among the states of the European Community [the more advanced experience of regional integration to date] it is not clear what preserving the "existence of the state" will mean in the years after 1992."[107]

Neoliberal institutionalism allows the analysis of regional integration to supersede the strait-jacket of the relative gains hypothesis, while recognising the importance of systemic constraints on state behaviour. The centrality of relative gains concerns can be challenged from a neoliberal institutionalist perspective. Although relative gains concerns may inhibit co-operation, there is no reason to believe that states will always seek relative gains, even if "in some circumstances, relative gains can help explain certain aspects of international behaviour."[108]

Regional hegemons play an important role in all the contemporary examples of the new regionalism, among other reasons because "the dynamic gains from regional blocs–enlarged size of the market and economies of scale– are more likely to occur if the bloc has at least one "big brother" as a member.[109]

Using a neoliberal institutionalist framework, one may argue that regional hegemons operate as the "central government" of regional regimes, by providing leadership, and willing to enter into agreements in which they make initial sacrifices for future gains, "precisely because they expect to have considerable control over the behaviour of [their] partners in the future: they can make life difficult for them if they fail to live up to their obligations. The smaller states, at the same time, know that the hegemon is likely to enforce a general pattern of rules."[110]

Brazil has been playing such a role in Mercosur, and could potentially play the same role in a future South American Free Trade Area (SAFTA). From this perspective, Mercosur can be seen as an assertion of Brazilian regional hegemony rather than as a step toward Western hemispheric integration under US leadership. The prospects for the emergence of SAFTA depend to a significant extent on whether Brazil can consolidate its hegemonic role in Mercosur and effectively exercise regional hegemony in the subcontinent or whether US hegemony in the Western Hemisphere completely overshadows and neutralises Brazilian hegemony in South America (see chapters 5 and 6).

The title of Robert Keohane's book, *After Hegemony*, summarises the challenge to characterise the new regionalism in the era of globalization. Is there room for regional co-operation/integration in a world increasingly dominated by globalization? Stephen Haggard has shown that it has not been easy for the United States to promote the concept of "deep integration" in the developing world,[111] which helps to explain the diversification of US foreign economic policy in the 1990s. If as neoliberal institutionalism claims, we live in a world in which no single international hegemon can provide the collective goods of economic and military security, the formation of "regional orders" becomes attractive. Yet despite scholarly attempts to reconcile them, regional orders coexist in an uneasy balance with "globalization." In the case of Latin

America, there is a long history of regional and subregional economic integration efforts, which as Yale Ferguson notes have managed to survive by adopting new forms:

> A remarkable feature of the integration process in Latin America has been a form of "spill-around," an apparent impasse in one organisation's leading to the creation of yet another institution. The integration ideal has often faltered, but never died–it has been reborn again and again in different guises.[112]

If Ferguson's assessment is correct, one should not hastily assume that the Brazilian SAFTA proposal would not materialise, just because of the Brazilian economic crisis of early 1999. On the contrary, it might well be reborn, in a different guise, in the first decade of the new millennium.

Notes

1   See Lowenthal, A., 1976, "The United States and Latin America: Ending the Hegemonic Presumption," in *Foreign Affairs*, vol. 55 (October), pp. 199-213, p. 201. For example, Peter H. Smith claims that "since World War II, ... the general trend has *always* been for the United States to exert a great degree of influence over Latin American countries, but the level of this influence revealed some oscillation (up, down, up) from the mid-1950s to the present time," Smith, P., 1996, "The United States, Regional Integration, and the Reshaping of the International Order," p. 30, in Nishijima, S. & Smith, P. (eds.), *Co-operation or Rivalry? Regional Integration in the Americas and the Pacific Rim*, Boulder (CO), Westview Press, pp. 27-51.

2   See Hollist, W. & Nielson, D., 1998, "Taking Stock of Inter-American Bonds: Approaches to Explaining Co-operation in the Western Hemisphere," in *Mershon International Studies Review* 42 (2), pp. 257-81.

3   On "unbundled territoriality," see Ruggie, J., 1993, "Territoriality and Beyond: Problematizing Modernity in International Relations," *International Organization* vol. 47 (Winter), pp. 139-174, p. 171. On "open regionalism" see Palmer, N., 1991, *The New Regionalism in Asia and the Pacific*, Lexington (MA), DC Heath and Co.

4   See e.g., Kaiser, K., 1968, "The Interaction of Regional Subsystems: Some Preliminary Notes on Recurrent Patterns and the Role of the Superpowers," *World Politics*, vol. 21 (1), pp. 84-107; Ayoob, M., 1985, "The Primacy of the Political: South Asian Regional Cooperation (SARC) in Comparative Perspective," *Asian Survey*, vol. 25 (4), pp. 443-457.

5   See Kaiser, K., 1968, *op. cit.*, p. 84.
6   See e.g., Palmer, 1991, *op. cit.*
7   See Haas, E., 1975, *The Obsolescence of Regional Integration Theory*, Institute of International Studies, University of California, Berkeley.
8   On the distinction between the global economy and the international economy, see Cox, R., 1993, "Structural Issues of Global Governance: Implications for Europe," in Gill, S. (ed.), *Gramsci, Historical Materialism and International Relations*, Cambridge (UK), Cambridge University Press, pp. 259-289. "These developments together constitute a *global economy*, i.e. an economic space transcending all country borders, which co-exists still with an *international economy* based on transactions across country borders and which is regulated by inter-state agreements and practices." (p. 260).
9   See Rodrik, D., 1997, *Has Globalization Gone Too Far?*, Washington DC, Institute for International Economics.
10 See Ruggie, J., 1993, *op. cit.*, p. 171.
11 See Luttwak, E., 1990, "From Geopolitics to Geo-Economics: Logic of Conflict, Grammar of Commerce," *The National Interest* (Summer), pp. 17-23, p. 19.
12 Poulantzas, N., 1979, *Classes in Contemporary Capitalism*, London, Verso, p. 73. It is worth noting that as Don Marshall points out, "Capital has always been an a-spatial phenomenon, never truly subordinated by legally fixed territorial boundaries. Indeed caution is required in identifying the restructuring processes as evidence of newness." Marshall, D., 1996, "Understanding Late-Twentieth-Century Capitalism: Reassessing the Globalization Theme," *Government and Opposition*, vol. 31, pp. 193-205.
13 See e.g., Hoffmann, S., 1993, "Goodbye to a United Europe?" *New York Review of Books*, vol. 27 May, pp. 27-31, p. 30.
14 Hurrell, A., 1992, "Latin America in the New World Order: A Regional Bloc of the Americas?" *International Affairs*, vol. 68 (1), pp. 121-139, p. 133.
15 There is no room for regionalization as an independent variable in the most extreme forms of the globalization thesis. If globalization explains everything then regionalization can only be dependent on the overarching and irresistible process of globalization, driven by the information revolution. See Friedman, T., 1999, *The Lexus and the Olive Tree*, New York, Farrar Straus Giroux.
16 See Bienefeld, M., 1996, "Is a Strong National Economy a Utopian Goal at the End of the Twentieth Century?" in Boyer, R. & Drache, D. (eds.), *States against Markets: The Limits of Globalization*, London, Routledge, p. 436.
17 For example, James H. Mittelman argues that "any imputed conflict between regionalism and globalization is more theoretical than real, for political and economic units are fully capable of walking on two legs. If globalization is understood to mean the compression of the time and space aspects of social

relations, then regionalism is but one component of globalization," Mittelman, J., 1994, "Rethinking 'the New Regionalism' in the Context of Globalization," paper presented at the Annual Meeting of the International Studies Association (ISA), Washington, DC, March.

18 See e.g., Thurow, L., 1992, *Head to Head: The Coming Economic Battle among Japan, Europe, and America*, New York, Warner Books, p. 16; Luttwak, E., 1990, *op. cit.*; Krugman, P., 1991, "Regional Blocs: The Good, the Bad and the Ugly," *The International Economy*, vol. 5 (6), pp. 54-56.

19 See Fishlow, A. & Haggard, S., 1992, *The United States and the Regionalization of the World Economy*, Paris, OECD.

20 See Garnaut, R., 1994, "Open Regionalism: Its Analytic Basis and Relevance to the International System," *Journal of Asian Economics*, vol. 5 (2), p. 273. See also Ohmae, K., 1995, *The End of the Nation State: The Rise of Regional Economies*, New York, Free Press.

21 Thompson, W., 1973, "The Regional Subsystem: A Conceptual Explication and a Propositional Inventory," *International Studies Quarterly*, (March), pp. 89-117, p. 93.

22 Young, O., 1969, "Professor Russett: Industrious Tailor to a Naked Emperor," *World Politics*, vol. 21 (April), pp. 487-488.

23 See Bélanger, L., Cooper, A., Mace, G. & Monfils, J., 1999, "Middle Powers and Regional Trade Cooperation: Argentina, Brazil, Canada, Mexico, and the Setting of the FTAA Negotiation," paper presented at the Annual Meeting of the International Studies Association, Washington, DC, 16-21 February.

24 See chapter 5.

25 See Mols, M., 1993, "The Integration Agenda: A Framework for Comparison," pp. 51-75, in Smith, P. (ed.), *The Challenge of Integration: Europe and the Americas*, New Brunswick (NJ), Transaction Publishers, p. 56.

26 See ibid. See also Sandholtz, W., Borris, M., Zysman, J., Conca, K., Stowsky, J., Vogel, S. & Weber, S., 1992, *The High Stakes: The Economic Foundations of the Next Security System*, New York, Oxford University Press, p. 174.

27 Mols, M., 1993, *op. cit.*, p. 57.

28 Ibid., p. 59. An example is the "Canberra Process" of Pacific-Asian economic Cupertino. See Palmer, 1991, *op. cit.*, pp. 186-190.

29 See Sandholtz *et al.*, 1992, *op. cit.*, p. 182; Luttwak, 1990, *op. cit.*

30 Whiting, Jr., V., 1993, "The Dynamics of Regionalization: Road Map to an Open Future?" p. 17, in Smith, P. (ed.), *The Challenge of Integration, op. cit.*, pp. 17-43.

31 Luttwak, 1990, *op. cit.*, p. 21.

32 On "mercantilist regionalism" and "benign regionalism" see Sandholtz *et al.*, 1992, *op. cit.*, pp. 174-175.

33 See Layne, C., 1993, "The Unipolar Illusion; Why New Great Powers Will Rise," *International Security*, 17 (4), pp. 5-51.

34 See Falk, R., 1997, "State of Siege: Will Globalization Win Out?" *International Affairs*, vol. 73 (1), pp. 123-136.
35 Clark, I., 1998, "Beyond the Great Divide: Globalization and the Theory of International Relations," *Review of International Studies*, vol. 24, pp. 479-498, p. 479. The classical locus of neorealist theory is Waltz, K., 1979, *Theory of International Politics*, Reading (MA), Addison-Wesley.
36 See Solingen, E., 1998, *Regional Orders at Century's Dawn: Global and Domestic Influences on Grand Strategy*, Princeton (NJ), Princeton University Press; Lake, D. & Morgan, P. (eds.), 1997, *Regional Orders: Building Security in a New World*, University Park (PA), Pennsylvania State University Press.
37 Luttwak, 1990, *op. cit.*, pp. 20-21.
38 See Johnson, H., 1991, *Dispelling the Myth of Globalization: The Case for Regionalization*, New York, Praeger; Weiss, L., 1998, "Globalization and the Myth of the Powerless State," *New Left Review*, vol. 213 (September/October), pp. 3-27.
39 See the compelling analysis of George Soros, one of the big beneficiaries of globalization. Soros, G., 1999, *The Crisis of Global Capitalism: Open Society Endangered*, New York, Public Affairs.
40 See Friedman, 1999, *op. cit.* As Nicholas Lemann points out, "Friedman is probably the most sanguine of the major writers on globalization ... He is quick to stipulate, too, that the triumph is not just of a particular form of social and economic organisation, but of a particular country, ours. As one of his interview subjects puts it, 'Globalization is Americanization.' We already dominate the world in almost every sense, and we will continue to do so, and to Friedman that's great." Nicholas Lemann, "A Theory of Everything: Thomas Friedman Goes Global," *The New Yorker*, 10/5/99, p.88.
41 See Sandholtz, W., *et al.*, 1992, *op. cit.*, pp. 186-187.
42 Bhalla, A. & Bhalla, P., 1997, *Regional Blocs: Building Blocks or Stumbling Blocks?*, New York, St. Martin's Press p. 21.
43 Smith, P., 1996, *Talons of the Eagle: Dynamics of US-Latin American Relations*, New York, Oxford University Press, p. 315.
44 See Ruggie, 1993, *op. cit.*
45 See Mols, M., 1996, "Regional Integration and the International System," p. 18, in Nishijima, S. & Smith, P. (eds.), *Cooperation or Rivalry?*, *op. cit.* pp. 9-26.
46 Hurrell, A., 1995, "Regionalism in Theoretical Perspective," in Fawcett L. & Hurrell, A. (eds.), *Regionalism in World Politics: Regional Organization and International Order*, New York, Oxford University Press, p. 57.
47 "An amalgamated security community exists whenever there is the 'formal merger of two or more previously independent units into a single larger unit, with some type of common government after amalgamation.' Deutsch offers the United States as an instance. Alternatively, a pluralistic security community

retains the legal independence of separate governments," Adler, E. & Barnett, M., 1998, "Security Communities in Theoretical Perspective," in Adler, E. & Barnett, M. (eds.), *Security Communities*, Cambridge (UK), Cambridge University Press.

48   Caporaso, J. & Keeler, J., 1995, "The European Union and Regional Integration Theory," in Rhodes, C. & Mazey, S. (eds.), *The State of the European Union: Building a European Polity?*, vol. 3, Boulder (CO), Lynne Rienner, p.31.

49   See Haas, E., 1968, *The Uniting of Europe: Political, Social, and Economic Forces 1950-1957*, Stanford (CA), Stanford University Press.

50   Keohane, R. & Hoffmann, S., 1994, "Institutional Change in Europe in the 1980s," p. 249, in Nelsen, B. & Stubb, A. (eds.), *The European Union: Readings on the Theory and Practice of European Integration*, Boulder (CO), Lynne Rienner, pp. 237-255.

51   See e.g., Hettne, B., 1998, "Regionalism and the New Third World," in Poku, N. & Pettiford, L. (eds.), *Redefining the Third World*, Basingstoke (UK), Macmillan Press.

52   See Wallace, W., 1995, "Regionalism in Europe: Model or Exception?" in Fawcett, L. & Hurrell, A. (eds.), *Regionalism in World Politics*, chap. 7, pp. 201-227.

53   Ibid., p. 208.

54   Binder, L., 1958, "The Middle East as a Subordinate International System," *World Politics*, vol. 10 (3), p. 410.

55   See Lake, D. & Morgan, P., 1997, "The New Regionalism in Security Affairs," in Lake, D. & Morgan, P. (eds.), *Regional Orders, op. cit.* p. 12.

56   See Petras, J. & Morley, M., 1992, *Latin America in the Time of Cholera: Electoral Politics, Market Economics, and Permanent Crisis*, New York, Routledge, chap. 3, "US Policy Toward Latin America: Military Intervention, Client regimes, and Economic Pillage in the 1990s," pp. 47-78.

57   See chapters 5 and 6.

58   See Castañeda, J., 1990, "Latin America and the End of the Cold War," in *World Policy Journal* 7 (3), p. 477.

59   See Tulchin, J., 1995, "The United States and Latin America in the World" p. 332, in Martz, J. (ed.), *United States Policy in Latin America: A Decade of Crisis and Challenge*, Lincoln (NE), University of Nebraska Press. "These possibilities present Latin America with a fearsome challenge and represent a historic opportunity. Never before have the nations of Latin America had a similar chance to define their roles in the world community and to contribute, in a meaningful and substantial fashion, to the shaping of the Hemispheric community. They must act, and act soon, or the opportunity may pass, and a new framework will be imposed on them which could reduce their autonomy to less than it is today or than it has been in the past ... More than at any time since their independence the nations of Latin America have the opportunity to take their

destiny into their own hands," Tulchin, J., 1997, "Hemispheric Relations in the 21st Century," *Journal of Interamerican Studies and World Affairs*, vol. 39 (1), pp. 33-43.
60 See Hornbeck, J., 1998, *A Free Trade Area of the Americas: Toward Integrating Regional Trade Policies*, pp. 16-18. Congressional Research Service Report, National Law Center for Inter-American Free Trade, http://natlaw.com/pubs/spmxcu8.htm
61 See Castañeda, 1990, *op. cit.*, pp. 474-475.
62 Van Klaveren, A., 1993, "Why Integration Now? Options for Latin America," p. 118, in Smith, P. (ed.), *The Challenge of Integration: Europe and the Americas, op. cit.*
63 Whiting, Jr., V., 1993, "The Dynamics of Regionalization: Road Map to an Open Future?" in Smith, P. (ed.), *The Challenge of Integration: Europe and the Americas, op. cit.*, p. 17.
64 See Manzetti, L., 1993/94, "The Political Economy of Mercosur," *Journal of Interamerican Studies and World Affairs*, vol. 35 (4), pp. 120-29.
65 See Whiting, Jr., V., 1993, "The Dynamics of Regionalization," *op. cit.*, p. 42.
66 Dos Santos, T., 1970, "The Structure of Dependence," *The American Economic Review*, vol. 60 (May), pp. 231-236.
67 See Frank, A., 1969, *Capitalism and Underdevelopment in Latin America*, New York, Monthly Review Press, p. 3, 11.
68 Cardoso, F., 1973, "Associated Dependent Development: Theoretical and Practical Implications," in Stepan, A. (ed.), *Authoritarian Brazil*, New Haven (CAT), Yale University Press, p. 149.
69 Jaguaribe, H., 1973, *Political Development: A General Theory and a Latin American Case Study*, New York, Harper & Row, pp. 378-379.
70 On the FTAA negotiations, see chapter 4.
71 See Milner, H., 1991, "The Assumption of Anarchy in International Relations Theory: A Critique," *Review of International Studies*, vol. 17, pp. 67-85.
72 Milner, H., 1998, "Rationalizing Politics: The Emerging Synthesis of International, American, and Comparative Politics," *International Organization*, vol. 52 (4), pp. 759-786, p. 761.
73 As Goldstein points out, the European Parliament "might some day operate as a true legislature passing laws for all of Europe. At present it operates more as a watchdog over the Commission, with little power to legislate," Goldstein, J., 1999, *International Relations*, New York, Longman, p. 436.
74 Unemployment in Argentina was already high before the Brazilian crisis. According to a May 1999 estimate, Argentina's Gross Domestic Product will shrink by 1.5% in 1999, instead of growing by more than 3%. "Now private economists are hazarding that the contraction could exceed 2%," "Argentina: Budget Cuts Trigger Dual response," *Latin American Weekly Report*, 11/5/99, p. 206.

75 See Krauss, C., 1999, "Argentines Suffering From Brazil Crisis," *New York Times*, 8/2/99.
76 See e.g., Grandi, J. & Bizzózero, L., 1997, "Towards a Mercosur Civil Society: Old and New Actors in the Sub-regional Fabric," *Integration and Trade*, vol. 3 (1), pp. 31-46, p. 32.
77 Solingen, 1998, *op. cit.*, p. 150.
78 For a radical critique of the "global logic of liberalization" including free trade, see Nader R., *et al.*, 1993, *The Case Against Free Trade: GATT, NAFTA, and the Globalization of Corporate Power*, San Francisco (CA), Earth Island Press; Mander, J. & Goldsmith, E. (eds.), 1996, *The Case Against the Global Economy*, San Francisco (CA), Sierra Club Books. The capitalist critique appears in Soros, 1998, *op. cit.*
79 Solingen, 1998, *op. cit.*, p. 151.
80 See Grandi & Bizzózero, 1997, *op. cit.*, p. 36.
81 Pereyra, L.V., 1999, p. 9, "Toward the Common Market of the South: Mercosur's Origins, Evolution, and Challenges," in Roett, R. (ed.), *Mercosur: Regional Integration: World Markets*, Boulder (CO), Lynne Rienner, pp. 7-23.
82 Solingen recognises that "levels of [regional] co-operation decrease somewhat where a weak internationalist coalition (as in Brazil in 1992-94) faces a strong internationalist neighbour (as in Argentina in the same period). But she fails to recognise the weight of Brazil as the regional hegemon setting the pace of sub-regional integration in the same years. See Solingen, 1998, *op. cit.*, p. 68.
83 See Schwartz, G., 1996, "Brazil, Mercosur and SAFTA; Destructive Restructuring or Pan-American Integration?" in Smith, P. & Nishijima, S. (eds.), *Cooperation or Rivalry?*, *op. cit.*, p. 132.
84 Solingen, 1998, *op. cit.*, p. 150.
85 See Poulantzas, N., 1970, *Political Power and Social Classes*, London, New Left Books.
86 Sandholtz, W. & Zysman, J., 1989, "1992: Recasting the European Bargain," *World Politics*, vol. 41 (1). Brackets added.
87 Solingen, 1998, *op. cit.*, p. 157. Although the neoliberal "internationalist" model still enjoys legitimacy among regional elites, it may face *democratic* challenges, particularly in cases of severe economic and political crisis, as in Venezuela, following the election of Hugo Chávez to the presidency in the fall of 1998.
88 Van Klaveren, 1993, *op. cit.*, p. 119.
89 See Wendt, A., 1992, "Anarchy is What States Make of It: The Social Construction of Power Politics," in *International Organization* 46 (Spring), pp. 391-425. See also Wendt, A., 1999, *Social Theory and International Politics*, New York, Cambridge University Press.

90 See Deutsch, K., 1957, *Political Community and the North Atlantic Area*, Princeton (NJ), Princeton University Press; Haas, E., 1958, *The Uniting of Europe*, Stanford (CA), Stanford University Press.
91 Hurrell, A., 1995, *op. cit.*, pp. 64-65.
92 Wendt, A., 1994, "Collective Identity Formation and the International State," in *American Political Science Review*, vol. 88 (2) (June), p. 385.
93 Hurrell, A., 1998. "An Emerging Security Community in South America?" in Adler, E. & Barnett, M. (eds.), *Security Communities*, *op. cit.*, p. 260.
94 Ibid., p. 252; Hurrell, A., 1994, "Regionalism in the Americas," In Lowenthal, A. & Treverton, G. (eds.), *Latin America in a New World*, Boulder (CO), Westview Press, pp. 167-190.
95 Hurrell, 1998, *op. cit.*, p. 253.
96 Wendt, 1994, *op. cit.*, p. 392.
97 Caporaso, J., 1996, "The European Union and Forms of State: Westphalian, Regulatory or Post-Modern?" *Journal of Common Market Studies*, vol. 34 (1), pp. 29-52. p. 33.
98 See Taylor, P., 1991, "The European Community and the State: Assumptions, Theories and Propositions," *Review of International Studies*, vol. 17, pp. 109-125; Milward, A., 1992, *The European Rescue of the Nation-State*, London; Moravcsik, A., 1999, *The Choice for Europe: Social Purpose and State Power from Messina to Maastricht*, Ithaca (NY), Cornell University Press.
99 See Poulantzas, 1979, *op. cit.*, p. 73. For a critique of the strong version of globalization, see Hirst, P. & Thompson, G., 1996, *Globalization in Question: The International Economy and the Possibilities of Governance*, Cambridge (UK), Polity Press, esp. chap. 1, "Globalization: a Necessary Myth?" pp. 1-17; Weiss, L., 1998, *op. cit.* See also Douglas, I., 1997, "Globalization and the End of the State?" *New Political Economy*, vol. 2 (1), pp. 165-77.
100 Haas, E., 1967, "The Uniting of Europe and the Uniting of Latin America," *Journal of Common Market Studies*, vol. 5 (4), pp. 315-343. Haas comments may sound very pessimistic today: "Europe is divided by language and religion, but united by regionally similar social and economic conditions and institutions; Latin America is united merely by language and religion. For automatic integration this is not enough, as the history of the continent since 1810 seems to emphasise," (p. 333). Yet his point is well taken against the excessive optimism of contemporary constructivists. The danger of eurocentrism becomes evident when one considers that in spite of monetary union, no member government of the EU has shown any specific inclination to abandon its sovereignty. The European experience shows that economic integration does not necessarily lead to political integration; each regional integration experience has unique characteristics that cannot be extrapolated to other regions. See Katzenstein, P.,

1996, "Regionalism in Comparative Perspective," *Cooperation and Conflict*, vol. 31 (2), pp. 123-159.
101 Odell, J., 1986, "Growing Trade and Growing Conflict Between Latin America and the United States," in Middlebrook, K. & Rico, C. (eds.), *The United States and Latin America in the 1980s: Contending Perspectives on a Decade of Crisis*, Pittsburgh, University of Pittsburgh Press, p. 261.
102 Cox, R., 1992, "Global Perestroika," in Miliband, R. & Panitch, L. (eds.), *Socialist Register 1992*, London, Merlin Press, pp. 30-31.
103 Panitch, L., 1994, "Globalization and the State," in Miliband, R. & Panitch, L. (eds.), *Socialist Register 1994: Between Globalism and Nationalism*, London, Merlin Press, p. 71.
104 Krasner, S., 1983, "Structural Causes and Regime Consequences: Regimes as Intervening Variables," in Krasner, S. (ed.), *International Regimes*, Ithaca (NY), Cornell University Press, p. 1.
105 Axelrod, R., 1984, *The Evolution of Cooperation*, New York, Basic Books; Goldstein, 1999, *op. cit.*, pp. 104-109.
106 Hurrell, 1998, *op. cit.*, p. 251. Before 1995, several analysts were sceptical as to the ability of Argentina and Brazil to overcome their trade disputes and agree on a common external tariff. For example, Luigi Manzetti wrote: "The common external tariff remains a sticky issue with the potential for disruptive consequences" and wrongly predicted that Paraguay could abandon Mercosur because of doubts regarding the real benefits of the regional agreement for its economy. See Manzetti, L., 1993, "The Political Economy of Mercosur," *Journal of Interamerican Studies and World Affairs*, vol. 35 (4), p. 126.
107 Goldgeier, J. & McFaul, M., 1992, "A Tale of Two Worlds: Core and Periphery in the Post-Cold War Era," *International Organization*, vol. 46 (2), pp. 467-492, p. 478, note 48. On institutionalism, see Finnemore, M., 1996, "Norms, Culture, and World Politics: Insights from Sociology's Institutionalism," *International Organization*, vol. 50, pp. 325-347.
108 Snidal, D., 1993, "Relative Gains and the Pattern of International Cooperation," p. 173, emphasis added, in Baldwin, D. (ed.), *Neorealism and Neoliberalism: The Contemporary Debate*, New York: Columbia University Press.
109 Bhalla, & Bhalla, 1997, *op. cit.*, p. 199.
110 Keohane, R., 1984, *After Hegemony: Cooperation and Discord in the World Political Economy*, Princeton (NJ), Princeton University Press, p. 180.
111 See Haggard, S., 1995, *Developing Nations and the Politics of Global Integration*, Washington, DC, Brookings Institution, chap. 1, "Deep Integration and the Developing World," pp. 1-14.

112 Ferguson, Y., 1984, "Cooperation in Latin America: The Politics of Regional Integration," Lincoln, J.K. & Ferris, E.G. (eds.), *The Dynamics of Latin American Foreign Policies: Challenges for the 1980s*, Boulder (CO), Westview Press, p. 53.

2 From Old Style Integration to the New Regionalism in the 1990s: A Future Unlike the Past?

Introduction

The dream of Latin American integration goes back to the Congress of Panama, organised in 1826 by Simón Bolívar, and the four Spanish American congresses that followed, in a failed attempt to create a political confederation of the Latin American republics. By the mid 1880s the image of a united Latin America had given way to the idea of inter-American or *hemispheric co-operation* and to the rhetoric of "Pan-Americanism." However, despite numerous setbacks Bolivar's vision of Latin American integration has never died. In his judgement, regional unity was an absolute necessity for the future of Latin America. Can the dream become a reality in the era of globalization?

The purpose of this chapter is twofold: (1) to examine the transition from the old Latin American regionalism of the 1960s and 1970s to the new regionalism of the 1990s; (2) to debunk the assumptions of the neoliberal literature on the subject. Was the old regionalism really a failure? What are the prospects for success of the new regionalism? Can the current experiments of autonomous "open regionalism" (Mercosur, the Andean Community) be preserved, eventually leading to an autonomous South American Free Trade Area (SAFTA)?

The Latin American Free Trade Association (LAFTA)

In February 1960 seven Latin American countries signed the Treaty of Montevideo, establishing the Latin American Free Trade Association, to increase trade between the contracting parties, to establish "gradually and progressively, a Latin American common market," and to pool their efforts "to achieve the progressive complementarity and integration of their economy on the basis of an effective reciprocity of benefits."

The idea of Latin American economic integration had been born during the 1950s in the "think tanks" of the United Nations Economic Commission for Latin America and the Caribbean (ECLAC) led by the commission's executive secretary, Raúl Prebisch. The rationale behind LAFTA was ECLAC's centre-periphery view of international economic relations, according to which the deterioration in the terms of trade placed the countries of the periphery (such as the Latin American nations) in a perennial disadvantage vis-à-vis the core countries of the world capitalist economy (the US, Western Europe, and Japan). According to Prebisch, Latin America's role in the periphery of the world economy denied it an equal share in material and technological progress, condemning it to perpetual underdevelopment. The only way out of secular economic stagnation due to declining foreign exchange earnings was to accelerate the process of import-substitution industrialisation (ISI)–which began in the 1930s during the great depression–while seeking new markets for traditional exports of primary products and diversifying exports. Extending ISI to the regional level would stimulate the abandonment of a traditional primary commodity export trade, while solving the foreign exchange constraints of purely "national" ISI development strategies. Moreover, regional integration would help modernise the Latin American economies, creating incentives for rapid industrialisation.

Import-substitution industrialisation was the response of the largest Latin American countries to the severe shortage of foreign exchange produced by the world economic crisis of 1929-1933. The literature makes the distinction between the "easy" phase of import-substitution industrialisation (from the 1930s to the late 1950s) and the "exhaustion" of import-substitution in the early-to-mid 1960s which is associated with the first wave of military "bureaucratic-authoritarian" regimes (Brazil, 1964, Argentina, 1966) and the adoption of a more "open" model of economic development in which "free trade" and transnational corporations began to play a crucial role.[1] The Latin American Free Trade Association (LAFTA) corresponds to the last stage of the "easy" phase of ISI. The standard explanation for the "old regionalism" represented by LAFTA is that national ISI had run its course by the mid 1950s. Therefore, an enlarged regional market protected by extra-regional trade barriers would continue to provide a stimulus to ISI.[2] Regional integration was aimed at achieving the *advantages* of ISI on a regional scale.

On the other hand, regional economic integration in Latin America was not only driven by economic factors. The Cuban revolution of 1959 was perceived by national elites and the US government as a potential threat to regional stability making it imperative to promote economic growth and development to avoid the emergence of a "second Cuba." The adoption of the "Charter of Punta del Este" (1961) after the signing of the Treaty of Montevideo in 1960 and the formal endorsement of a Latin American common market by US president Johnson at the first Summit of the Americas in Punta del Este (1967) must be seen in that context.

According to the Treaty of Montevideo, LAFTA would become a free trade area (*not* a customs union) by 1973 through periodically negotiated tariff reductions. The Treaty provided for (1) a general liberalisation program, consisting of national schedules and a common schedule. Tariff reductions were neither lineal nor automatic; they were negotiated product by product; (2) a special regime applicable to the so-called "lesser developed countries" (Bolivia, Paraguay, Uruguay, Ecuador); (3) agreements on complementarity by industrial sector, and (4) resolutions of harmonisation and co-ordination of policies of industrial and agricultural development and of policies relating to goods, services, and capital imports.

LAFTA had three institutional organs: a Conference of Contracting Parties and an Executive Committee, both assisted by a Secretariat. The Conference was the highest organ of the Treaty; it met in ordinary sessions once a year and in extraordinary sessions at the request of the Executive Committee. In 1965, LAFTA's Council of Ministers was created, to speed up the process of regional integration.

In its first two years of existence, LAFTA members made 7593 tariff concessions under the national tariff schedules. However, the process of tariff reductions significantly slowed down in the mid-to-late 1960s and only 224 additional tariff concessions were made in the decade of the 1970s under the national schedule.

LAFTA made little progress partly because of the different levels of economic development among the eleven contracting parties. By 1980 only 14 percent of annual trade among members could be attributed to LAFTA agreements, and it was the richest states (Argentina, Brazil, Mexico) which were receiving most advantages. Although the first Common List was quickly approved in 1964, the second Common List, set for 1967, failed to win acceptance on schedule. In the 1970s, there was a stalemate in negotiations. Critics argued that negotiations on a country-by-country and item-by-item basis had to be replaced by a system of automatic tariff reductions, applicable either to all countries or to groups of countries.

The Latin American Integration Association (LAIA/ALADI)

In August 1980 a new Treaty of Montevideo was signed by all LAFTA members to institute the Latin American Integration Association (LAIA/ALADI). In some ways, LAIA was a continuation of LAFTA, with certain aspects of the old treaty incorporated into the new one. On the other hand, however, the 1980 treaty introduced significant changes in both the concept and operation of economic integration. Instead of across-the board tariff cuts, the treaty envisaged an area of economic preferences, made up of several mechanisms: a regional tariff preference scheme, regional-scope agreements, and partial-scope agreements, the most dynamic and innovative element of ALADI.

The new Montevideo Treaty adopted a more modest and flexible approach to regional integration. All quantitative and temporal targets to achieve intra-regional free trade were abandoned. The purpose was to create an "area of economic preferences" as part of a gradual movement towards the eventual integration of the whole region. Member states were free to sign bilateral trade agreements with a partial scope. According to Genberg and De Simone, "LAIA moved away from a strategy of import substitution toward the promotion of already existing bilateral trade relations, thereby increasing the differences between countries in preferential trade and in market access."[3]

The three basic functions of the Latin American Integration Association (LAIA) are: the promotion and regulation of reciprocal trade, the creation of economic complementation, and the development of co-operative actions leading to enlarged markets. In response to the criticism that LAFTA only benefited the largest countries, the status of "lesser developed" countries was more fully recognised and more extensive provisions in their favour were incorporated.

The Treaty provides for three types of agreements:

1) The *Regional Tariff Preference* is the multilateral mechanism for tariff reductions. Preferences would be different for different economic sectors, and member countries would be permitted to exclude certain commodities. The most developed countries (Argentina, Brazil, Mexico) would be allowed the fewest number of exceptions, intermediate countries (Chile, Colombia, Peru, and Uruguay) more exceptions, and the least developed (Bolivia, Ecuador, Paraguay), the most exceptions.

2) *Agreements of Regional Scope* are those in which all member countries participate. Examples: trade, economic complementation, agricultural, scientific and technological co-operation, promotion of tourism, environmental preservation.

Two important financial agreements were inherited from LAFTA:

a) The 1965 Treaty on Reciprocal Payments and Credits, signed by the central banks of all the contracting parties and the Dominican Republic, provides for reciprocal credit lines between banks to finance trade flows.

b) The Multilateral Agreement of Support for the Attenuation of Transitory Deficiencies in Liquidity, or Santo Domingo Agreement (1969). It created a common fund to help member countries overcome short-term difficulties in settling multilateral accounts.

3) *Partial-Scope Agreements.* Only some member countries participate. The renegotiation of the tariff cuts agreements reached during the two decades of LAFTA belongs to this category.

All agreements between pairs or among groups of countries are open to eventual multilateralization, although the extension of benefits does not occur automatically to the rest, as it happened under LAFTA by application of the most favoured nation (MFN) clause. The adherence of other member countries must be negotiated.

Partial-scope agreements open up the possibility of deepening the process of regional integration; they must provide for differential treatment according to the three categories of countries recognised by the Treaty.

LAFTA contemplated differential treatment only for "lesser developed" members; ALADI recognises three different levels of economic development: "most developed," "intermediate," and "least developed." Moreover, Resolution 71 (III) recognises a special category of countries with an "insufficient market," characterised by the "narrowness of their national markets for the development of certain industrial activities." Colombia, Chile, Peru, Uruguay, and Venezuela belong to this group.

Although there have been several rounds of negotiations to deepen the regional tariff preference zone, the results have not been deemed satisfactory by an evaluation requested by the heads of state of the *Rio Group*.[4] According to this report, the Regional Tariff Preference had "a limited impact on intra-regional trade, as a result of the little significance of its magnitude, its limited scope of application, the indiscriminate adoption of non-tariff restrictions; the extent and negative commercial impact of the list of exceptions; the delay in implementing the Treaty on the part of some parties, and the absence of an evaluation on the part of the political organs of the Association."[5]

Intra-regional exports for LAIA/ALADI declined from a maximum of 16.4 per cent of total exports in 1981 (on the eve of the debt crisis) to only 12 percent of the total for the 11 member states in 1987. Yet the decline must be attributed to the Latin American debt crisis, which severely affected all integration efforts in Latin America–not only LAIA/ALADI. Latin American imports fell by 40 percent in the four years after 1981, with intra-regional imports falling as fast as extra-regional imports.[6] By 1990, the share of intra-regional exports of ALADI was about 13 percent of total exports, close to the level of 1970. Yet with a partial recovery in the early 1990s (increasing foreign investment, lower interest payments, and some renewal of private bank lending) intra-regional exports have significantly increased, particularly among the Mercosur countries (see chapter 3). In fact, as Ffrench-Davis points out, "total intra-regional exports of Latin America doubled in the four years 1990-94. By 1994 reciprocal trade covered 22 percent of total exports of goods, capturing nearly two-thirds of the increase in exports of the region between 1990 and 1994."[7] Whether this trend will continue after the Asian economic crisis of 1997 and the Brazilian economic crisis of 1999 is an open question.

Old Style Integration: Success or Failure?

Current assessments of the "old" regionalism in Latin America are very negative, blaming import-substitution industrialisation (ISI) and a "closed" model of development for the failure of LAIA/ALADI, the Andean Pact, and the Central American Common Market. For example, according to Alberto van Klaveren,

> Deadlines for the removal of barriers to intra-regional trade were typically postponed; most of the liberalisation schemes were limited in terms of product coverage and preferences given; implementation of the agreements was almost always partial, and initial liberalisation was followed by delays, reversals, and impasses.[8]

By contrast, the "new regionalism" is presented as outward looking, much more ready than the old regionalism to eliminate both tariff and non-tariff barriers to trade, and designed to achieve integration with the world economy rather than protection from it.

I will argue that ISI is not "guilty" of having caused the failure of early regional integration efforts in Latin America. ISI has been unfairly demonised by the literature on the new regionalism. The claim that the old regionalism failed because of the adoption of an inward-looking development strategy (ISI) is an ideological construct aimed at justifying the "need" for the neoliberal model of economic development in the 1990s (the so-called "Washington Consensus"). The region has paid a high price to achieve "economic stability" following the neoliberal model, an important component of which is "open regionalism" and "free trade": worsening social conditions and absolute poverty for 44 percent of the Latin American population.[9] Who benefits from subregional and regional economic integration? The social aspects of creating free trade areas and customs union are neglected in the pro-globalization literature on Latin American integration.

What was wrong with ISI? The dominant interpretation is that LAFTA failed because of the inadequacies of the ISI model of economic development. From this perspective, regionalism in Latin America faced severe crises in the late 1970s and the 1980s because regional integration could not offset the disadvantages of ISI: the "excessive" protection of domestic industries, their loss of competitiveness, and growing indebtedness.[10]

The ISI model of economic development was not a panacea. Yet, can one argue that the Latin American regional integration efforts of the 1960s and 1970s failed *because* of the ISI model of economic development? If an inward-looking development strategy was so bad, how does one explain the amazing dynamism of trade flows in the Central American Common Market between 1960 and 1968, and the medium to high rates of economic growth in most Latin American countries, notably the Mexican and Brazilian economic "miracles" in the 1970s? As Albert Fishlow (a critic of ISI) recognises, "From 1953 to 1973, Brazil and Mexico increased their share of regional income from 43 to 54 percent, reflecting their relatively higher rates of growth."[11]

According to Sidney Weintraub, ISI was "bad" because it "punished" consumers and importers of intermediate products necessary for efficient production, and because "the punishment inflicted within countries did not necessarily benefit the protected producers within the same countries."[12] Granting that one of the shortcomings of LAFTA was the unequal distribution of benefits for some countries (the more advanced ones) and costs for other countries (relatively less developed countries such as Bolivia and Ecuador) it is not true that these deficiencies "destroyed" the old subregional integration efforts. A more plausible explanation is that they were destroyed by the way in which the United States managed the debt crisis of 1982 (see below) not by any inherent flaw in the inward-looking development strategy.

As Albert Hirschman points out, the distinction between "outward-looking" and "inward-looking" phases of economic development carries a value-judgement in the English literature: positive, in the case of "outward-looking"; negative in the case of "inward-looking." In Spanish, "*desarrollo hacia adentro*" has a positive connotation because, instead of autarchy and introversion, it evokes the image of opening up the interior and the domestic market.¹³ The literature on the "new regionalism" claims that "open regionalism" is "good" because it is "outward-looking," i.e., it is designed to achieve integration with the world economy instead of protection from it; whereas the "old regionalism" was "bad" because it was "inward-looking" and based on ISI (a "bad" idea).

Other scholars argue that ISI had many *advantages*, and was very successful. ISI was an *autonomous* development strategy that increased national welfare and greatly diversified the Latin American economies while providing important sources of jobs and income. As Robert Alexander points out, the ECLAC-Prebisch program for import-substitution development in Latin America was a success in the sense that it achieved most of its objectives: (1) several countries were able "to produce within their borders the majority of their basic consumption and construction goods; (2) various countries became self-sufficient in many products of heavy industry, and (3) the larger economies of the region and some of the intermediate ones had the potential to significantly diversify their exports, so that their affluence no longer needed to depend on the vagaries of one particular product market.¹⁴

The conventional explanation for the emergence of the "new regionalism" is (1) that ECLAC's "integration industry" idea was flawed from the very beginning because of asymmetries inside LAFTA between the more advanced member states (Argentina, Brazil, Mexico) and the less developed ones, such as Bolivia and Ecuador,¹⁵ and (2) that it was wrong for the Latin American countries to undertake an autonomous development strategy, aimed at creating a heavy industrial base. Isaac Cohen goes as far as claiming that ISI was a wrong development strategy while recognising that it brought about "almost thirty years of sustained economic expansion!"¹⁶ Moreover, the pro-Washington consensus literature of the early 1990s claims that the Latin American countries finally came to their senses and changed their view regarding the role of trade policy in a development strategy:

> From being conceived as the extension of domestic import substitution strategies to a regional level, regional integration efforts are now perceived as a component of an overall outward-oriented strategy that can contribute to enhanced export growth for the region as a whole, without discriminating excessively against other trade partners.¹⁷

Yet are ISI and enhanced export-growth incompatible? The strategy of "import protection for export promotion" was basically sound, as shown by the fact that LAFTA/LAIA *did* contribute to industrialisation and *did* lead to export diversification into manufacturing. A careful reading of Prebisch's writings shows that for him, an *efficient* ISI was *not* incompatible with an outward-oriented strategy.[18] Prebisch argued that promoting exports of industrial products to the centres of the world capitalist economy was a necessity for peripheral countries, in order to break their dependency relationship with the developed countries. The Brazilian case shows that ISI and an export-oriented development strategy are quite compatible. As a "global trader" Brazil has diversified its export profile since 1985, with a growing participation of Latin American markets (especially the Mercosur countries) a markedly declining share of US markets and a growth in European and Asian markets.[19] The EU and the United States account for, respectively, 31 and 20 percent of Brazil's exports and 22 and 23 percent of its imports. The other countries of Latin America account for 15 percent of exports and 17 percent of imports. Asia's participation in Brazil's international trade has grown from less than 10 percent in 1980 to nearly 17 percent in 1990. Brazil's strategy for trade liberalisation and economic integration can only be understood in that context. Although one may argue that domestic corruption and inefficiencies have hampered the positive impact of ISI on Brazil's economic growth, the real challenge is to answer the question: Is there room for a combined ISI/export-led development strategy in the era of globalization? Subordinated regionalism does not provide a good answer; autonomous regionalism, even if more open than the old regionalism, is a meaningful answer; to better absorb the shocks caused by globalization while responding to the challenge of achieving international competitiveness vis-à-vis other regions.

The inward-looking strategy of economic integration followed by the old regionalism (best represented by LAFTA) is often accused by neoliberal US economists (and the dominant pro-globalization discourse) of having led to "excessive protection" and "trade diversion." Yet the United States practises trade diversion, as shown by the fact that Mexico has become the US's largest trading partner.[20] As Andrew Axline points out, trade diversion can be considered beneficial for developing countries, because it may become "an important tool of development strategy that may have reached its limits at the national level." Trade diversion may allow LDCs to expand production, "as firms attempt to supply other countries' markets... In terms of opportunity costs this represents a rational strategy since growth benefits may be reaped without sacrificing alternative uses of resources, and the developmental gains in the form of savings of scarce foreign exchange and expansion of production ...outweigh the costs in the form of national income foregone by protectionism..." From this perspective, successful ISI at the regional level "allows for a more efficient combination of factors of production."[21]

The literature on the new regionalism often blames ISI, the "excessive" role of the state in the development process (statist industrial policies) and highly expansionary fiscal and monetary policies for the failure of old style integration.[22]

Yet the reliance on "the markets" by most countries of the region in the 1990s, following the prescriptions of globalization fundamentalism, has not been a panacea. The "neoliberal consensus" that today prevails in Latin America has three main elements: macroeconomics stability (smaller fiscal deficits), a diminished government role in the economy (privatisation, deregulation) and greater openness to the outside (free trade and an "open" approach to foreign capital). Chile was the most extreme case of reaction against ISI when the so-called "Chicago boys" gained control of economic policy in 1974. As a result of their "free trade" policies, the home products, textiles, and a wide range of domestic industries disappeared, creating massive long-term unemployment. As Alexander points out, the "Chicago boys" were willing "to sacrifice a third to a half of [Chile's] industrial sector in the name of 'economic orthodoxy' and to accept the unemployment of a quarter of the labor force rather than have those people employed in producing goods that could not compete with imports. This was [their] definition of 'economic rationality'."[23]

An alternative to the dominant neoliberal interpretation is that LAFTA failed not because the development model (ISI) was wrong, but because it didn't go far enough (as envisaged by ECLA); and it didn't go far enough because doing so would have threatened US exports to the region, thus confirming the hypothesis that Washington promotes free trade and the "free market" doctrine in a one-sided manner, only to advance US business interests.[24] Moreover, the South American military governments embarking on the neoliberal experiments of the 1970s and 1980s saw regional integration as another form of protectionism and rejected it on ideological grounds. The abolition of LAFTA in 1980 and its replacement by the much weaker ALADI/LAIA is directly related to the "opening up" of the Latin American economies to the international market since the mid-seventies. As Diana Tussie has shown, LAFTA was destroyed by unilateral trade liberalisation measures undertaken by the "first generation" of neoliberal policy-makers in the mid-seventies (Chile under the "Chicago Boys") and late-seventies (Argentina under the Martinez de Hoz economic policies).[25]

Although the LAFTA countries were unable to meet the targets for intra-regional trade liberalisation set by the Treaty of Montevideo, intra-regional trade grew in both absolute and relative terms: "The share of *intra-LAFTA trade* in total trade of member nations nearly doubled between 1962-1964 (7.6 percent) and 1979-1981 (13.7 percent)."[26] On the other hand, the share of *intra-LAFTA exports* in total exports "rose from 7.7 percent in 1960 to 9.9 percent in 1970 and 13.6 percent in 1980, before falling to 8.3 percent in 1985. In a few cases (e.g., Argentina, Bolivia, Chile, Paraguay and Uruguay), intra-regional trade came to occupy a significant (greater than 20 per cent) share of total trade" (see table 2.1).[27]

Critics often ignore LAFTA's significant success (considering the limitations of the product-by-product approach) in liberating intra-regional trade in the 1960s. For example, Sebastian Edwards recognises that the total number of tariff concessions granted by LAFTA members on their "national lists" more than doubled between 1962 and 1968, but he quickly points out that they "almost stagnated from then on."[28]

On the other hand, critics ignore the lack of material (instead of purely rhetorical) support on the part of the United States and international financial institutions, such as the International Monetary Fund, for Latin American integration. The Alliance for Progress, and the Punta del Este Charter (its legal instrument) recognised the Montevideo Treaty and the General Treaty on Central American Integration as efficacious instruments for accelerating Latin American development. At the summit conference of Western Hemisphere presidents in Punta del Este, Uruguay, in April 1967, US President Johnson formally endorsed the commitment of the Latin American countries to turn all of Latin America into a common market by no later than 1985. Yet no action in support of LAFTA on the part of the US was forthcoming. Moreover, international development and financial institutions in which the US has a decisive weight remained aloof or hostile to Latin American integration. The World Bank and its subsidiaries, the International Development Association and the International Finance Corporation, ignored LAFTA's existence in their lending activities and their technical assistance to the area. And the International Monetary Fund (IMF) openly opposed the creation of regional payment mechanisms, even in the most innocuous form of a clearinghouse.[29]

As Miguel Wionczek wrote in 1965,

> Any review of LAFTA's achievements and shortcomings must be based on a recognition that the Treaty of Montevideo was the beginning of a process, not the end; and that that process would have to go on for many years before sure foundations had been laid for a common market in Latin America.[30]

Table 2.1 Intra-regional Exports of LAFTA/LAIA Countries (in $US million and as a percentage of total exports)

Country	1960 $ m	1960 %	1970 $ m	1970 %	1980 $ m	1980 %	1985 $ m	1985 %
Argentina	170.3	15.8	365.8	20.6	1850.5	23.1	1485.5	17.7
Bolivia	8.3	12.2	20.3	8.9	380.4	36.7	403.0	60.0
Brazil	88.5	7.0	304.0	11.1	3,459.0	17.2	2,233.0	8.7
Chile	33.0	6.7	152.0	12.2	1,117.0	23.0	546.9	14.1
Colombia	6.2	1.3	54.5	7.5	551.3	14.0	288.3	8.1
Ecuador	8.1	7.7	20.2	9.6	439.7	17.7	132.6	4.6
Mexico	8.1	1.1	92.7	7.1	608.0	4.0	596.0	2.7
Paraguay	8.9	33.0	24.5	33.1	140.6	45.3	83.4	27.4
Peru	36.8	8.5	63.6	6.1	590.9	15.1	357.8	12.0
Uruguay	3.3	2.5	29.2	12.5	393.4	37.2	237.8	28.0
Venezuela	195.7	7.8	137.3	4.3	1,396.0	7.3	761.0	5.4
Total	567.2	7.7	1,264.1	9.9	10,926.8	13.6	7,125.3	8.3

Source: Bulmer-Thomas, V., 1997, "Regional Integration in Latin America Before the Debt Crisis: LAFTA, CACM and the Andean Pact," in El-Agraa, A. (ed.), *Economic Integration Worldwide*, New York, St. Martin's Press, Table 9.2, p. 236. Reproduced by permission of Macmillan Press Ltd., Basingstoke, Hampshire, UK. © Macmillan Press Ltd 1997.

Similarly, before his retirement from the post of Executive Secretary of ECLA, Raul Prebisch warned, "it would be a mistake to consider that the instruments established under the Treaty [of Montevideo] are not intrinsically efficacious. They are; but important policy decisions are required before this efficacy can be reflected in concrete achievements capable of withstanding whatever factors may make for stagnation in the near future."[31]

Economic Integration in Latin America and the Debt Crisis

The old regionalism lost dynamism and suffered a serious crisis in the early 1980s under the pressure of balance of payments difficulties which became a full blown debt crisis in August 1982 when Mexico declared that it was unable to pay the interest on its external debt.

Explaining the Debt Crisis

The Latin American economies had registered impressive rates of economic growth in the 1960s and 1970s. As Cardoso and Fishlow point out, for the region as a whole, "economic growth accelerated from 5.2 percent per year in the decade 1953-1963 to 6.4 percent in 1963-1973" and "the more successful countries were able to sustain a large public presence while also giving greater scope to market signals and the opportunities afforded by continuing expansion of international markets."[32]

The Latin American countries withstood the first oil shock of 1973-1974, but at the expense of increased external indebtedness.[33] Many people wondered until when these countries would be able to implement IMF-sponsored austerity programs which asked them to increase their debt burden and to adopt policies which generated negative growth and unemployment, as a condition for receiving IMF funds. The severe world recession in 1980-1982 affected the prices of Latin American exports, which went down due to a drastic reduction of the aggregate demand of the central countries.[34] Latin America's terms of trade declined by 7 percent in 1981, by 5 percent in 1982 and by slightly over 7 percent in 1983. Moreover, there was little or no economic growth in Latin America in 1980-1982 after having averaged about 5.5 percent per year in the 1970s.[35] Several additional factors contributed to aggravate the situation, especially a steep rise in real interest rates (a consequence of the tight monetary policies of the Reagan administration) which not only contributed to current account deficits but also had immediate adverse effects on the debt-service ratio, i.e., interest payments as a percentage of exports.[36] These were particularly large among the major Latin American borrowers. High real interest rates and a shortening of debt maturities caused the total debt-service ratio (total debt service as a percentage of exports) of the 21 Latin American countries to climb from 50 percent in 1979 to 75 percent during 1982.

The "scissors effect" of higher interest rates and lower export earnings (because of OECD recession) had a devastating effect on the Latin American economies. The region registered negative rates of economic growth during most of the 1980s. In that decade, Latin America went from being a net importer of capital to becoming a net source of capital for the developed world. It is estimated that in the 1982-1990 period the Latin American countries transferred a net amount of about $220 billion of domestic savings to Northern developed countries in order to meet their contractual obligations. Facing a drastic reduction of voluntary capital inflows, the largest Latin American debtors were compelled to significantly slash imports (from $98 billion in 1981 to $59 billion in 1984) to have enough foreign exchange to pay the interest on the debt, which was consuming between one-third and one-half of their export earnings. Even Chile, the "role model" for market reforms and the strongest supporter of free trade in the region, tripled its import tariffs.

The standard explanation for the debt crisis is that the problem originated in the dominant role in credit markets of the newly industrialising countries (such as Mexico, Brazil, Argentina, and Venezuela) in the aftermath of the first oil-price shock (1973-1974). "They accounted for over two-fifths of the increase in all developing-country debt between 1973 and 1976. Mexico and Brazil, together, accounted for about a quarter."[37] These countries would have become "accustomed" to borrow funds that were easily available in the Euromarkets. This would have tempted them to embark on an "irresponsible" strategy of economic development and industrialisation based on public indebtedness. Although this explanation is based on real data,[38] it tends to underestimate the role of the above mentioned external causes of the problem; as if only the debtor countries were responsible for the debt crisis. If Argentina, Brazil and Mexico were eager to borrow, private international banks were eager to lend. Latin American debt with private banks reached enormous proportions because of the willingness of the banks in question to finance most of the region's deficit on current account from 1974 on. It was the world recession, rather than the "irresponsibility" of the Latin American countries what aggravated their debt difficulties. Since mid-1982, both the recession and economic policies in the industrialised countries put the debtor countries in the difficult situation of having to increase their trade surpluses, under very unfavourable international conditions, in order to service the debt. The reduction in absolute terms of the net flow of capital into the periphery, which was especially severe in the case of the non-petroleum exporting countries of Latin America such as Brazil, was closely interwoven with the "unexpected" duration of the recession in the advanced capitalist countries.[39]

The debt crisis was blamed on the Latin American countries not only because of their high levels of external borrowing but also for having chosen the "wrong" development strategy, based on import-substitution industrialisation (ISI). Instead of being pursued through local savings and domestic capitalisation, ISI was dependent on high levels of foreign capital (indebted industrialisation) and led to increasing fiscal deficits under corrupt authoritarian regimes. There is no doubt that the bureaucratic-authoritarian military regimes of the 1960s and 1970s were corrupt, and that a significant portion of external borrowing was aimed at arms purchases and nationalist projects, such as the nuclear programs.[40]

The Devastating Impact of the Debt Crisis

As of 1988 the Latin American foreign debt amounted to $400 billion, with the largest amounts being those contracted by Brazil, Mexico, Argentina, Chile, Venezuela, and Peru. Out of the seventeen most indebted countries in the world, twelve are in Latin America. The annual interest service for 1986-1987 averaged 33 percent of the total export earnings, while the total debt amounted to well over four times the total export earnings. IMF stabilisation programs exacerbated the social problems caused by high unemployment, the bankruptcy of domestic industry, and the collapse of domestic and regional markets. The burden of poverty and social inequity produced by the debt crisis has been summarised by Enrique Iglesias, president of the Inter-American Development Bank:

> Although poverty has always existed in Latin America, perpetuated by traditional growth patterns, it was aggravated by the crisis of the 1980s. Stagnation swelled the ranks of the so-called informal sectors of the region's economies, with the proportion of the poor rising from 41 to 44 percent over the last decade, affecting living conditions for nearly 183 million Latin Americans in 1989, as compared with 136 million in 1980.[41]

Moreover, the debt crisis brought about accelerating inflation and economic stagnation, a significant decline in real domestic investment, education, and health expenditures, the deterioration of the national infrastructure, and the lag in technological development.[42] Intra-regional trade (excluding fuels) fell by 50 percent or more between its 1980-1981 peak and 1983. By 1984, the share of intra-Latin American exports reached its lowest value since 1970.[43]

Both the redefinition of the role of the state in economic development and the emergence of a new regional consensus on the advantages of competition, market orientation and openness date back to the economic "structural adjustment" policies adopted in the mid-1980s as a response to the debt crisis. Structural adjustment led to the shrinkage of the state and the destruction of several branches of the state apparatus that until then had been considered useful for the attainment of societal goals.[44] The logic of the market was now expected to be the central engine of economic growth and development. Whether the new model of "open regionalism" of the late 1980s and early 1990s is part of this process is an open question. The more the state shrinks, the greater "open regionalism" following the market logic? Or does the "new regionalism put a brake on the shrinkage of the state? Does it "save" the state by redefining its role in a regional framework?

There are two interpretations of the debt crisis in the literature:

1) Those who argue that it was good, because it compelled the Latin American countries to abandon the import-substitution model of economic development, while adjusting to the "new economic realities" of the world economy. Critics of old style integration in Latin America argue that LAFTA/LAIA failed because ISI led to excessive protectionism. Instead of practising free trade the old regionalism only practised "a small volume of managed trade, operated selectively."[45] This is the gist of the neoliberal model: "protectionism is bad; free trade is good." Yet one may argue that tariff and non-tariff protection in the 1960s and 1970s was part of a development strategy that *did work*, by comparison to the stagnant growth rates of the 1980s and 1990s.

2) A second school of thought argues that the debt crisis was bad because it forced the Latin American countries to open up their economies for "private foreign pillage" paying the heavy price of dismantling the state and its social safety nets while adopting anti-popular policies (such as the layoffs of hundreds of thousands of public-sector employees) and renouncing to an autonomous model of economic development in exchange for a vague promise of an active insertion into the international (global) economy.

Those who defend the advantages of the neoliberal model of the 1990s tend to overlook the fact that (as we have seen) the debt crisis was largely due to factors outside of (and outside the control of) Latin America. Moreover, the US exercised enormous bilateral pressure on the Latin American countries for the adoption of the austerity programs imposed by the International Monetary Fund, even though they caused economic paralysis, poverty and unemployment. The debt crisis had a "disciplinary" effect on most Latin American leaders, who concluded that they had "no alternative" but to accommodate their domestic policies to the new international economic environment. As Barry Gills points out, "such policies were not necessarily 'the people's choice'."[46]

The Latin American Response to the "Debt Trap"

At first, the Latin American debtor countries made an attempt to develop an autonomous response to the debt crisis. The debt problem went well beyond the realm of economics. It was a *political* problem that required a *political* solution. At the Quito Conference in January 1984, they prepared a bold Plan of Action, claiming that it was "imperative that any external debt arrangements and negotiations... should harmonise the requirements of debt servicing with the development needs and objectives of each country, by minimising the social cost of the adjustment processes under way."[47]

In 1984, a debtors' cartel was a real possibility; there was great uncertainty about the ability of the Latin American countries to continue servicing their debt. At the beginning of the debt crisis (in 1982-1983) default by the larger debtors (Argentina and Brazil) could have triggered a world economic crisis and the survival of the largest northern creditors. Yet a debtors' cartel did not come into existence, among other reasons because the governments of the largest debtors were subject to enormous diplomatic pressures from the US government.[48] At the Tenth Annual Economic Summit of developed countries, which took place in London in 1984, the North refused to undertake government-to-government negotiations with the Southern debtors thus defusing the Latin American claim that the debt issue was a *political* problem requiring a *political* solution. Instead, the IMF and the banking community would deal separately with each country on a case-by-case basis. In the end, the individual debtor countries negotiated with a cartel of private creditor banks led by a Steering Committee. As Levinson explains,

> The Steering Committee informally co-ordinated with the [US] Treasury and the [US] Fed. The IMF designed the policy conditionality, which the debtor country was obligated to follow and which represented a consensus view between the IMF staff and that of the Treasury and the Fed.[49]

Why didn't the Latin American governments form a debtors' cartel to obtain a meaningful moratorium (e.g., five years) to pay the interest on the debt, that was consuming the great bulk of their export earnings? Besides US pressure, the Latin American governments faced a collective action problem. As Guillermo O'Donnell points out, to get out of the "debt trap" the Latin American countries had to weigh "the immediate and tangible advantages of receiving side payments ["bribes not to act in accordance with the interests of the debtors as a group"] against the medium term benefits of forming a debtors' cartel.[50] The banks succeeded in implementing a strategy of "divide and conquer" by rewarding co-operative countries with lower interest rates and easier repayment terms while isolating recalcitrant governments (such as Argentina in early 1984) and holding out the incentive of better terms of repayment for those governments willing to comply with IMF imposed austerity measures as a condition to reschedule interest payments and obtain new credits from the banks.

The inability of the Latin American countries to agree on a unified course of action placed the initiative in the hands of the US and the private banks. The US imposed the IMF management of the debt crisis instead of government to government negotiations, as requested by the Latin American governments. The Baker Plan (1985) recognised that the Latin American debtor countries faced crises of solvency, not just liquidity. The plan was based on the idea that these countries could not service their debts if they could not grow, and that they could not grow if they did not get better terms for debt repayment and enough inflows of new credits. The plan asked the World Bank to play a major role in the resolution of the debt crisis and called for new loans of $20 billion to those Latin American countries that were willing to implement "market based" economic reforms. Yet the Baker Plan was too little too late. As Shepherd points out, "the fact that Baker did not take stronger steps to persuade the banks to lend more money provides evidence that continued lending was never a strong commitment of the US government. The stability of the banking sector was still the overriding concern."[51]

The $20 billion offered by the Baker Plan proved to be unavailable, and after Brazil unilaterally declared a moratorium on interest repayments in 1987 the private banks withdrew support for the Baker Plan. Once the banks managed to set apart enough reserves to reduce their exposure to a default by the largest debtors, the Brady Plan (1989) offered partial debt relief to selected countries such as Mexico and Costa Rica, without providing an overall, lasting solution to the problem. After the Brady Plan, the Latin American debt crisis was effectively over for the banks, but not for Latin America. Although the Latin American economies sluggishly resumed economic growth in the early 1990s, they are still heavily indebted; most of the debt has been rescheduled, not reduced. The end of the Cold War opens up the possibility for the South American countries to solve their collective action problems through autonomous regional integration (SAFTA), to face up to the threats represented by financial globalization, capital mobility, and capital flight.[52]

The Neoliberal Model and the New Regionalism

After the initial shock caused by the debt crisis and under enormous pressure from the US-led international financial institutions (IMF and World Bank) and the private banks, one Latin American country after another gradually introduced free market oriented economic policies, including unilateral trade liberalisation and export promotion. Export-led growth would be the new engine of development. As a result of the triumph of neoliberal economics, fundamental market-oriented economic reforms were undertaken in the major countries of the region. The strategy of import-substitution industrialisation was blamed for all the "inefficiencies" of the Latin American economies. If Latin America was in trouble, it was the Latin Americans' own fault; they had to implement "structural adjustment" programs if they wanted to receive new capital inflows and a reasonable rescheduling of their foreign debt.[53]

Was the conversion to free market reforms inevitable? The adoption of neoliberal economic reforms is presented in the literature as both inevitable and desirable. As we have seen in chapter 1, the "inevitability assumption" is an important component of globalization fundamentalism. President Menem of Argentina is quoted as claiming that "no alternative remained" to the policies he chose.[54] The conversion to market economics by new civilian governments in the late 1980s and early 1990s is presented as inevitable given the "macroeconomics excesses" of the ISI era. Presumably, such "excesses" would be magically corrected by the logic of the market. The neoliberal model would rectify the "inefficiencies" of the old development model. The Latin American governments were expected to completely revise their trade policies, looking outward, not inward, for markets. According to the so-called "Washington Consensus", policies of import-substitution and state capitalism were wrong because they "implied that, in any regional trade arrangement, the partners would be buying from each other at far higher prices than they would pay for the same goods imported from the industrial nations."[55] From this perspective, the "old regionalism" was bad because it was more "trade diverting" than "trade creating." Yet as we have seen, trade diversion is not necessarily bad, and can even be considered beneficial for underdeveloped countries. After all, the northern countries practised ISI and "trade diversion" when they protected their own manufacturing sector at earlier stages of their development.

Isaac Cohen argues that the Latin American countries did well in embracing the neoliberal model because "the slump of the 1980s revealed some of the most striking social and economic shortcomings of defensive nationalism."[56] Yet the Latin American "lost decade" of the 1980s was not caused by ISI (Cohen's "defensive nationalism"), or by mistaken regional integration policies. The bureaucratic-authoritarian military regimes of the 1970s were certainly responsible for fiscal deficits and unnecessary military expenditures. Yet their policies of indebted industrialisation would have *not* resulted in the severe slump of the 1980s hadn't it been for the draconian US-sponsored IMF stabilisation programs (basically aimed at protecting US banks) implemented by their civilian successors in the 1980s.

Cohen celebrates the end of the search for a "third way" between socialism and capitalism in Latin America arguing that the emergence of "a new, more positive form of nationalism" is good, whereas the "old" defensive nationalism of the ISI era was "bad." Similarly, Sebastian Edwards considers the Latin American reforms of the 1980s and early 1990s as "impressive," arguing that "by 1992 the [neoliberal] reforms were beginning to bear fruit, as more and more countries began to recover and to experience higher rates of growth."[57] Yet the inability of the neoliberal model to promote *sustained* growth became evident after the Asian crisis of 1997-1998 when even Brazil, the largest economy in the region, fell victim to radical financial liberalisation and the vagaries of short-term mobile capital.

There are several problems with the celebration of the introduction of neoliberal reforms in Latin America. Clarifying these problems is essential to determine whether the new regionalism is just an instrument to "manage" economic reforms or, alternatively, an autonomous response to the emergence of regional trading blocs in other parts of the world (see chapter 3). Edwards argues that the "old" inward-oriented development model in Latin America was a failure by comparison to the export-led model of development in East Asia. Yet East Asia is less of a "model" after the Asian crisis of 1997 that has shown the vulnerabilities of "open" models of economic development to financial crashes.

Second, Cohen blames the inward-oriented development model for the persistence of poverty in the region, without recognising, as Enrique Iglesias does, that the implementation of the neoliberal model, which began during the "lost decade" of the 1980s, has only exacerbated the problem. For whom have "structural adjustment" programs been successful? As Walden Bello points out,

> Judged by its ostensible objectives–resolving the debt problems of Third World economies and bringing about renewed and sustained growth while reducing poverty and unemployment–structural adjustment has been a resounding failure.[58]

Chile is often presented by those who celebrate the introduction of neoliberal reforms in the region as the success story of the New Latin American consensus and a "role model" for the rest of Latin America.[59] Yet even in Chile economic structural adjustment has had a devastating impact on income distribution:

> Not surprisingly, between 1980 and 1990, the proportion of families below "the line of destitution" had risen from 12 to 15 percent and of those living below the

poverty line (but above the line of destitution) from 24 to 26 percent. This meant that at the end of the Pinochet era, some 40 percent, or 5.2 million people out of 13 million were now classified as poor in a country that had once boasted a large middle class.[60]

Third, the world financial crisis of 1997-1999 has revived the search for a "third way" between unfettered market liberalism and the now discredited socialist route to economic development. This is a search for "capitalism with a human face" (social justice) similar (even if not equal) to the search for a "third way" that Cohen quickly dismisses together with the concept of "defensive economic nationalism." Rather than a "religious conversion," the adoption of the neoliberal model by Latin American elites in the late 1980s and early 1990s can be seen as the product of a cost benefit analysis, summarised in Menem's claim that he had "no alternative" but to adopt in Argentina the economic reforms "suggested" by the Washington Consensus. From this perspective, it is too simplistic to see Mercosur (and other examples of the "new regionalism") as simply facilitating the "thorough" insertion of the Southern Cone economies in the new "global" economy. There is more to Mercosur than being an instrument to manage neoliberal economic reforms. The "open" side of Mercosur should not obscure the fact that it is a new form of defensive regionalism. Arguably, globalization has shifted relative gains concerns to the inter-regional level.[61] The new regionalism of the 1990s pools sovereignty to achieve defensive economic goals at the regional level. It can be seen, as a new form of *defensive* economic "nationalism" that has more in common with the "old" nationalism than globalization fundamentalists would have us believe. As Robert Wade notes, regional variations will be crucial in defining the world economy in the new millennium, that may be characterised by "many capitalisms" rather than by an overarching "globalization" model.[62]

Fourth, the Asian crisis of 1997-1998 has challenged the assumption that there is no alternative to unrestrained neoliberal, market-dominated development. The threat of a world slump produced a backlash in Asia and revived the search for alternatives to the neoliberal model in Latin America.[63] A regional backlash against globalization is not likely in the near future; the new class of "transnational capitalists" in the region still obtains substantial benefits from globalization. Yet Brazilian President Cardoso has publicly called for a new "Southern Consensus" and several Asian governments challenged in the second quarter of 1998 IMF-prescribed austerity programs, expanding domestic demand and introducing several restrictions on the free movement of capital across national borders. Most notably, Malaysia imposed exchange controls on September 1, 1998, in response to speculative attacks on its currency. This shows that the neoliberal model has more serious problems than the ones examined by Sebastian Edwards in his analysis of the Mexican *peso* crisis of 1994.[64]

"Prudent macroeconomics management" may not be enough to deal with the challenge of mobile capital flows. According to recent press reports, Argentina and Brazil are sympathetic with the European Union's proposal to build a new "global architecture" dividing the world into monetary zones to protect individual countries from attacks on their currencies by mobile capital that can now so easily go in and out of a country. As of this writing (June 1999) the Argentine-Brazilian effort to revive Mercosur (see chapter 3) seems to suggest that both countries are moving in the direction of a subregional (or South American) monetary union, along the lines of the EU proposal.

Conclusion: "Open Regionalism" and the New Regionalism: A Future Unlike the Past?

The dominant rationale for the "new regionalism" in Latin America is the concept of "open regionalism." It is often defined as part of the broader neoliberal agenda of economic reforms inspired by the "Washington Consensus," with five characteristics:
1) Outward-oriented, "open" policies to reduce official and non-official barriers to trade.
2) Open to foreign investment, capital, and technology.
3) Market-driven.
4) Favouring across-the-board, automatic tariff reductions, instead of the selective, piecemeal approach of the old regionalism.
5) Clearly available opportunities for accession by non-members.[65]

"Open regionalism" is a fuzzy concept. The central premise is that regional arrangements should serve as "springboards" to integrate member states in the global economy. Closer economic integration among neighbours is seen as a lever to boost Latin American exports to world markets. The concept was first used to analyse economic co-operation in the Asia-Pacific region and then applied by ECLAC to describe regional integration in Latin America in the early 1990s.[66] Yet it is not clear whether "open regionalism" only applies to free trade areas or also to customs unions (FTAs with a common external tariff),[67] and whether it is fundamentally different from "discriminatory" integration, since by definition regional trade agreements give preferences to members as against non-members. Customs unions and free trade areas are permitted under GATT article XXIV. However, as a recent study points out, "most existing and potential regional agreements are *against* GATT rules" which "are not enforced because much of the motivation for regional blocs is political rather than economic."[68]

Some writers claims that free trade areas can complement World Trade Organisation (WTO) multilateralism[69] if they are "open," leaving their members outward-looking, multilaterally oriented, and active participants in the WTO; while resulting in net trade creation rather than net trade diversion and without provoking other countries to form their own regional groupings for purely defensive reasons.[70]

Yet the achievement of genuinely "open" regionalism proved to be a "daunting task" in Latin America.[71] The socio-economic hardships imposed by neoliberal readjustment programs created difficulties to lower trade barriers among parties, as shown by the Argentine-Brazilian trade disputes in Mercosur, and its difficulties to negotiate a common external tariff without establishing important exceptions for certain countries and certain "strategic" goods and services (see chapter 3). Openness to new members also created problems of implementation, since none of the new subregional agreements had transparency accession clauses; and most importantly, "there would be scant motivation to share existing benefits with non-member countries if the integration scheme were working well."[72] The typical example is Mexico's obvious lack of interest in extending NAFTA to other Latin American countries, thus losing its privileged exclusive access to the lucrative US market. In the process, "open" regionalization became "bounded" regionalization as subregional integration agreements in South America consolidated themselves (particularly Mercosur) and the US failed to impose a hub-and-spoke structure (with the US/NAFTA as the hub) to the FTAA negotiations.[73]

Neoliberal scholars present the "open regionalism" of the 1990s as part of the broader agenda of economic reforms of a new Latin American consensus on the advantages of free markets, privatisation of public enterprises, and export promotion policies. Yet Chile, considered the "role model" of the emerging "consensus," practised unilateral trade liberalisation policies well into the 1990s and only joined Mercosur (as an associate member) in 1996. On the other hand, Brazil continued to stress import-substitution industrialisation as a development strategy in the first half of the 1990s, while selectively adopting certain elements of the "Washington Consensus." Moreover, as we have seen, in the original ECLA doctrine of regional integration, ISI and enhanced export growth are not incompatible. The Brazilian proposal for a

South American Free Trade Area (SAFTA) is not in principle incompatible with "open regionalism" defined as closer South American economic co-operation as a lever to boost South American exports to world markets.

Although originally inspired by the neoliberal model, the new regional integration efforts in Latin America acquired a life of their own as they began integrating with each other *around* the United States, *not* with the United States. The neoliberal model envisaged an US-centred (or NAFTA-centred) hemispheric free trade agreement. Yet as we will see in chapter 4, between the Summits of the Americas in Miami (December 1994) and Santiago (April 1998) the US-centred hub-and-spoke model lost clout and Mercosur's independent diplomacy threatened the US bid to be at the centre of the FTAA negotiations. Now the new subregional arrangements have the potential to become autonomous trading blocs and/or merge into a South American Free Trade Area (SAFTA) if the FTAA does not come into existence. Part of the reason they have acquired a life of their own is that the Latin American countries have shown greater interest in trade liberalisation than the United States.[74]

Analysts could not foresee in the late 1980s the emergence of a new regionalism. On the contrary, the bleak picture created by the debt crisis led some scholars to believe that LAIA/ALADI would suffer a slow death, becoming totally irrelevant because of its "inherent weaknesses."[75]

The revitalisation of old regional integration agreements, with ambitious time frames, and the creation of new ones, such as Mercosur, took analysts by surprise. These agreements involve not only trade liberalisation but also a whole set of complex issues, such as harmonisation of macroeconomics policies. Both Mercosur and the revived Andean Community (AC) intend to establish common markets.

The new movement toward regional integration has sometimes been described as simply resulting from the adoption by the Latin American elites of free-market oriented economic policies. According to Stephan Haggard, "In Latin America, wide-ranging economic reforms *preceded* the consideration of regional integration agreements; this was no less true in Mexico and NAFTA than for the rest of the hemisphere."[76] Yet as we will see in the next chapter, it is a mistake to equate Mexico's motivations to join NAFTA (the paradigmatic example of "open regionalism") with those of the rest of Latin America. For one thing, the Latin American countries did not at first request to join NAFTA. On the contrary, they signed an array of bilateral trilateral, and multilateral, criss-crossing agreements among themselves. Secondly, as we have seen, there is a long history of regional integration efforts in Latin America. The economic reforms of the second half of the 1980s did not cause the new regionalism, even if they affected the ideology behind it. It is impossible to understand the new regionalism without situating it in a historical context. Moreover, an excessive emphasis on market reforms as the independent variable has led some analysts to an "end of history" argument; there is no room for autonomous trading blocs if globalization is unstoppable and irreversible.[77]

The first example of the new regionalism, the Argentine-Brazilian Treaty of 1988 (to create a common market in ten years) was signed in the middle of the "lost decade" of the 1980s. Argentina and Brazil were particularly affected by the debt crisis. Yet Mercosur was not "imposed" by the International Monetary Fund (IMF.) Even if it adopted the rhetoric of "open regionalism" it is an autonomous endeavour. The uniqueness of Mercosur and the meaning and prospects of the new regionalism in South America form the subject matter of the next chapter.

Notes

1 See e.g., Hirschman, A, 1979, "The turn to Authoritarianism in Latin America and the Search for Its Economic Determinants," in Collier, D. (ed.), *The New Authoritarianism in Latin America*, Princeton (NJ), Princeton University Press, pp. 61-98.
2 Wionczek, M., 1970, "The Rise and the Decline of Latin American Economic Integration," in *Journal of Common Market Studies* 9, pp. 49-66, p. 60.
3 Genberg, H. & De Simone, F.N., 1993, "Regional Integration Agreements and Macroeconomic Discipline," p. 173, in Anderson, K. & Blackhurst, R. (eds.), *Regional Integration and the Global Trading System*, New York, Harvester/Wheatsheaf.
4 The 14-member *Rio Group* is an important mechanism for political consultation among South American leaders. Originally known as the *Group of Eight*, it was created in December 1986 as a follow-up to the Contadora Initiative, between Argentina, Brazil, Colombia, Mexico, Peru, Uruguay, Venezuela, and Panama. Chile, Ecuador, Bolivia, and Paraguay became members in October 1990. After its first presidential summit (Acapulco, November 1987), the *Group of Eight* focused on the best ways to achieve full conditions for lasting peace and security in Latin America.
5 Evaluation requested by the Presidents of the Rio Group in the Caracas Declaration, ALADI Report CR.DL, March 15, 1991. My translation.

6   See Bulmer-Thomas, V., 1997, "Regional Integration in Latin America Before the Debt Crisis: LAFTA, CACM and the Andean Pact," p. 249, in El-Agraa, A. (ed.), *Economic Integration Worldwide*, New York, St. Martin's Press, pp. 230-252.
7   Ffrench-Davis, R., 1995, "Trends in Regional Cooperation in Latin America: The Crucial Role of Intra-Regional Trade", p. 90, in Teunissen, J. (ed.), *Regionalism and the Global Economy: The Case of Latin America and the Caribbean*, The Hague, FONDAD, pp. 90-118.
8   See Van Klaveren, A., 1993, "Why Integration Now? Options for Latin America," p. 115, in Smith, P. (ed.), *The Challenge of Integration: Europe and the Americas*, New Brunswick (NJ), Transaction Publishers, pp. 115-148.
9   See Iglesias, E., 1993, "The New Latin America and the Inter-American Development Bank," *The Washington Quarterly* 16, p. 118.
10 Grugel, J., 1996, "Latin America and the Remaking of the Americas," p. 136, in Gamble, A. & Payne A. (eds.), *Regionalism and World Order*, London, Macmillan Press, pp. 131-167.
11 Fishlow, A., 1990, "The Latin American State," *Journal of Economic Perspectives* 4 (3), pp. 61-74, p. 63.
12 Weintraub, S., 1993, "Western Hemisphere Free Trade: Probability or Pipe Dream?" pp. 14-15, in Weintraub, S. (ed.), *Free Trade in the Western Hemisphere, The Annals of the American Academy of Political and Social Science*, 526 (March), pp. 9-24.
13 Hirschman, 1979, *op. cit.*, p. 73, note 20.
14 Alexander, R., 1995, "Import Substitution in Latin America in Retrospect," p. 163, in: Dietz, J. (ed.), *Latin America's Economic Development: Confronting Crisis*, Boulder (CO), Lynne Rienner, pp. 159-166.
15 See Weintraub, 1993, *op. cit.*, p. 15.
16 See Cohen, I., 1993, "A New Latin American and Caribbean Nationalism," p. 43, in Weintraub, S. (ed.), *Free Trade in the Western Hemisphere, op. cit.*, pp. 36-46.
17 Edwards, S., 1993, "Latin American Economic Integration: A New Perspective on an Old Dream," in *The World Economy* 16 (3), pp. 317-338, p. 324.
18 See Salazar-Xirinachs, J., 1993, "The Integrationist Revival: A Return to Prebisch's Policy Prescriptions?" in *CEPAL Review* 50, pp. 21-40.
19 See Schwartz, G., 1996, "Brazil, Mercosur and SAFTA: Destructive Restructuring or Pan-American Integration," p. 143, in Nishijima, S. & Smith, P. (eds.), *Cooperation or Rivalry? Regional Integration in the Americas and the Pacific Rim*, Boulder (CO), Westview Press, pp. 129-149.
20 When NAFTA entered into force in 1994 the members of the Association of Southeast Asian Nations (ASEAN) were concerned about the prospects for a "Fortress North America" that would thwart the future growth of their economies: "Asian countries argue that the principle of 'open regionalism'

behind NAFTA is protectionism under another name." Roett, R., 1993, "Why Integration Now? US Interests and Purposes," in Smith, P. (ed.), *The Challenge of Integration, op. cit.*, p. 97.
21 Axline, W.A., 1977, "Underdevelopment, Dependence, and Integration: The Politics of Regionalism in the Third World", in *International Organization*, 31 (1), pp. 83-105, pp. 84-85.
22 See e.g., Weintraub, 1993, *op. cit.*, p. 14; Hufbauer, G. & Schott, J., 1994, *Western Hemisphere Economic Integration*, Washington, DC, Institute for International Economics, p. 64.
23 Alexander, 1995, *op. cit.*, p. 160.
24 See Petras, J. & Morley, M., 1992, *Latin America in the Time of Cholera*, New York, Routledge; Richards, D., 1997, "Dependent Development and Regional Integration: A Critical Examination of the Southern Cone Common Market," *Latin American Perspectives*, vol. 24 (6), pp. 133-155.
25 See Tussie, D., 1982, "Latin American Integration: From LAFTA to LAIA," *Journal of World Trade Law*, vol. 16 (September/October), p. 410.
26 Ffrench-Davis, R., 1995, *op. cit.*, p. 94, emphasis added.
27 Bulmer-Thomas, 1997, *op. cit.*, p. 236.
28 Edwards, S., 1993, *op. cit.*, p. 320.
29 Wionczek, M., 1966, "The Latin American Free Trade Association: Toward Economic Cooperation," in *International Political Communities: An Anthology*, Garden City (NY), Anchor Books, pp. 322-323.
30 Ibid., pp. 323-324. See also Denham, R., 1969, "The Role of the US as an External Actor in the Integration of Latin America", *Journal of Common Market Studies*, vol. 7 (3), pp. 199-216, esp. p. 207.
31 Prebisch, R., 1964, "Toward a Dynamic Development Policy for Latin America," p. 89. Quoted in Wionczek, 1966, *op. cit.*
32 Cardoso, E. & Fishlow, A., 1989, "Latin American Economic Development: 1950-1980," NBER Working Paper No. 3161, p. 14.
33 Brazil was particularly affected by the sharp rise in the price of oil in 1973-74 and again in 1979-80.
34 "From 1973 to 1979 real growth in industrial countries averaged 3.2 percent annually. It then fell to 1.2 percent in 1980-81 and -0.3 percent in 1982," International Monetary Fund, *World Economic Outlook*, 1983. Quoted in Cline, W., 1983, *International Debt and the Stability of the World Economy*, Cambridge (MA), MIT Press.
35 See Iglesias, E., 1985, "External Debt Problems of Latin America," in Wionczek, M. & Tomassini, L. (eds.), *Politics and Economics of External Debt Crisis: The Latin American Experience*, Boulder (CO), Westview Press, pp. 73-96. See also *The Economist*, 6/3/82, pp. 16 and 80, and *World Financial Markets*, June 1983, p. 7. For example, 1983 was Brazil's third year

of recession and GDP dropped 3.9 percent. Industrial production declined 7.9 percent and in 1984 it was only at 1977 levels.
36 "Real interest rates, which had fluctuated between +2 and -2 percent for nearly a decade, rose sharply, ranging between +5 and +10 percent during 1981-1982," Weinert, R., 1983, "Banks and Bankruptcy," *Foreign Policy* (Spring), pp. 138-149.
37 Fishlow, A., 1985, "Coping with the Creeping Crisis of Debt," p. 104, in Wionczek & Tomassini, *op. cit.*
38 See Lipson, C., 1981, "The International Organization of Third World Debt," in *International Organization*, vol. 35 (4), pp. 603-631.
39 See Iglesias, 1985, *op. cit.* The prolongation of the recession in the centre brought about a liquidity crisis there, which made itself felt in an upsurge of demand for credit. As this demand for credit coincided with stabilisation policies centring on monetary restrictions, it generated unusually high interest rates. Iglesias shows how "the real cost of credit for Latin America increased spectacularly between 1981 and 1982, while there was a sharp drop in export prices" (ibid. p. 79). Obviously, it was beyond the Latin American countries' reach to control these systemic, external factors.
40 There is a double standard in Northern criticism of the ISI development strategy, considering that Northern countries promoted local production of manufactured goods via protective trade barriers at earlier stages of their development; while spending significant percentages of their gross domestic products in military expenditures and arms purchases. As far as nuclear non-proliferation is concerned, the US policy was "do as I say, not as I do," continuing its nuclear energy program and nuclear weapons build up while condemning Argentina and Brazil for having independent nuclear energy programs.
41 Iglesias, E., 1993, "The New Latin America and the Inter-American Development Bank," in *Washington Quarterly* 16 (1), pp. 115-125, p. 118.
42 See Urquidi, V., 1993, "Free Trade Experience in Latin America and the Caribbean," in Weintraub, S. (ed.), *Free Trade in the Western Hemisphere, op. cit.*, pp. 63-64; Fishlow, A., 1990, "The Latin American State," *Journal of Economic Perspectives*, vol. 4 (3), pp. 61-74, p. 64.
43 See Ocampo, J., 1985, "Financial Aspects of Intra-regional Trade in Latin America," in Gauhar, A. (ed.), *Regional Integration: The Latin American Experience*, Boulder (CO), Westview Press, p. 114; Genberg, H. & De Simone, F., 1993, "Regional Integration Agreements and Macroeconomics Discipline," in Anderson, K. & Blackhurst, R. (eds.), *Regional Integration and the Global Trading System*, New York, Harvester/Wheatsheaf, p. 173.

44 See O'Donnell, G., 1994, "Some Reflections on Redefining the Role of the State," in Bradford, C. (ed.), *Redefining the State in Latin America*, Paris, Organization for Economic Cooperation and Development.
45 Urquidi, 1993, *op. cit.*, p. 62.
46 Gills, B., 1997, "Whither Democracy? Globalization and the 'New Hellenism'," in Thomas, C. & Wilkin, P. (eds.), *Globalization and the South*, New York, St. Martin's Press, p. 65.
47 "Plan of Action," Latin American Economic Conference, Quito, 9-13 January 1984, pp. 1-2, published by the SELA Permanent Secretariat.
48 This pressure has been documented by Jerome Levinson, on the basis of his personal experience as a former General Counsel to the Inter-American Development Bank (IADB). He gave details of US diplomatic pressure on the governments of presidents Alfonsin (Argentina) and Sarney (Brazil) at a talk at the University of Wisconsin-Madison, Fall 1990. See also Levinson, J., 1999, "The International Financial System: A Flawed Architecture," *Fletcher Forum of World Affairs*, vol. 23, pp. 10-14.
49 Ibid., p. 10.
50 See O'Donnell, G., 1985, "External Debt: Why Don't Our Governments Do the Obvious?" *CEPAL Review* 27, pp. 27-33.
51 Shepherd, M., 1994, "US Domestic Interests and the Latin American Debt Crisis," in Stubbs, R. & Underhill, G. (eds.), *Political Economy and the Changing Global Order*, New York, St. Martin's Press, p. 309.
52 See among others, Mahon, J., 1996, *Mobile Capital and Latin American Development*, University Park (PA), Pennsylvania State University Press; Haggard, S. & Maxfield, S., "The Political Economy of Financial Internationalization in the Developing World," pp. 209-239, in Keohane, R. & Milner, H. (eds.), 1996, *Internationalization and Domestic Politics*, Cambridge (UK), Cambridge University Press.
53 The first net positive transfer of funds (nearly $7 billion) to the region only occurred in 1991, thanks to an increase in the flow of foreign capital, combined with lower interest payments. See Iglesias, 1993, *op. cit.*, p. 116.
54 See *La Prensa* (Buenos Aires), 11/7/89, p. 4. Quoted in Mahon, 1996, p. 131, note 36.
55 Hufbauer & Schott, 1994, *op. cit.*, p. 65.
56 Cohen, I., 1993, "A New Latin American and Caribbean Nationalism," in Weintraub, S. (ed.), *Free Trade in the Western Hemisphere*, *op. cit.*, p. 37.
57 See Edwards, S., 1995, *Crisis and Reform in Latin America: From Despair to Hope*, New York, Oxford University Press, p. 6.
58 Bello, W., 1996, "Structural Adjustment Programs: 'Success' for Whom?" in Mander, J. & Goldsmith, E. (eds.), *The Case Against the Global Economy and for a Turn toward the Local*, San Francisco, Sierra Club Books, p. 293.

59 See Edwards, 1995, *op. cit.*, p. 53.
60 Bello, 1996, *op. cit.*, p. 291.
61 See Whiting, Jr., V., 1993, "The Dynamics of Regionalization: Road Map to an Open Future?" *op. cit.*, pp. 22-30.
62 See Wade, R., 1998-99, "The Coming Fight Over Capital Flows," *Foreign Policy*, vol. 113, pp. 41-54.
63 See Conger, L., 1998, "A Fourth Way? The Latin American Alternative to Neoliberalism," in *Current History* (November), pp. 380-384.
64 See Edwards, 1995, *op. cit.*, chapter 9, "The Mexican Crisis of 1994 and the Future of the Latin American Reforms," pp. 295-314.
65 See Saborio, 1992, *op. cit.*, p. 17; Smith, 1996, *op. cit.*, p. 307; Bhalla & Bhalla, 1997, *op. cit.*, p. 21.
66 See Garnaut, R., 1994, "Open Regionalism: Its Analytical Basis and Relevance to the International System," *Journal of Asian Economics*, vol. 5 (2), pp. 273-290; Economic Commission for Latin America and the Caribbean (ECLAC), 1994, *Open Regionalism in Latin America and the Caribbean: Economic Integration as a Contribution to Changing Production Patterns with Social Equity*, Santiago, Chile, United Nations.
67 Manfred Mols suggests that "open regionalism" only applies to "soft" integration via free trade areas, "which are regarded as better starting points for globalization than are nation-states acting alone... Self-sufficient blocs, closed common markets, exclusionary institutional frameworks, and monopolistic ways of representation vis-à-vis the external world are to be avoided," Mols, 1996, *op. cit.*, p. 19.
68 Committee for Development Planning, 1990, *Regional Trading Blocs: A Threat to the Multilateral Trading System?*, New York, United Nations, p. 25.
69 The WTO is the successor to the General Agreement on Tariffs and Trade (GATT).
70 See e.g., Lipsey, R., 1992, "Getting There: The Path to a Western Hemisphere Free Trade Area and Its Structure," in Saborio, S. (ed.), *The Premise and the Promise*, *op. cit.*, p. 98.
71 See Smith, P., 1996, *Talons of the Eagle*, *op. cit.*, p. 310.
72 Ibid.
73 See chapter 4. On the difference between "bounded regionalization" and "open regionalization" see Whiting, Jr., 1993, *op. cit.*, pp. 41-42.
74 See Bhalla & Bhalla, 1997, p. 155.
75 See Gordon Mace, 1988, "Regional Integration in Latin America: A Long and Winding Road," *International Journal*, vol. 43, pp. 404-427, p. 422.
76 Stephan Haggard, 1996, "The Political Economy of Regionalization in Asia and the Americas," pp. 8-9, in Van R. Whiting, Jr. (ed.), *Regionalization in the World Economy: NAFTA, the Americas and Asia Pacific*, New Delhi, Macmillan India.

77 Even Sebastian Edwards, a strong advocate of neoliberal reforms for Latin America, recognises that "there is little doubt that, as we approach the twenty-first century, the world economy is moving toward the formation of a small number of trading blocs," Edwards, S., 1995, *Crisis and Reform in Latin America, op. cit.*, p. 142.

3 Mercosur: Building Block or Stumbling Block towards a Free Trade Area of the Americas?

Introduction: What is "New" in the New Regionalism?

There is a growing literature on the new regionalism in Latin America and other parts of the Third World. There is a sense that the new regionalism is different from the old regionalism but as Percy Mistry points out, much of the literature is ambiguous and confusing:

> What is also striking is that in discussing the new, open regionalism (and whether it is a threat or not to multilateralism), different sources appear to be talking about entirely different concepts. There is an absence of definitional focus on what the new regionalism actually is.[1]

The absence of definitional focus is reflected in the variety of terms used to describe the new regionalism: "deep integration" (as opposed to "shallow integration"); "open regionalism"; "soft regionalism," "market integration." The problem is compounded by the dominance of economic arguments. As Percy Mistry points out, "trade economists have monopolised debate on regional integration since the invention of Vinerian analysis in the early 1950s."[2] Consequently, mainstream analyses of the new regionalism excessively focus on the "trade creation/trade diversion" issue, thus neglecting the *political* dimensions of the new regionalism. Yet as Mistry also notes, the new wave of regional integration efforts is probably not just a passing fad: states are turning to regionalism "as a practically more realistic and more feasible approach" even if it is sub-optimal according to neoliberal trade theory.

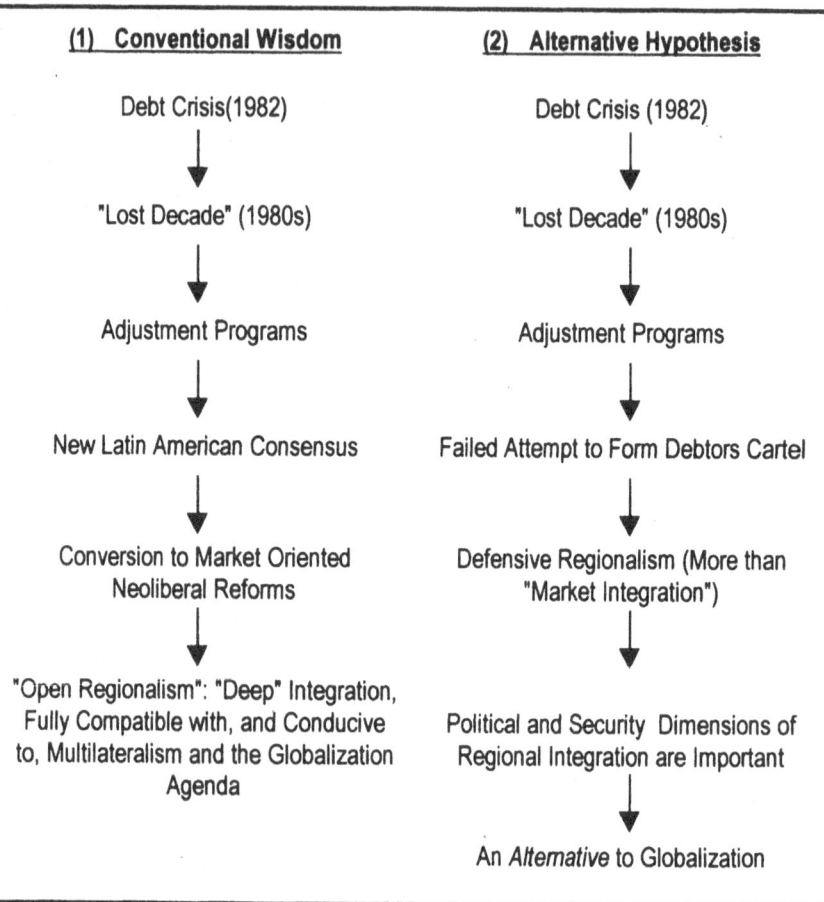

Figure 3.1 Two Views of the New Regionalism

The monopoly of the debate on the new regionalism by trade economists has focused on the question of whether the new regionalism is compatible or antithetical (if not dangerous) to multilateralism.[3] As Mistry points out: "The literature still tends to assume that regionalization is *per se* bad and multilateralization is *per se* good."[4] Economists distrust regionalism because trading blocs are potentially "trade diverting" and incompatible with WTO (World Trade Organization) rules. Globalization fundamentalism and the "inevitability assumption" have led some scholars to interpret the new regionalism as just an (important) aspect of globalization, or as an accessory to the global logic of economic liberalisation (see chapter 1). The unilinear logic of the conventional wisdom on this subject is presented in figure 3.1. An alternative hypothesis, however, is that the new regionalism is not just driven by the "logic of the market" and has an autonomous political dynamics of its own (summarised in the Latin American claim that there is "life after debt") that goes beyond the logic of globalization and could lead to a renegotiation of the rules of the game in the international political economy. As Mistry points out, one could argue that "the new regionalism is being resorted to because the old multilateralism does not seem to work any longer; at least not for the benefit of most of its members."[5] If this alternative hypothesis is correct (see figure 3.1) the new regional integration agreements can be seen as an alternative to globalization rather than as potential building blocks to a new multilateralism; there is no guarantee that they will "land" in a new multilateralism and not become rather permanent rival trading blocs.

1. Mercosur, the New Approach towards Regional Integration in South America

On March 26, 1991, the heads of state of Argentina, Brazil, Paraguay, and Uruguay met in the Paraguayan capital to sign the Treaty of Asunción. The purpose of the meeting was to establish "a common market that must be ready to function by 31 December 1994, and will be called the Common Market of the South (Mercosur)."[6] The rationale for such an ambitious project is stated in the preamble to the treaty. Mercosur was a response to the "evolution of international events, especially the consolidation of major economic blocs, and the need to occupy an appropriate place in the international community."[7]

This chapter examines Mercosur's prospects for survival in the complex dynamics between globalization and regionalization. The first section summarises the history, achievements, and limitations of Mercosur as an inter-governmental organisation. Next, I discuss two alternative models of Mercosur and its internal contradictions since it became an imperfect customs union in January 1995. Section 3 considers the issue of "open regionalism" and the Brazilian proposal to create a South American Free Trade Area (SAFTA). Section 4 estimates whether a "perverse" diversion of trade is developing in Mercosur. Section 5 analyses Mercosur's international relations and its independent approach to the FTAA negotiations. The concluding section examines the future of Mercosur after the Brazilian economic crisis of January/February 1999.

Whether regional blocs are building blocks or stumbling blocks in post-GATT multilateral trade liberalisation is a controversial issue among economists.[8] At the Second Summit of the Americas (Santiago, Chile, April 1998) 34 heads of government in the Western hemisphere formally launched negotiations to create a "Free Trade Area of the Americas" (FTAA) by 2005. These negotiations compel the Latin American countries (with the exception of Mexico) to decide whether they are ready to pay the price of weakening, or even renouncing, to their autonomous subregional integration schemes in exchange for gaining unlimited access to the big US market. The FTAA process creates a particularly excruciating dilemma for Mercosur, because it is already a customs union and has gone a long way toward the formation of an autonomous regional trading bloc. Will Mercosur accommodate US demands during the negotiations to create the Free Trade Area of the Americas (FTAA)? Will Mercosur become a protectionist trading bloc, thus becoming an obstacle to the successful negotiation of an FTAA? Would Mercosur survive the establishment of an FTAA in 2005?

Mercosur drew on integration efforts going back to the 1960s (see chapter 2). The four Mercosur countries (Argentina, Brazil, Paraguay, and Uruguay) embrace an area larger than the continental United States, with 50 percent of the population, 58 percent of the gross domestic product and 40 percent of the total foreign trade of the Latin American Integration Association (LAIA). Mercosur is the third largest trading bloc of the world (after the EU and NAFTA); its four member states have a combined population of 200 million and an aggregate GDP of over US$ 800 billion. Like NAFTA, which followed the Canada-US Free Trade Agreement, Mercosur resulted from specific steps taken by Argentina and Brazil in the mid-1980s: the bilateral 1986 Program for Economic Integration and Cooperation (PEIC, PICAB, in Spanish) and the Treaty for Integration, Cooperation, and Development (TICD) signed in November 1988 with the purpose of creating a binational common market in ten years. Several factors contributed to the *rapprochement* between Argentina and Brazil, including the transitions to democracy in both countries in the 1980s, and the adoption of neoliberal policies of economic adjustment aimed at stabilising their economies in response to the debt crisis (see chapter 2).

The Treaty of Asuncion has three fundamental components: First, it calls for the total liberalisation of trade among member countries. Second, it envisions the establishment of a common external tariff (CET) and a common trade policy vis-à-vis outside parties. Third, it promotes the co-ordination and harmonisation of macroeconomics policies in order to eliminate asymmetries that might distort the operation of the common market.

The Mercosur partners had agreed in the Treaty of Asuncion to create a common market by 31 December 1994. However, at the Colonia Presidential Summit in Uruguay (January 1994) the four heads of state decided that at the end of 1994 Mercosur would become just a customs union, thus postponing the creation of a common market beyond the end of the century.[9]

In August 1994 a presidential summit in Buenos Aires defined the main features of the transition to a common market, beginning on January 1, 1995. This summit can be seen as a turning point in the evolution of Mercosur, or as Juan Manuel Rodriguez puts it, the "last opportunity" to save the regional arrangement from extinction. By January 1, 1995 Mercosur was a free trade area, covering 95 percent of intra-regional trade; and an imperfect customs union, with a common external tariff covering about 85 percent of goods traded by the bloc with third countries. Thus, Mercosur emerged as the second largest customs union in the world.[10]

Mercosur survived the regional financial crisis triggered by the bungled devaluation of Mexico's currency in December 1994 which uncovered the structural weaknesses of open regionalism based on structural adjustment and the neo-liberal economic model known as the "Washington Consensus."

Both Argentina and Brazil resisted external pressures to devalue their currencies and the stage of consolidation of Mercosur began with the Protocol of Ouro Preto, signed by the four presidents on 17 December 1994. This agreement confirmed the setting up of a customs union as of January 1995 and Mercosur became an important actor in the world stage, with international juridical personality and the power to sign trade agreements with other countries and international organisations, such as the European Union. On the other hand, Mercosur remained an inter-governmental rather than a supranational organisation, with the following decision-making bodies:

1) The *Common Market Council*, made up of the four ministers of foreign affairs and four economy ministers, is the legal representative of Mercosur. The Council formulates policy, and negotiates and signs agreements with third countries, groups of countries and international organisations.

2) The *Common Market Group* is Mercosur's executive agency, with four representatives from each member country. It submits draft decisions to the Council and adopts the measures necessary for implementing its decisions.

3) "The *Mercosur Trade Commission* includes representatives from all four countries and is responsible for submitting new regulations to the Group, or modifications to trade and customs policy."[11] The Commission can establish technical committees responsible for analysing specific topics and recommending solutions to trade disputes.

According to the Treaty of Asuncion (Annex III) the parties to a controversy would submit their dispute to the Common Market Group which could "establish or call panels of experts or qualified groups to provide technical assessment." The Protocol of Brasilia (December 1991) maintained this system, and there is no permanent body (similar to the European Court of Justice) that can issue final decisions in controversies regarding the construction and application of Mercosur law; or condemn a member state for not complying with its obligations.

At Ouro Preto, the Mercosur partners decided that the system of voting by consensus in the above mentioned institutions would be continued. Therefore, controversies must be handled through diplomatic channels and personal diplomacy between the four heads of state at summit meetings.

Mercosur's "supranationality deficit" has been criticised by scholars who have suggested that it should adopt the EU's system of qualified majority voting, recognising the relative weight of each country in the integration process. There has been talk about establishing a permanent Secretariat. A permanent supra-national court for Mercosur has also been proposed, to issue final interpretations of Mercosur law.[12]

2. Mercosur's Asymmetries and Internal Contradictions: The Two Models of Mercosur

Mercosur is largely dependent on Brazil and Argentina, whose economies are much larger than those of Uruguay and Paraguay. Brazil is the dominant country in Mercosur, with 80 percent of the subregion's population and 65 percent of the subregional domestic product. Argentina follows with 16.9 and 32.3 percent, respectively. At the other extreme, Paraguay and Uruguay represent 2.4 and 1.1 percent, respectively, of the population and 1.6 and 1.8 percent respectively of the domestic product (see table 3.1).

These asymmetries have had an impact on the evolution of Mercosur whose survival has been challenged several times by trade disputes between Argentina and Brazil; whereas the subregional grouping has become a necessity for Paraguay and Uruguay, given their limited domestic markets and their trade dependence on their giant neighbours.

The Argentine-Brazilian axis contributes to 98 percent of industrial production and to 93 percent of Mercosur trade. Pronounced asymmetries also appear at the level of the strategic projection of member states' business enterprises. By late 1994 about 500 Brazilian companies had established themselves in Argentina in a variety of areas, from the food industry to insurance, construction, automobiles, and banking, whereas only 20 Argentine companies had managed to establish themselves in Brazil.[13]

Because of the asymmetries between Brazil and its smaller neighbours Mercosur has been particularly vulnerable to macroeconomics "squalls," as in 1995, during the financial crisis triggered by Mexico's devaluation of the peso (the "tequila effect"). Brazil was never seriously committed to the "deepening" of subregional integration and rather saw Mercosur as an instrument to consolidate its hegemony in South America, while being in a better position to negotiate with the US-led NAFTA bloc.[14] Brazilian policymakers and corporate leaders "reached a broad consensus in support of Mercosur"[15] only after Argentina, Paraguay, and Uruguay agreed to make concessions on the common external tariff.

During the four-year transition period to complete a free trade area (1991-1994) the structural asymmetries between Brazil, on the one hand, and Argentina, Uruguay, and Paraguay, on the other, were exacerbated by the divergent macroeconomics policies of Argentina and Brazil. While Argentina decided to fight inflation by adopting a currency board and pegging the peso to the dollar Brazil was still suffering hyperinflation and was not yet committed to unambiguous trade liberalisation. The gap between both countries' macroeconomics policies was narrowed with the election of Fernando Cardoso as President of Brazil and the adoption of the *Real Plan* in mid-1994, which successfully eliminated hyperinflation and stabilised the local currency. The presidential summits of Fortaleza in December 1996 and of Asunción in July 1997 decided to deepen the customs union, enlarge Mercosur, and advance toward the creation of a "regional identity": administrative headquarters in Montevideo, protocols on education and

Table 3.1 Mercosur and Latin America: Basic Data (1994 figures)

	Argentina	Brazil	Paraguay	Uruguay	Mercosur	Latin America
Population (millions)	34.7*	159	4.8	3.2	206.9**	453.1
Urban Population (percent)	87.1	78.2	49.4	86.0	79.2	74.0
GDP (millions of 1990 dollars)	205.5	412.7	6.9	11.3	664.1**	1,185.7
GDP per capita (thousands of 1990 dollars)	6,066	2,596	1,450	3,576	3,210**	2,617
Rate of GDP growth (1990-94)	7.6	2.2	2.8	4.2	2.7	3.7
Rate of GDP growth (1994)	7.1	5.6	3.3	4.7	6.0	5.0
Manufacturing GDP (%)(in 1993)	28.2	26.3	11.3	21.6	26.7	24.8
Primary Sector GDP (%)(in 1993)	7.9	9.7	29.1	13.4	9.5	9.4

Source: Inter-American Development Bank; World Bank; World Development Report (1997).
* In 1995
** In 1996

cultural integration, and a Mercosur logo.

Yet, as Felix Peña points out, "the vitality of integration does not result so much from an abstract notion of common interests as from the constant exercise of co-ordinating some very real national interests."[16] Since 1991, Mercosur has oscillated between two alternative models of development and regional integration. The first model follows neo-classic orthodoxy and the fundamentalist approach to globalization. From this perspective, Mercosur is a transitory area of trade preferences, in which the markets reflect, without state interference, the centripetal forces of geography and the globalization of world order. For the second model Mercosur is an area of trade preferences in which governments and social and economic agents agree on active policies and strategies. As Aldo Ferrer points out, the purpose of this model is to accomplish development goals and an "intra-regional equilibrium" which are "unachievable when left to the free operation of the market."[17]

For the first model, trade liberalisation is more an end in itself than an industrial policy instrument. Mercosur is just a temporary stage toward the full insertion of member states in the globalized economy and the full acceptance of the "sovereignty of the market." For the second model, Mercosur is "here to stay" as an instrument through which member states agree on active policies to promote economic development, autonomous industrialisation, and sustainable integration.

The Foz de Iguazu Declaration of 30 November 1985 and the Bilateral Integration Treaty between Argentina and Brazil signed in 1988 were inspired by the second model. This treaty and its forerunner, the 1986 Program for Economic Integration and Co-operation, were aimed at promoting active industrial and technological policies at the regional level, with the Argentine and Brazilian states playing an active role in orienting markets and promoting bilateral integration. This approach inspired the establishment of a binational centre for biotechnology, and was reflected in the 24 sector-by-sector protocols on capital goods, agribusiness, and the automotive sector.

Yet the first model became dominant when the Buenos Aires Act of July 1990 replaced an integration strategy based on intrasectoral specialisation with a program of across-the-board, progressive, linear and automatic tariff reductions for most of the bilateral trade. Eight months later this principle would be incorporated to the Treaty of Asuncion.

The rationale for Mercosur was the notion of "open regionalism." Unlike the protectionist, inward-oriented model of regional integration of the 1960s and 1970s, "open" regionalism is often presented as part of a broader agenda of economic reforms. Both President Menem of Argentina and Collor de Melo of Brazil adopted the free market economic policies known as the "Washington Consensus," including opening up the economy to foreign investment, privatisation of state enterprises, and full reliance on market forces to allocate resources. Divergent macroeconomics policies in Argentina and Brazil (arising from different approaches to economic development and different foreign policies vis-à-vis the US) were an important obstacle for implementing this model. Argentina seriously considered joining NAFTA in 1994, a step that would have destroyed Mercosur. While "the lowering of trade tariffs became an integral part of antihyperinflation policy in Argentina, ... Brazil used that approach only marginally as part of long-term industrial policy."[18] In 1991-1994, while Brazil's inflation was accelerating, that in Argentina was declining. Some experts argued that because of this divergence it was virtually impossible for Argentina and Brazil to have a common market and most difficult to establish a customs union, although they could still have a free trade area while keeping an independent trade policy toward non-members.[19]

However, against these predictions, Mercosur made significant progress in liberating intra-regional trade in 1991-1994 and managed to establish the customs union on schedule, adopting a common external tariff beginning January 1, 1995. Since then, Mercosur has become a very successful trading bloc and an actor to be reckoned with in the global arena. Trade within Mercosur has grown fourfold from US$ 5.2 billion in 1991 to US$ 20.3 billion in 1997.[20] Mercosur has now a permanent decision making structure, including an administrative Secretariat, and it has become a major player in multilateral and inter-regional trade negotiations (see section 5).

What model of Mercosur will prevail is an open question. The re-election of Brazilian President Cardoso in November 1998 (under the shadow of severe economic conditions) and the neoliberal economic policies supported by the Frepaso/Radical Party alliance in Argentina seem to suggest that for the moment both countries will continue implementing the "free market" anti-inflationary model, although they may place some restraints on the fundamentalist vision of globalization, especially as far as its negative social consequences are concerned.[21]

The Asian crisis has had a contradictory impact on Mercosur. On the one hand, it has exacerbated old sources of trade disputes, such as the auto industry controversy of 1995, while creating new ones. In June 1995 there was a short "trade war" between Argentina and Brazil, when due to its persistent trade deficit Brazil imposed a temporary quota for imports of motorcars and reduced from 18 percent to 2 percent the tariff on imports of capital goods, components, and raw materials for the sector, thus matching the benefits of the regime granted by Argentina to automobile manufacturers operating in Argentina. There have been conflicts over the sugar industry (protected by Argentina) and it was difficult to negotiate the common external tariff because of Brazil's desire to continue protecting its capital goods, informatics, and telecommunications industries.

Argentina sells 30 percent of all its exports to Brazil, and is sensitive to any changes in its trade regime. Brazil's fiscal adjustment program, which was a requirement to attract a US sponsored 30 billion dollar loan in late 1998, has underlined the tension latent in Argentine-Brazilian trade relations.

In an attempt to counter the impact of the Asian financial crisis, the Brazilian government established an import licensing system for industrial imports, such as toys and electrical goods thus affecting Argentine manufacturers, who have asked the Menem government to make a complaint to Mercosur's Trade Commission. More than 50 percent of Argentine exports to Brazil are manufactured goods. Brazil has also threatened to go to arbitration over Argentina's 23 percent tariff on sugar and Argentina's anti-dumping actions against Brazilian steel. In the past, these controversies have been solved through direct negotiations between the two presidents. Yet the stakes are higher since the Asian crisis, particularly for Argentina, because of its "Brazil-dependency." According to the *Union Industrial Argentina*, 70 percent of Argentina's manufactured exports to Brazil, worth US$ 3 billion are endangered by Brazil's recent protectionist measures. Although the neoliberal model of "open regionalism" seems to have prevailed over a strategy of "sustainable integration" Mercosur has developed a strategy of "multiple alliances" since 1995, thus becoming an actor in the world arena (see section 5).

For Mercosur, deepening subregional integration may become a strategy for survival if there is a full-fledged world slump at the beginning of the new millennium. The four Mercosur partners have already accomplished the first two steps envisaged in the Treaty of Asunción: a free trade area and an imperfect customs union. Yet they have made little progress in the intermediate stages for the formation of a common market (a common trade policy, free circulation of goods, services and production factors) and no progress in the co-ordination of macroeconomics and sectoral policies. Although there has not been much progress either in the ongoing negotiations for a Free Trade Area of the Americas (FTAA) Mercosur runs the danger of extinction if those negotiations are successfully concluded by 2005. If Mercosur wants to survive as an independent entity after the emergence of an FTAA it must become a full customs union on schedule and then move toward a "real" common market.[22]

3. Mercosur and SAFTA: Open Regionalism or Autonomous Trading Bloc?

The model for an open free trade policy is unilateral trade liberalisation, of which Chile in Latin America is a typical example. After withdrawing from the Andean Pact in 1976, Chile decided to stay away from Latin American subregional integration schemes while becoming not only the "model" of neoliberal free market adjustment but also a "global trader" establishing trade links with the Asia-Pacific Economic Co-operation Forum (APEC) and signing bilateral trade agreements with several Latin American countries, including Mexico. Chile lobbied the US to sign a free trade agreement in 1992 and was a serious candidate to join NAFTA after the first Summit of the Americas (Miami, 1994) but it was rebuffed by the US, despite Canadian Prime Minister Chretien's famous statement in Miami: "For one year now, we have been the three amigos. Starting today, we will become the four amigos."[23]

For a while, joining NAFTA seemed to be the best trade strategy for Chile and the rest of Latin America. Yet as US President Clinton failed to obtain from the US Congress "fast-track" authority to negotiate free trade agreements the NAFTA option lost clout and the discourse on regional integration shifted from the "extension of NAFTA" and "NAFTA plus" scenarios to SAFTA, "the most ambitious conceivable model for regional integration without the United States."[24]

The proposal for a South American Free Trade Area (SAFTA) was first outlined by Brazilian President Itamar Franco in September 1993 and was presented to a meeting of ALADI in February 1994. The goal of SAFTA was to create a free trade zone for "substantially all trade" within the subcontinent, through a linear, automatic, and progressive schedule of liberalisation over the ten-year period from 1995 to 2005. By launching SAFTA Brazil was promoting a concept of ALADI without Mexico, "a scheme that would be free of US interference and in which the hegemonic role would inevitably be played by Brazil."[25]

The SAFTA proposal had several purposes: 1) to dissuade Argentina from joining NAFTA; if Argentina did so, reducing trade barriers below the levels provided for by Mercosur would harm the interests of Brazil, Paraguay and Uruguay in specific markets; 2) to capitalise on the experience of Mercosur which had led to a significant growth of intra-group trade (see above); 3) to accumulate negotiating power for future negotiations between Mercosur and NAFTA for the establishment of a Free Trade Area of the Americas (FTAA).

SAFTA is considered a feasible option for the South American countries due to the lack of progress in the FTAA negotiations.[26] Hollist and Nielson even talk about "Mercosur and the *emerging* South American Free Trade Area (SAFTA)."[27] SAFTA is closely associated with Mercosur and the leading role of Brazil. Although the idea of SAFTA was launched before the Protocol of Ouro Preto (December 1994) laid the basis for the consolidation of Mercosur, its feasibility critically depends on the success of ongoing free trade negotiations between Mercosur and the Andean Community. The impulse for SAFTA comes from Mercosur and Brazil, the regional hegemon.

There are two possible "readings" of SAFTA. First, as Sidney Weintraub points out, with the failure on the part of the US to extend NAFTA to Chile, the notion of a South American Free Trade Area took "a life of its own."[28] Originally, SAFTA could be seen as a Brazilian strategy to delay Hemispheric trade talks until the deepening and widening of Mercosur attracted more countries on its side of the negotiating table with the US. The SAFTA proposal had clearly both political and economic dimensions: to revive an old Brazilian geopolitical project of South American as opposed to Latin American integration.

An alternative "reading" of the SAFTA proposal is that Brazil was never really interested in deepening subregional integration with its three smaller Southern Cone neighbours. Intra-regional trade has significantly grown in the last decade and Brazil is more tied in to Mercosur than in 1991. Yet Brazil is still a "global trader": as of 1995 only 11.7 percent of its total trade was with its Mercosur partners, against 27.4 percent for Argentina, 47 percent for Uruguay and 66.4 percent for Paraguay.[29]

Table 3.2 Mercosur: Exceptions to the Common Trade Policy

	Argentina	Brazil	Paraguay	Uruguay
Capital Goods				
Tariff positions	Approx. 1100	Approx. 1100	Approx. 1100	Approx. 1100
Maximum CET	14%	14%	14%	14%
Convergence	1-1-2001	1-1-2001	1-1-2006	1-1-2006
Computers and Telecom				
Tariff positions	Approx. 400	Approx. 400	Approx. 400	Approx. 400
Maximum CET	16%	16%	16%	16%
Convergence	–	–	–	–
National Lists				
Tariff position*	300 / (206)	300 / (0)	399 / (288)	300 / (362)
Products**	R/F: Chemical products; Precision instruments; Steel products; Textiles & footwear; Food products; Rubber F: Mach. and Equip.; Paper; Furniture; Toys; Plastics; Lumber; Transportation Mat..	R/F: Chemicals; Foods F: Mach. and Equip.; Footwear; Petroleum Products; Transportation R: Paper and Cardboard Leather and Furs; Textiles	Chemical products; Mach. and equip.; Toys; Steel; Pharmaceuticals; Textiles & footwear; Foods; Plastics and rubber; Glass and ceramic manufactures; Paper and cardboard	R/F: Steel products; Paper and cardboard R: Chemical products; Mach. and equipment.; Pharmaceuticals; Textiles & Plastics and rubber; Leather and furs; Textiles
Sugar	Common Trade Policy by 2001			
Automotive	Common Trade Policy by 2000			

*The exceptions to the CET resulting from the automatic tariff reduction regime do not count for purposes of the limit established (indicated in parenthesis.) These positions must converge to the agreed upon CET in 1999 for Argentina and Brazil, and a year later for Paraguay and Uruguay. The number of position included is the maximum allowed.

**R: Rising tariff convergence. F: Falling tariff convergence. All of Paraguay excepted products have rising convergence.

Source: INTAL, Mercosur Report No. 1 (July/December 1996), Table IV.1, p. 31. Reproduced by permission of Institute for the Integration of Latin America and the Caribbean (INTAL): Inter-American Development Bank, Buenos Aires, Argentina. Prepared on the basis of Decisions 7/94, 19/94, 29/94, and 16/96, Resoluciones 48/94 and 124/94 and exemption national lists.

From this perspective, SAFTA would be a Brazilian strategy to avoid the deepening of Mercosur, including the creation of a supranational institutional structure. If SAFTA comes into existence, Mercosur could be forced to lower the level of its common external tariff or it might even disappear absorbed by SAFTA as a free trade area, especially if countries strongly committed to the neoliberal model, such as Peru, boycott the establishment of a "reasonable" common external tariff. The problem with this scenario is that external factors such as a deepening of the world economic crisis leading to "beggar-thy-neighbour" policies might lead to a deepening of Mercosur and/or SAFTA thus compelling Brazil to accept supranationality as a necessity. As Roberto Bouzas points out, "if the [Mercosur] customs union and an 'expanding' agenda are to be successfully pursued, a gradually larger share of issues will have to be dealt with by supranational mechanisms rather than inter-governmental negotiations."[30] Of course, the effect of the world economic crisis cuts both ways. On the one hand, it puts pressure on the Mercosur partners to take "deepening" more seriously, accelerating the constitution of a common market and perhaps a common currency. On the other hand, however, a world economic slump might lead to the disintegration of Mercosur if Argentina and Brazil are unable to overcome their trade disputes, exacerbated by the world financial crisis.[31] In turn, whether the first or the second alternative comes into existence depends on whether one considers internal pressures for Co-operation more important than environmental constraints that could convert the "tit-for-tat" of Mercosur's December 1998 summit into a self-destructive zero-sum game between Argentina and Brazil.[32]

Mercosur is generally considered as an example of "open regionalism,"[33] different from the "discriminatory regionalism" of past regional integration efforts in Latin America (LAFTA/ALADI; the Andean Pact, the Central American Common Market). Although the "second model" of Mercosur (see section 2) was abandoned in the early 1990s for a four-year program of linear and automatic trade liberalisation, one may argue that Mercosur does not meet all the criteria for "open regionalism."[34] First, it does not meet the requirement of easy accession by non-members. According to article 20 of the Treaty of Asuncion, ALADI countries could apply for membership in Mercosur only five years after the Treaty came into effect. Second, the goal of achieving a customs union at a fixed date (January 1, 1995) made it difficult for Mercosur to be truly "open." As Nofal points out, by becoming a customs union, the group would behave "as a trading bloc in the sense that it [would] have a common trade policy, and any changes in that policy [would] have to be negotiated jointly by the member countries."[35] Although Mercosur is still an incomplete customs union, in the absence of an FTAA by 2005, Nofal's prediction would be confirmed and the free-trade winds in the Western Hemisphere would die away as both NAFTA and Mercosur (or SAFTA) would become protectionist trading blocs.[36]

4. A "Fortress Mercosur"? The "Trade Creation" vs. "Trade Diversion" Debate

After Mercosur became an imperfect customs union in January 1995, a lively academic debate began about the prospects for a "fortress Mercosur." Was Mercosur more "trade diverting" than "trade creating," using the classical distinction made by Jacob Viner?[37] According to *The Economist*, the answer is negative because even though "some of the rise in trade within Mercosur represents a diversion of trade from outside sources" (e.g., Brazil's decision to buy oil from Argentina rather than Iraq) "the rise in intra-group trade has gone hand-in-hand with an accelerating rise in Mercosur's trade with the rest of the world."[38]

Alexander Yeats argued in 1996 that Mercosur was more "trade diverting" than "trade creating."[39] According to Yeats, the rise in intra-Mercosur exports was in sectors for which it did not have a comparative advantage. Therefore, a "perverse" diversion of trade was developing in Mercosur that was harmful to member states and the world community at large.[40] For example, Argentina and Brazil were increasingly trading with each other capital intensive goods (such as cars and car parts) a fact that could only be explained by the high trade preferences that they had granted to each other in the auto sector. He presented this as "the most convincing, and disturbing, evidence produced so far concerning the welfare reducing effects of regional trade arrangements."[41]

Economists are divided on this issue. Supporters of the Yeats thesis argue that during the transition period to complete a free trade area, intra-regional exports grew more rapidly relative to exports to the rest of the world. As table 3.3 shows, for the subregion as a whole, intra-regional exports rose from 9.1 percent of total exports in 1990 to 18.6 percent in 1994.

Table 3.3 Mercosur: Intra-zonal Exports in US$ Million (as percentage of total exports, 1990-1994)

	1990	1991	1992	1993	1994
Argentina	1,833 (14.8)	1,978 (16.5)	2,327 (19.0)	3,684 (28.1)	4,740 (30.0)
Brazil	1,320 (4.2)	2,309 (7.3)	4,098 (11.4)	5,394 (13.9)	5,918 (13.6)
Paraguay	379 (27.4)	259 (23.1)	246 (22.7)	276 (16.7)	377 (21.7)
Uruguay	712 (42.1)	679 (42.3)	689 (38.3)	1,019 (58.8)	716 (37.4)
Total	4,244 (9.1)	5,225 (11.3)	7,360 (14.5)	10,376 (18.8)	11,751 (18.6)

Source: Bulmer-Thomas V., 1997, "Regional Integration in Latin America since 1985: Open Regionalism and Globalization," in El-Agraa, A. (ed.) *Economic Integration Worldwide,* New York, St. Martin's Press, Table 10.2, p. 258. Reproduced by permission of Macmillan Press Ltd., Basingstoke, Hampshire, UK. © Macmillan Press Ltd 1997.

The low ratio of intra-regional exports to total exports for Mercosur as a whole by comparison to individual countries is a consequence of the low ratio in the case of Brazil: 4.2 percent in 1990 and still 13.6 percent in 1994, compared to 30 percent for Argentina and 37.4 percent for Uruguay in the same year. This is a consequence of the asymmetry between the size of the Brazilian market and that of its smaller partners (see table 3.1).

The main argument in defence of the "open" nature of Mercosur is that its member-states have unilaterally reduced tariffs to third parties since the late 1980s (the average Mercosur tariff on manufactures fell from 25 percent in 1990 to 12 percent in 1995) and that they all have adopted the Uruguay Round commitments to trade liberalisation.

Argentina's *Secretaría de Relaciones Economicas Internacionales*, Robert Devlin, Miguel Rodriguez Mendoza, and Isaac Cohen rebutted the Yeats thesis in a special issue of *Boletim de Integracao Latino-Americana* (December 1996). According to Devlin,

The story of trade diversion must be examined not from the angle of Mercosur's exports, but from the angle of Mercosur's imports, i.e., intra-Mercosur imports relative to imports from the rest of the world. Imports, not exports, should be examined because if preferences divert trade, their application in favor of a few selected partners should be reflected by a "crowding out" of imports from other, presumably more efficient, sources.[42]

From this perspective, there was no trade diversion. As Devlin notes, although the share of intra-Mercosur imports in the subregion's total imports rose from 15 percent to 19 percent, imports from the rest of the world also rose. In the case of NAFTA, from 23 percent to 24 percent of total imports; in the case of the European Union, from 23 percent to 29 percent, and in the case of Japan and the Newly Industrialising Countries from 8 percent to 11 percent.[43]

Preferential trade liberalisation in 1991-1994 within Mercosur raised intra-regional trade in automobiles, chemicals, and transport equipment. With regard to these capital-intensive goods, intra-regional trade may have been expanding at the expense of inter-regional trade, thus confirming the Yeats thesis. Yet, there is no evidence to suggest that the rise in intra-regional imports has been at the expense of imports from outside Mercosur. Both intra-regional imports and from outside Mercosur rose by as much as 180 percent between 1990 and 1995 compared with a 50 percent increase in total exports during the same period.[44]

Other economists have argued that intra-Mercosur trade *has* generated trade diversion, although recognising that it is difficult to estimate its magnitude. According to Renato Baumann, trade diversion is more important for Brazil, a major exporter with high tariff barriers, than for Argentina (see table 3.4). Also, it is more relevant for the latter than for Paraguay and Uruguay, probably because the two smaller Mercosur partners have always been dependent on trade with their larger neighbours.

Other estimates seem to suggest that there has been moderate trade diversion in the cases of Argentina and Brazil, considering the level of the common external tariff finally adopted at Ouro Preto (an arithmetic average of 11.14 percent for 85 percent of tariff items) and the "special arrangements" for the remaining 15 percent of tariff items (including capital goods, computers, and telecommunications equipment, sugar, and automobiles (see table 3.2).[45]

Table 3.4 Estimates of Trade Diversion in Mercosur

		Trade diversion	
	Number of product groups	Relative magnitude of diversion	
		In Intra-zonal exports (%)	In total exports (%)
Argentina	21	25	4
Brazil	98	77	8
Paraguay	--	--	--
Uruguay	3	3	1

Source: Baumann, R., 1993, "Integration and Trade Diversion," in *CEPAL Review*, No. 5 (December). Obtained from Bhalla, A. S. and Bhalla, P., 1997, *Regional Blocs: Building Blocks or Stumbling Blocks?* London, Macmillan Press, Table 6.4, p. 148. Reproduced by permission of Macmillan Press Ltd., Basingstoke, Hampshire, UK. © A. S. Bhalla and P. Bhalla 1997.

Because of Brazilian objections, Mercosur's common external tariff (CET) was only nominally close to the "ideal" CET recommended by neoliberal economists. For example, Sebastian Edwards echoed Yeats's attack on Mercosur when he wrote that "for the case of Argentina, joining a trade agreement with a Brazilian-level common external tariff is likely to result in significant 'trade diversion' that would more than offset any benefits derived from trade creation."[46] Although Brazil made concessions on the CET agreed upon at Ouro Preto, the list of temporary exceptions was important; the CET was set at 11 different levels, from 0 to 20 percent. Each country was allowed to exempt 300 items (399 for Paraguay) and the final "convergence" CETs for imported capital goods (14 percent by 2001) and telecommunications equipment (16 percent by 2006) were higher than the "ideal" CET recommended by Edwards (Argentina's average tariff of 10 percent, because it was the least protectionist). Hence, one may argue that there has been moderate trade diversion for the two largest Mercosur partners, more for Brazil than for Argentina, considering the higher level of protection of its domestic industry.[47]

5. Mercosur as an International Actor: Relations with Other Latin American Countries, NAFTA, and the European Union

Despite the rhetoric of openness, Mercosur was conceived from the beginning as an instrument to increase the Southern Cone countries' bargaining power vis-à-vis northern regional economic blocs in the post-Cold War international environment.[48]

After becoming an imperfect customs union in 1995, Mercosur began projecting itself as an important actor in the world stage. The first step was the widening of Mercosur to reach other South American countries. Mercosur plays an essential role in intra-Latin American trade relations:

> Mercosur countries contribute approximately 40 percent of total LAIA two-way trade flows, while intra-Mercosur trade amounts to over two-thirds of intra-LAIA export-import trade. This makes Mercosur a key player in the process of preferential trade liberalisation in the Western Hemisphere.[49]

As we will see in chapter 4, the course of the FTAA negotiations between the Summits of the Americas in Miami (December 1994) and Santiago, Chile (April 1998) strengthened Mercosur's negotiating position while weakening the ability of the US to successfully negotiate an agenda that would protect its "national interest." After the meeting of the Western Hemisphere's trade ministers at Belo Horizonte, Brazil, in May 1997 Mercosur's "building blocks" approach gained strength. It then became clear that the Free Trade Area of the Americas would not result from the progressive enlargement of NAFTA. By the time of the Santiago Summit, the US found itself sitting down to negotiate an FTAA with a united South American bloc, with Mercosur as its "hard core."

Chile was reluctant to join Mercosur when it was formed in 1991 because it did not want to commit itself to a common external tariff higher than its own tariff rate of 11 percent. Yet as the US proved unable to deliver on its promise to admit Chile to NAFTA, Mercosur became an increasingly attractive alternative for Chile.[50] After two years of negotiations, Chile and Mercosur signed, in July 1996, an agreement to form a free trade area beginning in October 1996. Bolivia and Mercosur signed a similar treaty that entered into force in January 1997. Both Chile and Bolivia are now associate members of Mercosur and regularly attend its summit meetings. Peru sought similar status at the Belo Horizonte trade ministerial meeting (May 1997) and

Venezuela may become an associate of the Southern Cone grouping soon. Colombia and Ecuador are interested in joining Mercosur and negotiations are under way for an Andean Community/Mercosur free trade area. If that happens, Mercosur, instead of NAFTA, would become the pole of attraction for a Free Trade Area of the Americas.

In the absence of US leadership in the FTAA negotiations the South American countries have decided to keep all the options open, multiplying the linkages between them and upgrading their bilateral and subregional agreements. Between the two summits of the Americas Brazil took advantage of the vacuum in US leadership on the FTAA project to reach out to other South American countries so as to establish SAFTA. The SAFTA proposal became increasingly attractive as a NAFTA-centred model for trade liberalisation in the Americas lost clout.

The uncertainties surrounding the FTAA process gave new force to the prospect of a strengthened commercial alliance among the countries of South America, centred on Mercosur, for which the EU is the main external economic partner. Mercosur sells 27 percent of its total exports to the European Union, 17 percent to the US, and 5 percent to Japan. On the other hand, 26 percent of Mercosur imports come from the EU, 23 percent from the US, and only 5 percent from Japan. One may argue that the FTAA makes little sense for Mercosur as a group.[51] As Bouzas notes, for Uruguay and Paraguay "the main issue is subregional trade liberalisation. Their main incentive vis-à-vis the US is defensive: to make sure that preferences in the subregional market are not being unilaterally eroded."[52] For Brazil, the FTAA would make sense if it could gain real access to the US market for its manufactured products, which seems problematic given the lack of fast track authority for the US president and the protectionist mood in the US Congress. Market access is not an essential issue in US-Argentine trade relations.

On the other hand, both Mercosur and the EU have strong incentives to sign a comprehensive free trade agreement. According to a study made by Brazil's Fundacao Getulio Vargas, Mercosur would benefit more from a free trade agreement with the EU than through the FTAA. For example, Argentina would stand to gain the most from a Mercosur-EU accord, with 6.71 percent growth of its GDP–versus a mere 0.68 percent from the FTAA.[53]

The EU clearly wants to take advantage of the stalemate in the FTAA negotiations between the US and Latin America to make economic advances in the region. Although EU exports have grown significantly, they have been losing their relative market position to US exports, due to the proximity of the US to Latin America and an aggressive, government-driven export promotion strategy on the part of the US. The EU has signed framework co-operation agreements with Mercosur (15 December 1995) and Chile (21 June 1996) and has regular ministerial meetings with the Rio Group (to which belong all four Mercosur partners). On 10 June 1997, the EU began formal talks for a political, trade, and economic agreement with Mexico. After French President Chirac visited the four Mercosur countries and Bolivia (March 1997) he proposed a European-Latin American Summit which took place in Rio de Janeiro, Brazil, in June 1999. Although Mercosur-EU free trade negotiations were formally launched at the summit, it was expected that they would proceed slowly after a meeting in Brussels in November 1999 to discuss the format and timetable of negotiations. The main obstacles are EU barriers to agricultural and industrial products, which account for the lion's share of Mercosur's exports to Europe. On the other hand, the two regions have multiple historical, cultural and social affinities and linkages; even in the absence of an FTA the framework co-operation agreement with the EU opens up the possibility of Mercosur-EU co-operation in other areas, such as technology transfers.[54]

6. Conclusion: Will Mercosur Survive the Brazilian Economic Crisis?

Mercosur's record is on balance highly successful; it has gone a long way toward becoming an autonomous trading bloc. The linear and automatic elimination of intra-regional tariffs during the transition period (1991-1994) was completed on schedule, and contrary to pessimistic forecasts,[55] a customs union was born on January 1, 1995 which will be fully implemented with the end of temporary exceptions and special regimes in 2001 and 2006. The four Mercosur partners have taken important steps to deepen subregional integration, including the decision to start talks aimed at freeing trade in services over a ten-year period, and the opening of a formal Mercosur headquarters in Montevideo in December 1997. Mercosur has made considerable progress in projecting itself internationally, both within and beyond the Western Hemisphere.

Although the US still exercises considerable influence over the Southern Cone politics and economics, the future of Mercosur is not necessarily tied up to the prospects for concluding the FTAA negotiations on schedule (by

2005), which essentially depend on NAFTA-Mercosur inter-bloc discussions and Brazil/US negotiations. As progress is made in completing Mercosur as a customs union, it will be able to negotiate the FTAA with NAFTA from a position of strength.

The Asian economic crisis of 1997 and the world financial crisis of 1998 have had a negative impact on the Latin American economies, slowing down regional integration efforts. As of this writing (August 1999), the Brazilian government's decision to devalue the *real* in January 1999 (in spite of an US-sponsored IMF bail out of US$ 30 billion dollars) shows that the world economic and financial crisis is not over. Progress in world trade has come to a halt.[56] The US has been unable to impose its agenda for a new round of global trade negotiations. The EU for now is dedicated to itself and the Brazilian devaluation has generated strong domestic pressures for protectionism in Argentina while reviving Argentine-Brazilian trade disputes.[57] Mercosur's survival will depend on the ability of both countries to successfully resolve, as in the past, their "mini-trade wars."

Whether and how Mercosur solves the dilemma of "widening vs. deepening" will have an impact on different scenarios for the future. Mercosur must decide whether it wants to consolidate itself as a trading bloc. After the Brazilian devaluation, the co-ordination of macroeconomics policies becomes a necessity and it will probably revive the debate on a common currency. While Brazil has more incentives for widening (the SAFTA proposal) and is reluctant to agree to deepening because of fears of loss of sovereignty; Argentina has shown an interest in deepening, including the creation of supranational institutions,[58] and moving toward the common market, the most difficult stage of the integration process. For example, "although the four Mercosur countries now issue a special businessman's visa, Uruguay and Argentina will resist giving the mostly poor and unskilled citizens of Brazil's northeast the right to work, let alone settle, in their richer countries."[59]

The future of Mercosur is heavily dependent on the convergence of interests between Argentina and Brazil. If they can overcome their trade conflicts, Mercosur will be able to consolidate itself to the point of having become irreversible. Both countries have gone a long way toward bilateral and subregional integration and the costs of breaking down the agreement would outweigh the benefits. The Brazilian economic crisis revives the image of Latin American finance ministers travelling to Washington to ask for help during the debt crisis of the 1980s. Yet the international and regional environments have changed and it would be more difficult for the US to take advantage of a world financial crisis to reassert its hegemony over the Southern Cone. US President Clinton expressed support for Mercosur when he travelled to Brazil and Argentina in 1997. Moreover, according to some analysts, the impact of the Brazilian crisis on the Argentine economy could be less severe than the "Tequila effect" of the Mexican devaluation of the peso in 1995.[60]

Since its inception, Mercosur has faced two obstacles to become a successful common market: the initial low level of intra-regional trade and the pronounced economic asymmetries among its four partners. The first problem has been largely overcome with a dramatic five-fold increase in intra-Mercosur trade between 1990 and 1997 (see section 2 and table 3.3).[61] Brazil has become the main market for Argentine exports, which represented one-third of its total exports in 1995; Argentina has become the second market for Brazil, compared to the 10th place it had in 1990. During most of the 1990s, intra-Mercosur trade grew more rapidly than Mercosur's trade with the rest of the world. For example, Argentina's exports to the subregion more than doubled, while exports to the rest of the world rose by only 4.5 percent. Brazil's exports to Mercosur more than quadrupled, and increased by only 25 percent to the rest of the world. Only Paraguay's exports to the subregion showed no increase during the tariff reduction period.[62]

The second problem has been difficult to overcome and lends itself to charges of Brazilian "subimperialism" in the region. Yet, despite economic asymmetries and Argentine Brazilian trade disputes Mercosur has been a success story because of the unprecedented level of *political* and diplomatic co-operation among member states. At the 12th Mercosur Summit, the four presidents reaffirmed their commitment to the deepening and enlargement of Mercosur while confirming that it is a "strategic alliance" to face up to the challenges of globalization. The four countries have vowed that Mercosur will stay in being, even if a Free Trade Area of the Americas (FTAA) is formed after 2005.

Early assessments of the future of Mercosur were pessimistic, arguing that the deepening of integration was too dependent upon strong presidential leadership.[63] Yet, the latter was very effective in saving Mercosur in prior Argentine-Brazilian trade disputes. For example, the mini-trade war over the automobile sector in 1995 (see section 2) was only solved after direct talks between presidents Cardoso of Brazil and Menem of Argentina. In the end, despite the imbalances in macroeconomics policies, the "Mercosur spirit" would prevail (for example, in dealing with the Mexican "tequila effect" early in 1995). By 1996-1997 Mercosur had become a reality that surpassed the most optimistic expectations: in the area of trade, a 44 percent expansion within the bloc (from US$ 14 billion to US$ 21 billion) between 1995 and 1997; while trade between the bloc and the rest of the world grew by 17 percent.

Yet the adoption of "open regionalism" and a dependent model of regional integration have been a serious limitation for the consolidation of Mercosur. In 1991 Argentina and Brazil abandoned the model of autonomous and sustainable integration of the Treaty for Integration, Co-operation and Development (TICD, 1988) and its forerunner, the 1986 Program for Economic Integration and Co-operation (PEIC) which included sectoral agreements on capital goods. The TICD envisaged not only a free trade area but also the co-ordination of monetary, fiscal, exchange, and capital policies with the objective of forming a common market. Although the latter was the ultimate goal of the Treaty of Asuncion, in practice, trade liberalisation became an end in itself rather than an industrial policy instrument. Therefore and in spite of the rhetoric on Mercosur as a "political project," the four member states were left at the mercy of external forces and factors. By linking regional integration to globalization Argentina and Brazil became vulnerable to external crises and did not pursue the minimum of "developmental protectionism" that would have allowed them to overcome technological obsolescence and become competitive in world markets. Although Brazil supported the model of "sustainable integration" during the trade liberalisation period (1991-1994), it then accepted the idea of fully linking subregional integration with globalization. As a result, although Mercosur became an international actor with the Protocol of Ouro Preto (December 1994) its "consolidation" was not complete: the trade aspects of integration became *the* absolute priority in the process of building Mercosur while Argentina and Brazil abandoned the goal of a common industrial policy. As Rodríguez points out, the productive complementation of national economies was not even given second place in the subregional integration project.[64]

On the other hand, the absence of a common monetary policy weakens the construction of Mercosur and threatens its very existence, as shown by the crisis provoked by the Brazilian devaluation of January 1999. The international financial crisis and the impending recession in most South American countries gives the US more leverage in the FTAA negotiations and might speed up their conclusion on schedule, by 2005. However, the US position has been weakened by the inability of President Clinton to obtain fast-track authority from the US Congress. If Mercosur survives its present crisis, in the absence of fast-track authority it may be difficult for the next US administration to "lock in" the concessions made by the South American countries in the first stage of negotiations, which will end on 31 October 1999.

The resolution of the Mercosur crisis created by the Brazilian devaluation will be affected by the ongoing Mercosur/European Union negotiations to create a free trade area between both regional blocs. If there is progress in that direction, it would be more difficult for the US to reassert its hegemony over South America. In a world economy divided into competing trading blocs South America is not necessarily condemned to greater integration with the Western Hemisphere hegemon (the US) and could create its own autonomous trading bloc to maximise the subcontinent's relative gains and security vis-à-vis its regional competitors. A free trade area with the EU and a strategy of "multiple alliances" with other regional trading blocs (ASEAN, SADC) would strengthen Mercosur as an international actor allowing it to negotiate the FTAA with NAFTA from a position of strength.

Yet there are two problems with this scenario. First, the international financial crisis of 1997-1998 has slowed down trade negotiations between subregional blocs, while exacerbating intra-bloc conflicts. Mercosur and the Andean Community have not made progress in bloc to bloc negotiations, and a Mercosur-Mexico accord has made little headway, because of Brazilian objections. Argentina and Mexico have signed a free trade agreement, heightening tensions within Mercosur.[65] Second, the international financial crisis opens a window of opportunity for the US to revive the NAFTA-centred approach to Western Hemisphere integration and/or to reinvigorate the FTAA process. By granting the US president fast-track authority the US Congress could definitely "win" the Andean countries to the US side, thus practically destroying the prospects for a SAFTA.[66] However, the world financial crisis may exacerbate protectionist tendencies in the US. Fast-track authority for the US president is not a real possibility in the near future; even less so if the Democratic Party regains control of the US House of Representatives in the year 2000. In any case, SAFTA will not come into existence unless Argentina and Brazil are able to resolve their trade disputes and move toward the creation of a common market.[67] This would imply a radical departure from the model of "open regionalism" adopted in the

Buenos Aires Act (August 1994) and the Protocol of Ouro Preto (December 1994).

The US failed to prevent Mercosur from becoming a customs union in January 1995. Yet the US could succeed in freezing Mercosur as an *imperfect* customs union, especially if Argentina-Brazil trade disputes continue and Argentina makes progress in negotiating with the US the "dollarization" of the Argentine economy. On the other hand, if Brazil overcomes its present crisis it could still pursue its vision of South American capitalist development with itself at the centre while resisting US pressures to actually destroy Mercosur in the name of Western Hemisphere trade liberalisation. If there is a world slump in the first decade of the twenty-first century, in the absence of US leadership to complete the FTAA on schedule the South American countries may be hard pressed to achieve a consensus among themselves on trade issues and SAFTA may come into existence, with Mercosur at its core. In any case, if Mercosur is to survive the present crisis it will have to take serious steps toward both *widening* (the SAFTA proposal) and *deepening*, by co-ordinating macroeconomics policies, adopting a common currency, and building a permanent supranational structure to face up to the challenges of the new millennium.

Notes

1 Mistry, P., 1995, "Open Regionalism: Stepping Stone or Millstone toward an Improved Multilateral System?", p. 12, in Teunissen, J. (ed.), *Regionalism and the Global Economy: The Case of Latin America and the Caribbean*, The Hague (the Netherlands), Forum on Debt and Development.
2 Ibid., p. 14.
3 See e.g., Bhagwati, J., 1993, "Regionalism & Multilateralism: An Overview," in: de Melo, J. & Panagariya, A., *New Dimensions in Regional Integration*, CEPR, Cambridge (UK), Cambridge University Press.
4 Mistry, 1995, *op. cit.*, p. 15.
5 Ibid., p. 15.
6 "Text of Mercosur Common Market Treaty Released," *Foreign Broadcasting Information Service/Latin America*, 25/3/91, p. 2.
7 Ibid.
8 See e.g., Bhalla & Bhalla, 1997, and Krugman, 1991.
9 Rodriguez, J., 1995, *El Mercosur Después de Buenos Aires: La Ultima*

Oportunidad, Montevideo, Fundación de Cultura Universitaria/Centro Uruguay Independiente, p. 14.

10   It took eight years for the European Community (EC) to become a customs union in 1968; Mercosur achieved the same goal in less than four years.

11   See Arocena, M., 1997, "Common Market of the Southern Cone (Mercosur)," pp. 159-160, in Jatar, A. & Weintraub, S. (eds.), *Integrating the Hemisphere: Perspectives from Latin America and the Caribbean*, Washington, DC, Inter-American Dialogue.

12   See Regunaga, C., 1997, "Seguridad Juridica in Mercosur," *Comments on Argentine Trade*, vol. 79 (5), pp. 26-27.

13   The existence of a "big brother" is a characteristic of the emerging trading blocs: Germany in the EU, the US in NAFTA, South Africa in SADC, Nigeria in ECOWAS, and India in SAARC. See Bhalla & Bhalla, 1997, *op. cit.*, pp. 198-199.

14   This is shown by the clear opposition between Argentine and Brazilian priorities regarding SAFTA and NAFTA in 1994-1995. For Argentina: Mercosur first, then NAFTA and SAFTA. For Brazil: Mercosur, SAFTA, and then NAFTA. See Schwartz, G., 1996, "Brazil, Mercosur, and SAFTA: Destructive Restructuring or Pan-American Integration?" in Smith & Nishijima (eds.), *Cooperation or Rivalry? Regional Integration in the Americas and the Pacific Rim*, Boulder (CO), Westview Press, p. 139.

15   Motta Veiga, P., 1997, "Brazil's Strategy for Trade Liberalization and Economic Integration in the Western Hemisphere," in Jatar, A. & Weintraub, S. (eds.), *Integrating the Hemisphere, op. cit.*, p. 202.

16   Peña, F., 1995, "New Approaches to Economic Integration in the Southern Cone," *Washington Quarterly*, vol. 18 (3), pp. 113-122, p. 120.

17   Ferrer, A., 1997, "Los Dos Modelos de Mercosur: Integración Sostenible o Consenso de Washington," in *Encrucijadas*, University of Buenos Aires (UBA), pp. 9-25, p. 9, my translation.

18   Schwartz, 1996, *op. cit.*, p. 132.

19   See e.g., Nofal, M., 1994, "Mercosur and Free Trade in the Americas," in Weintraub, S. (ed.), *Integrating the Americas: Shaping Future Trade Policy*, New Brunswick (NJ), Transaction Publishers, pp. 137-167.

20   See *Latin American Special Report*, April 1998, p. 6.

21   See Rodrik, D., 1997, *Has Globalization Gone Too Far?*, Washington, DC, Institute for International Economics.

22   See Lavagna, R. & Giambiagi, F., 1998, "Mercosur: Hacia la Creación de Una Moneda Común," *Archivos del Presente* (Buenos Aires) (April-June), pp. 45-61, p. 49.

23 Quoted in Feinberg, 1997, *op. cit.*, p. 160.
24 Smith, P., 1996, *Talons of the Eagle, op. cit.*, p. 160.
25 Bulmer-Thomas, V., 1997, "Regional Integration in Latin America since 1985," *op. cit.*, p. 271.
26 "'Not much is happening in the FTAA. Things have slowed down enormously and people are disillusioned,' says Patricia Rich, a trade analyst with U.N. Economic Commission for Latin America and the Caribbean. 'Without fast track in the United States, the Latin American point of view is that let's push on with our own regional efforts'." Stinson, D., 1999, "Building Blocks," in "NAFTA: Five Year Anniversary," *Latin Trade* (January), pp. 40-47, p. 45.
27 See Hollist, L. & Nielson, D., 1998, "Taking Stock of Inter-American Bonds: Approaches to Explaining Cooperation in the Western Hemisphere," in *Mershon International Studies Review*, vol. 42 (2), pp. 257-281, p. 269.
28 Weintraub, S., 1997, "US-Latin American Economic Relations," *Journal of Interamerican Studies and World Affairs*, vol. 39 (1), pp. 59-69, p. 63.
29 See Acuña, E. S., 1997, *Mercosur: Entre el Regionalismo y el Continentalismo*, La Plata, Argentina, Universidad Nacional de La Plata, p. 25.
30 Bouzas, R., 1997, "Mercosur and Preferential Trade Liberalization in South America: Record, Issues and Prospects," pp. 58-89, in Lipsey, R. & Meller, P. (eds.), *Western Hemisphere Trade Integration: A Canadian-Latin American Dialogue*, New York, St. Martin's Press, p. 89.
31 On the prospects for a "great depression" early in the next century, see Wade, R. & Veneroso, F., 1998, "The Gathering World Slump and the Battle Over Capital Controls," in *New Left Review*, vol. 231 (September/October), pp. 13-42.
32 On the Mercosur summit in Rio de Janeiro (9-10 December 1998) see "Tit-for-tat between Main Partners Sours Mood for Mercosur's December Summit," *Latin American Weekly Report*, 24/11/98, p. 541.
33 See Peña, 1995, *op. cit.*; Mondino, G. & Reca, A., 1997, "Toward a Hemispheric Free Trade Area: the Case of Argentina," in Jatar, A. & Weintraub, S. (eds.), *Integrating the Americas, op. cit.*, pp. 177-196; Bouzas, 1997, *op. cit.*; Edwards, S., 1993, "Latin American Economic Integration: A New Perspective on an Old Dream," in *The World Economy*, vol. 16 (3), pp. 317-338.
34 See chapter 2.
35 Nofal, 1994, *op. cit.*, p. 153.
36 Mercosur will be a more perfect customs union in 2001, once tariffs on imported capital goods converge at a CET of 14 percent; it will become a full-

fledged customs union in 2006, when tariffs on computers and telecommunications equipment must converge at 16 percent (see table 3.2). See "What Mercosur Has Done," in "Remapping South America: A Survey of Mercosur," *The Economist*, 12/10/96, pp. 1-30, p. 5.

37 See Viner, J., 1950, *The Customs Union Issue*, New York, Carnegie Endowment for International Peace.
38 See "Remapping South America: A Survey of Mercosur," *op. cit.*, p. 6.
39 The Yeats thesis generated a major stir in Washington's academic and journalistic circles (the paper was leaked to the *Wall Street Journal* and the *Financial Times*) and a strong rebuttal from both the Argentine and Brazilian governments and Southern Cone scholars. See Cohen, 1996, and Devlin, 1996.
40 See Yeats, A., 1996, "Does Mercosur's Trade Performance Justify Concerns about the Global Welfare Reducing Effects of Regional Trading Arrangements? Yes!" unpublished World Bank Paper.
41 Quoted by Rodriguez Mendoza, M., 1996, "Which Mercosur Anyway?" *Boletim de Integracao Latino-Americana*. Special edition (December), pp. 20-26, p. 20.
42 Devlin, R., 1996, "In Defense of Mercosur," in *Boletim de Integracao Latinoamericana*, Special edition (December), p. 18.
43 Ibid.
44 See *The Financial Times*, 4/2/97.
45 See Benegas Cristaldo, G., 1994, *A la Búsqueda de Un Mercado Común. Mercosur: Creación de Comercio, Desviación de Comercio, e Implicancias de Políticas Públicas*, Asunción (Paraguay), Universidad Católica, chap. 6, pp. 89-121. Benegas Cristaldo considers four scenarios. The first two scenarios consider the average external tariff of the four Mercosur partners: 11.2 percent. Scenarios 3 and 4 assume a common external tariff of 35 percent (originally discussed between Mercosur and the GATT). The arithmetic average of the CET agreed upon at Ouro Preto (11.14 percent) is very close to her first two scenarios. Benegas Cristaldo's estimates of trade diversion as a percentage of total imports oscillate between 0.9 percent (scenario 2) and 20.9 percent (scenario 3) both in the case of Argentina. Although her scenarios 3 and 4 are unrealistic, her findings seem to confirm that the Yeats thesis is correct and there has been "moderate" trade diversion in Mercosur. The fact that capital intensive goods (automobiles, chemicals and transport equipment) are being produced under protectionist conditions (as temporary "exceptions" to the CET) points in the same direction. See Bhalla & Bhalla, 1997, *op. cit.*, p. 149.

46 Edwards, 1993, *op. cit.*, p. 327.
47 As Schwartz points out, since the 1980s Argentina de-industrialised its productive structure, while Brazil continued protecting its domestic industries through import substitution and a system of export promotion, a strategy in which Mercosur played an essential role. See Schwartz, 1996, *op. cit.*, pp. 131-133. Although the Argentine government emphatically denies it, there is something to the claim that Argentina would become "the granary" and Brazil "the factory" of Mercosur.
48 See the Preamble to the Treaty of Asunción, reproduced and translated in *Foreign Broadcasting Information Service, FBIS/Latin America*, 25/3/91, p. 2.
49 Bouzas, 1997, *op. cit.*, pp. 85-86.
50 In August 1997, Chilean foreign minister Jose Miguel Insulza proclaimed: "Mercosur is our FTA," adding that Chile was betting "on comprehensive integration with Mercosur, far beyond any interest it may have in a deal with NAFTA." See "Mercosur Approach to FTAA Advances," *Latin American Weekly Report*, 5/8/97, p. 364.
51 See Panagariya, A., 1996, "The Free Trade Area of the Americas: Good for Latin America?" *World Economy* (September), pp. 485-515, p. 505.
52 Bouzas, 1997, *op. cit.*, p. 85.
53 See "Should Mercosur Opt for Europe? Study Says Benefits Are Greater than in the FTAA," *Latin America Weekly Report*, 6/5/97, p. 206.
54 See Stahringer, O., 1996, "El Mercosur en Un Mundo en Bloques," p. 119, in Stahringer, O. (ed.), *El Mercosur en el Nuevo Orden Mundial*, Buenos Aires, Ediciones Ciudad Argentina.
55 See e.g., Manzetti, L., 1993/94, "The Political Economy of Mercosur," *Journal of Interamerican Studies and World Affairs*, vol. 35 (4), pp. 101-141, p. 131.
56 In November 1999, the World Trade Organization (WTO) organised a meeting in Seattle to launch a "Millennium Round" of global trade negotiations. Yet the conference collapsed in bitterness and discord without agreeing on a common agenda amid street demonstrations organised by environmental activists, labour rights groups, and other non-governmental organisations. See "The New Trade War," *The Economist*, 4/12/99, p. 25.
57 Paraguay has even threatened to withdraw from Mercosur if Argentina goes ahead with a plan to create a free-trade zone in the city of Clorinda, in the province of Formosa, right on the Paraguayan border. See "Paraguayan Flap over Free Zone," *Latin American Weekly Report*, 24/8/99, p. 386.
58 In December 1998 Argentina asked for a "big leap forward" moving Mercosur "upwards" from an intergovernmental organisation to a supra-

national one with a common currency and fully co-ordinated macroeconomics policies, while completing the customs union. See "Mercosur: Argentina Suggests a Big Leap Forward," *Latin American Weekly Report*, 1/12/98, p. 558.

59 "Remapping South America: A Survey of Mercosur," *op. cit.*, p. 27.

60 According to Norberto E. Sosa, chief economist at the Buenos Aires economic consulting firm Estudio Proeco, a maxi-devaluation in Brazil in 1998 (which actually happened in January 1999) would have left Argentina with a minimum of 1.3 percent growth in GDP for that year. The reason is that Argentina's fiscal and financial situation was much better in 1997-98 than in 1994. See Sosa, N., 1997, "The Effects of a Brazilian Maxi-Devaluation on Argentina," in *Comments on Argentine Trade*, vol. 79 (5), pp. 19-21.

61 See "Rise of the Subregional Blocs," *Latin American Special Report*, April 1998, SR-98-02, p. 6.

62 See Arocena, 1997, *op. cit.*, table 6, "Mercosur: Evolution of Trade in Goods, 1990-1994," p. 167.

63 See Manzetti, 1993, *op. cit.*, p. 131.

64 Rodríguez, J., 1995, *op. cit.*, p. 67. The remaining "industrial policy" (e.g., for the automotive industry; and the other temporary exceptions to the CET) is just for "training" purposes, so that temporarily protected domestic enterprises can enter in better conditions to the "rough sea" ("mar encrespado") of globalization. See Secretaría de Relaciones Económicas Internacionales, 1996, "El Mercosur: Regionalismo Abierto o Un 'Building Block'? Comentarios Acerca del Trabajo de Alexander Yeats," in *Boletim de Integracao Latino-Americana*, Special Edition (December), pp. 4-17, p. 13.

65 Brazil fears that Argentina is becoming a route through which Mexican products will be imported to Argentina for re-export to the rest of the Mercosur.

66 Arguably, "the United States' market matters far more to them than does the Brazilian one." See *The Economist*, 1996, "Remapping South America: A Survey of Mercosur," *op. cit.*, p. 28.

67 An interesting issue is whether a Mercosur common market would be compatible with the FTAA, if it comes into existence.

4 Between Two Summits: From a NAFTA-Centred FTAA to SAFTA

Introduction

At the Summit of the Americas held in Miami during December 1994 thirty-four American heads of state agreed in principle to conclude negotiations for a Free Trade Area of the Americas (FTAA) no later than 2005, with concrete progress by the turn of the century. The Miami Summit was praised as marking the beginning of a new era in US-Latin American relations, based on a common agenda of promoting democracy and free market economic reforms. Four years later at the Second Summit of the Americas held April 18-19, 1998 in Santiago, Chile, the hemispheric leaders formally launched the FTAA negotiations. If the FTAA comes into existence, it will be the world's largest free trade arrangement in history, with a combined GDP of over $9 trillion (with the $7 trillion US economy accounting for more than 75 percent of the total) and a potential market of 765 million people.

The purpose of this chapter is to examine the history of the FTAA negotiations between the two summits of the Americas, to assess the prospects for completion of the FTAA negotiations on schedule and to consider the compatibility of a future FTAA with Mercosur and NAFTA, the two largest subregional integration agreements in the Western Hemisphere. The chapter will also examine the incentives and disincentives, for both the US and the South American countries to join a Western Hemisphere Free Trade Area.

The US has strong commercial and political incentives to complete the FTAA on schedule. For the South American countries, the possibility of having unrestricted access to the US market is a strong incentive to join an FTAA, even in the case of Brazil, which has good reasons to slow down the pace of the FTAA negotiations.[1]

During 1996-1998, the course of the hemispheric negotiations to determine the structure and schedule of the FTAA process strengthened the bargaining power of the South American countries, especially Mercosur and its leader, Brazil; while weakening the ability of the United States to successfully negotiate an agenda that would protect its national interest, particularly after the US failure to incorporate Chile to NAFTA.

Between 1996 and 1998, Mercosur became the pole of attraction for a future South American Free Trade Area (SAFTA) (see chapter 3). Although the Brazilian proposal for a SAFTA was temporarily shelved by the Cardoso administration in 1995, the northward expansion of Mercosur with the adhesion of Chile, Bolivia, and Venezuela, and the successful completion of an Andean Community/Mercosur free trade accord would put SAFTA back in the South American agenda, especially if the FTAA negotiations are delayed due to the failure of the US president to obtain fast-track authority from the US Congress. In that scenario, SAFTA would de facto come into existence and Mercosur would be in a much stronger position to prevail in the FTAA negotiations.

NAFTA and Mercosur have played different roles during the FTAA negotiations. For the purposes of the FTAA, "NAFTA" does not really exist, since its member countries are negotiating individually. Before the Santiago Summit, there was a basic disagreement between the US and Mercosur on the format of the FTAA negotiations. The impasse on this issue at the May 1997 trade ministerial meeting in Belo Horizonte (Brazil) strengthened Mercosur's bargaining position vis-à-vis the United States. At that meeting, Brazil's foreign minister Luis Felipe Lampreia argued that "what is good for the US is not good for Brazil" while Brazil's president Fernando Henrique Cardoso said that hemispheric integration "depends on the willingness of the US, on the North's capacity to effectively open its markets in the sectors we need the most." The only concession the US got was a formal announcement that the heads of state and government *should* be ready to launch the FTAA negotiations at the second Summit of the Americas that took place in Santiago, Chile in April 1998. In the words of Argentine foreign minister Guido Di Tella, Latin America "lent a hand" to the Clinton administration with this face-saving compromise. The Clinton administration's lack of fast-track authority to negotiate the FTAA created a leadership vacuum that was quickly filled by Brazil reaching out to other South American countries so as to establish SAFTA to accumulate negotiating power for dealing with the "colossus of the North." In the absence of an FTAA, Mercosur could well strengthen links with Europe, while consolidating itself as an independent trading bloc, rather than passively accepting US hegemony as in the past.

The Enterprise for the Americas Initiative

On 27 June 1990, President Bush gave his "Enterprise Initiative for the Americas" speech, proposing the extension of a prospective North American Free Trade Area (NAFTA) further south, with the long-term objective of a hemispheric free trade area, "stretching from the port of Anchorage to the Tierra del Fuego." The proposal promised the creation of a US$1.5 billion investment fund, administered by the Inter-American Development Bank (IDB) to support market-oriented investment reforms (privatisation); "deeper tariff reductions" in the Uruguay Round of the GATT negotiations on products of special interest to the Latin American nations; a significant reduction on US government-owned official debt; and an end to "overrestrictive trade barriers that wall off the economies of our region from each other, and from the United States, at great cost to us all."[2]

The Enterprise for the Americas Initiative (EAI) was the first US attempt to elaborate a comprehensive policy agenda for the entire Latin American region since President Kennedy's ambitious Alliance for Progress. In contrast to the Alliance, which relied primarily on US aid, the EAI was based on the "trade not aid" formula, reflecting both the budgetary constraints of the 1990s and the neoliberal ideology of the "Washington Consensus."

Did the United States have the political will to deliver on the EAI? It has been argued that the EAI was a "rhetorical ploy" that was "designed in part to mollify the third countries [in Latin America] that [would] be most affected by NAFTA," considering that the EAI speech was given shortly after Mexico formally requested to negotiate a free trade area with the US and Canada.[3]

The implementation of the EAI faced from the beginning several problems. First, the Bush administration had to receive authority from Congress to reduce the official debt to the US of selected Latin American countries. Moreover, the Bush Initiative would only benefit the small countries with the largest portion of Latin American official debt to the US, that is a small portion of the Latin American total debt, about three quarter of which is commercial. The implementing legislative norms under consideration by Congress (H.R. 665 [Lagomarsino]; H.R. 964 [Fascell] required debtor countries to be making significant progress toward rescheduling arrangements with the International Monetary Fund, the World Bank or the International Development Association and to be implementing a "strong" free-market oriented economic and investment policy to be eligible for official debt reduction.

The "free market" doctrine proposed by Washington was supposed to be based on the concept of reciprocity: in exchange for opening up their economies and markets, the Latin American countries could expect equivalent US concessions in the form of opening the US market to Latin American products and capital funding for Latin American development. Yet in practice, as Petras and Morley point out, the Bush administration applied the free market doctrine in an extremely one-sided way: "taking advantage of large-scale deregulation of Latin economies without providing much in the way of capital resources or market opportunities" for the Latin American countries. The only "positive" aspect of the initiative was to encourage the foreign commercial banks that were owed the vast bulk of the hemisphere's debt to provide some debt relief "in return for an accelerated deregulation of markets."[4] The banks had already covered themselves from possible defaults by several Latin American countries, and were rapidly cutting back on their overall exposure in the region (see chapter 2).

President Bush's Fiscal Year 1992 budget proposed $410 million in budget authority for special assistance to Latin America under the Enterprise for the Americas Initiative. The petition included $100 million for an investment fund managed by the Inter-American Development Bank and $310 million in debt reduction for Latin America. These were exiguous figures, considering that at the end of 1989 total Latin American debt amounted to $428 billion and that in the 1980s (the so-called "lost decade") negative resource transfers from Latin America to the rest of the world averaged $30 billion annually. Resources transferred out as interest payments consistently exceeded new loans coming into the region in the 1980s. It was only in 1991 that Latin America received a net transfer of funds of nearly $7 billion, because of an increase in the flow of foreign capital, attracted by economic "restructuring" and "free market reform."

The most serious obstacle to a successful implementation of the Enterprise for the Americas Initiative is US foreign economic policy itself, which has been markedly protectionist in recent years. As Pierre Martin points out, although the United States still relies on multilateral trade negotiations, "a key development in the 1980s was the shift toward aggressive unilateralism, in sharp contrast with the central position of multilateralism in earlier post-war US trade policy."[5] The shift to Western Hemisphere regionalism in the early 1990s can be seen as a tactical move, prompted by the apparent movement of the world economy toward regional trading blocs: the "single market" decision in the European Community, leading to an enlarged European Union, and the possibility of an East Asian trading bloc led by Japan.

The protectionist portions of the US Trade and Tariff Act of 1984 were reinforced by the Trade Act of 1988 ("Special 301"), which entitles the US Trade Representative (USTR) to commence investigations, take legal actions, and provide for retaliation against countries which carry out unfair trading practices. Is the US prepared to renounce to unilateral trade barriers, such as legislated tariffs and quotas, and to impose strict limits to the application of unfair trade laws against Latin American countries? In their book, *Putting People First*, US President Clinton and vice-president Gore promise support for a strong "Super 301" and for a free trade agreement with Mexico, "so long as it provides adequate protection for workers, farmers, and the environment on both sides of the border."[6] They do not mention the Enterprise for the Americas Initiative, but stress that "no trade agreement should preclude the United States from enforcing non-discriminatory laws and regulations affecting health, worker safety, and the environment."

The Enterprise for the Americas Initiative can be seen as a bold attempt on the part of the US to "capture" the potentially advantageous Latin American market (with a population of around 430 million) without making major concessions on non-tariff barriers to trade. The US was ready to sign free trade agreements with subregional trade groupings, such as Mercosur, so long as they had escape clauses (e.g., safeguard clauses) that could be invoked to continue practising discriminatory trade policies.

Free trade with Latin America was the most important aspect of the Enterprise Initiative, and it was enthusiastically received by most Latin American leaders. The EAI was strongly supported by Mexican President Carlos Salinas, who had proposed a Mexico-US Free trade agreement in the Spring of 1990. The EAI can be seen as President Bush's answer to the Salinas proposal. Argentine President Carlos Menem said that Argentina was "passing through [its] most brilliant moment in [its] relations with the United States." Uruguayan President Luis Lacalle was even more enthusiastic: "When, after years of our complaining of neglect, the most important man in the world offers his hand, then I think we should grab it--and the arm and the elbow and the shoulder, too."[7] This attitude was a radical break with the past. Most Latin American countries were suspicious of free-trade theories emanating from the US after World War II:

> It was obvious, in their view, that free competition between large, technologically advanced companies from industrialised countries and young, weak industries in Latin America would simply permit the former to devour the latter.[8]

By mid-January 1992, the US had signed separate "framework agreements" (highly preliminary treaties committing only to hold future talks that might lead to free trade agreements) with two multilateral organisations (Mercosur and CARICOM) and 14 individual states. These instruments did not contain final concessions about substantive matters and only identified agendas of essential issues in the areas of trade and investment for further negotiations through special councils that would serve as consultative mechanisms. Less than three months after the signing of the Treaty of Asunción, which established Mercosur, the four participating countries (Argentina, Brazil, Paraguay, and Uruguay) signed an agreement with the United States in June 1991 to create a Consultative Council on Trade and Investment. An Annex to the agreement contains an "Immediate Action Agenda," including future negotiations toward a free trade general agreement between the parties. This accord, known in the US as the "Rose Garden Agreement" and in Latin America as the "Four plus One Agreement," is important to interpret the legal aspects and ideological commitments of the Treaty of Asuncion.[9]

As can be seen, the EAI had limited objectives. The proposal to create a free trade area "from Anchorage to Tierra del Fuego" was a long-term goal. Although the Bush Initiative laid the initial groundwork for discussing free trade with 32 of the 34 other American states (excluding only Cuba and Haiti) the US did *not* assume substantial commitments except "talking." Yet, the EAI paved the way for formal negotiations between the US, Mexico, and Canada. In May 1991, the US Congress approved authority for the US administration to conduct "fast-track" trade negotiations with its North American neighbours. After ratification by legislatures of the three governments, the North American Free Trade Area (NAFTA) entered into force in January 1994.

From the Enterprise of the Americas Initiative to the FTAA Negotiations

The first Clinton administration continued the traditional US policy of "benign neglect" toward Latin America. Although Clinton followed up the negotiations begun by Bush for a free trade agreement with Mexico and Canada, he did not set foot in Latin America or the Caribbean (outside of a few hours in Haiti) during his first term. Even after the Miami Summit, Clinton travelled repeatedly to Europe and the Middle East in 1995-96, but not to Latin America.[10]

The "regionalist turn" of US foreign economic policy in the 1990s can be explained for a number of reasons. Structural changes in the global economy, the uncertainties created by the stalemate with France during the Uruguay Round negotiations, and the possible emergence of protectionist trading blocs in Europe and East Asia probably played a role in convincing US policy makers that Western Hemisphere regionalism was the best strategy to deal with the challenges of globalization.

The decision to organise the First Summit of the Americas in Miami was made while US vice-president Gore was en route to Mexico to give a speech in relation to the passage of the NAFTA agreement in the US Congress. Despite Latin American enthusiasm with the idea, the Summit was poorly prepared. As Howard Wiarda points out, "once the Clinton administration had announced, and then issued invitations to, the summit, it then became so preoccupied with other matters that it tended to ignore the proposal for much of 1994. There was little high-level policy involvement; what planning there was took place largely at staff levels."[11] On the other hand, Clinton did match Bush's EAI rhetoric by formally calling for the establishment of an American Free Trade Area and boldly setting the year 2005 as the date of its commencement.

The FTAA process can be seen as a deliberate attempt by the United States to "normalise" the South American countries by peacefully integrating their economies into the global capitalist economy while accepting the fundamental tenets of "deep integration": 1) the effort to extend international rules from trade to investment (the inclusion of "trade" in services in a future FTAA); 2) rules governing intellectual property, differences in national standards, and financial, industrial, technology, competition, and environmental policies; and 3) the elimination of all domestic restraints on trade and investment.[12]

Initially, the FTAA proposal was conceived as an extension of the NAFTA model of free trade to the rest of the Western Hemisphere. In 1993, after meeting with Argentine President Carlos Menem in the White House, US President Clinton told the press:

> I have long thought that NAFTA should be a model for embracing all of Latin America's democracies and free market economies.[13]

Yet, the US lost credibility vis-à-vis its prospective South American partners by failing to deliver on the promise to incorporate "responsible" countries to NAFTA. A dramatic proof of the negative impact of US policy on South American expectations and behaviour is Chile's decision (at the Mercosur presidential summit in Montevideo, December 14-15, 1997) to co-ordinate with Mercosur its position in the FTAA talks that were formally launched the following April in Santiago, Chile, even though Chile is not yet a full member of the Southern Cone grouping.

As of early 1995, one could envisage two scenarios for the completion of an FTAA:

1) The disintegration of the subregional groupings analysed in chapters 2 and 3 (Mercosur, the Andean Community, the Central American Common Market, CARICOM) in the face of strong attraction by NAFTA. Individual members of those groupings would unilaterally attempt to negotiate the "best deal" with NAFTA at the expense of intra-regional co-operation. Argentina flirted with this scenario in 1994-1995.

2) The strengthening of subregional groupings as "preparatory steps" to entering NAFTA. As a group, countries would be in a better position to strike a good deal for accession to NAFTA.

In the aftermath of the Miami Summit (December 1994) accession to NAFTA was the "only game in town" and it was widely expected that Chile would sooner or later be admitted, after Canadian Prime Minister Chretién's famous statement at the closing session of the Summit: "For one year now, we have been the three amigos. Starting today, we will become the four amigos."

Most analysts recognised that a "hub-and-spoke" model, centred on NAFTA (and its core country, the US) was unfair for the Latin American countries, because the US would be placed in a superior bargaining position. By negotiating separate agreements with each of its smaller partners, the latter would have no chance to make common cause against the US in matters of common interest.[14]

Yet less than two weeks after the Miami Summit, the Mexican peso crisis and the adverse reaction it provoked in the US Congress and public opinion completely changed the parameters of the FTAA negotiations. Later on, the failure of the US government to incorporate Chile to NAFTA raised several questions: was the United States really committed to free and *fair* trade with its neighbours to the South? How far and how fast would the US actually travel down the road of hemispheric economic integration? Were the South American countries ready to follow US leadership in that area? Who would benefit from the FTAA?

Before the Miami Summit, the US government prepared a complex fourteen-point agenda, covering a wide range of problems in three issue-areas: (1) government corruption and drug trafficking; (2) promotion of free trade, based upon the principles of "open regionalism"; (3) a broad range of commitments in the areas of public health, education, resource management, and environmental protection.

The paramount concern of the Latin American countries in Miami was free trade and trade issues. As Peter Smith points out, "fearful of possible exclusion from the anticipated benefits of free trade with Canada and the United States, countries other than Mexico were overwhelmingly concerned with questions and anxieties about the terms, timing, and conditions for accession to NAFTA or to some form of Western Hemisphere Free Trade Area (WHFTA.) They were particularly insistent that the Miami gathering should establish a specific timetable for hemispheric integration."[15] Yet the 34 Western Hemisphere leaders in Miami only agreed to complete *negotiations* for an FTAA by the year 2005.

The Miami Summit had two important consequences for future US-Latin American relations.

First, the Miami meeting marked the beginning of the "Summit of the Americas Process," and the design of a mechanism, involving periodic meetings of the hemisphere's trade ministers, to negotiate the FTAA. A Second Summit of heads of state of the Americas took place in Santiago, Chile (April 18-19, 1998) and a Third Summit of the Americas will take place in Quebec, Canada, on 2001. The institutionalisation of Summitry in the Western Hemisphere is a new phenomenon that has been made possible by the common ground created by the transitions to democracy and the adoption of free market economic policies by all the Latin American countries, with the exception of Cuba.

Second, the governments in Miami agreed jointly to address 22 other issues besides free trade. For example, they announced their willingness to co-operate to defend democracy and human rights, alleviate poverty, upgrade education and health services, combat corruption, fight against drug trafficking, improve the status of women and indigenous groups, and protect the environment. Such an ambitious agenda, with 23 initiatives and more than 150 actions, was arguably too difficult to implement. For example, although an Inter-American Convention Against Corruption was signed in 1996 and progress was "good" on energy and pollution prevention, only modest progress was achieved in the areas of democracy and human rights, education, narcotics and money laundering, women's rights, capital market liberalisation, and trade.[16]

There are significant structural obstacles to successfully implement an FTAA: the extreme heterogeneity of the levels of development in the hemisphere, namely, the enormous gap between GDP per capita in the US and Canada, on the one hand, and the poorest countries in the Western Hemisphere, such as Haiti and Honduras, on the other. As Mace and Bélanger point out,

Strict application of a rigorous free trade agreement to the whole hemisphere would seriously harm Caribbean and Central American countries as well as certain South American countries, such as Bolivia, Ecuador, Paraguay, and Peru, which would require important structural adjustment in order to comply with such a treaty.[17]

Even the largest South American countries, Brazil and Argentina, would face the challenge of competing with US companies on a levelled playing field. This is the reason Brazil and its Mercosur partners made an effort to slow down the FTAA negotiations at the four trade ministerial conferences between the Miami and Santiago summits. The Mercosur governments fear that their local industries would be unable to compete with the more competitive US industries. How to administer regional asymmetries and their impact on the distribution of costs and benefits is one of the challenges of the FTAA process.

Who Benefits from the FTAA? Why Should the US and Latin America be Interested?

One may argue that the US has more to gain from an FTAA than the Latin American countries (with the exception of Mexico, who already has access to the US market). In any free trade agreement, the country that liberalises most is likely to lose. Since Latin American tariff barriers alone average four times US tariff barriers to Latin American products, it is unlikely that the Latin American countries stand to gain much from entering into an FTAA because it will give the US and Canada a much greater preferential market access than the latter are able to offer in return.

For the Mercosur countries, an FTAA would only make sense if the US seriously commits itself to eliminate its *non-tariff barriers*, such as customs procedures, investment restrictions, sanitary/phytosanitary measures, and technical standards. On the other hand, the bulk of Latin American exports to the US come from Mexico. While 76 percent of Mexican exports go to the United States, the rest of Latin America exports only 28 percent of its total exports to the "colossus of the North." In the post-Cold War era, South America has a clearly defined strategic interest in diversifying its economic relations. Unlike Mexico, most South American countries have most of their foreign trade with countries outside the hemisphere, and intra-South American trade has dramatically increased in the 1990s. If the FTAA comes into existence, they run the serious risk of uneconomic trade diversion through discriminatory liberalisation within the hemisphere. This is a serious danger for Mercosur for whom the European Union is a more important trading partner than the United States (see figure 4.1).

This helps to explain Mercosur's proposal at the Belo Horizonte Trade Ministerial (May 1997) to negotiate the FTAA in three stages, beginning with the elimination of non-tariff barriers (NTBs) which pose significant obstacles to Mercosur exports to the US market. Instead of the "early harvest" of tariff cuts that the US wanted by 2000, the negotiators will seek "business facilitation" steps by that date, such as standardised customs forms. Staggered negotiations in nine negotiating groups will give the four Mercosur partners some time to modernise their economies before embarking on open trade with the United States. Mercosur won two important diplomatic victories at the Second Summit of the Americas (Santiago, Chile, April 1998): the principle that subregional blocs may negotiate as such and the idea that FTAA negotiations would be conducted as a "single undertaking" instead of building on partial agreements, as the US wanted. The South American bloc was reinforced by Chile's decision to align itself with Mercosur at the Santiago Summit.

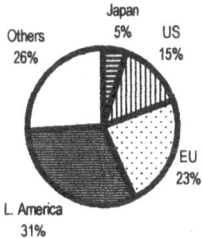
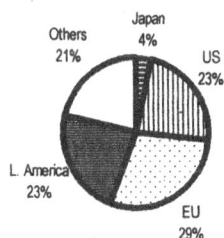

Who they sell to **Who they buy from**
(% of total exports)   (% of total imports)

Figure 4.1 Mercosur: Imports and Exports by Region
Source: Latin American Weekly Report, WR-97-43, 28 October 1997, p. 510-11. Reproduced by permission of Latin American Newsletters, London, England.

Why would the Latin American countries be interested in an FTAA? Because it would attract US investment to the region. More importantly, the FTAA would allow the Latin American countries to gain "real" access to the US market, insuring them against a resurgence of US protectionism and "locking in" the opening of the huge US market for Latin American exports, especially of manufactured goods. Yet since US tariffs are already very low for most Latin American goods, arguably "Latin America's *direct* gains from hemispheric free trade will not be great."[18]

The Latin American (especially South American) countries are particularly interested in gaining access to the US market for their manufactured products. The fastest growing export sector for the Latin American countries is manufacturing. Manufactured goods constituted 23 percent of US imports from Latin America in 1980 and 56 percent in 1989. From this perspective, the US is potentially more important for Latin America than Latin America for the US, considering that Latin American growth and development is still heavily dependent on external factors, as shown by the Brazilian crisis of January/February 1999.

The other possible advantage of the FTAA is that it would provide the Latin American countries with an "insurance policy" against the possible formation of competing trading blocs in the world economy. At least in theory, the FTAA would allow the South American countries to follow Mexico's example and "jump upon the economic bandwagon of North-North development."[19] Yet is being the junior partner of the "colossus of the North" really an advantage? Brazil has pursued the parallel track of the SAFTA proposal to have its own "insurance policy" and in 1994 it saw the creation of SAFTA as a precondition for hemispheric integration with the US through the FTAA.[20]

Trade between equals is not the same as trade between unequals. Because of the asymmetric nature of its relationship with the United States, Latin America may stand to lose *politically* from a free trade agreement with the "colossus of the North," for the reason pointed out by Albert Hirschman many years ago in his study of German trade pacts: "when a large, powerful country–for example, Germany or the United States–trade with a small, weak country, the gains to the latter come at the cost of its additional dependence on the former."[21]

For Latin America, the case against free trade with the United States stems from a long history of non-reciprocity in US policy toward the region.[22] While US exporters would immediately benefit from lower tariffs for the entry of their products in the Latin American markets, as Naim points out, "asymmetric competitive pressures make nearly all Latin exporters extremely vulnerable to charges of dumping lodged by US companies. This vulnerability tends to be higher for exporters of manufactured goods than for exporters of raw materials."[23] The real gains for Latin America would come from the elimination of US *non-tariff* barriers and countervailing duties on Latin American exports, especially of manufactured products. Brazil's protection of its pharmaceutical, telecommunications, and computer industries has been a source of trade conflicts with the US in the past,[24] the solution of which is a prerequisite for a successful implementation of a *fair* free trade agreement between the US (or NAFTA) and Mercosur.

The FTAA Negotiations: From Miami to Santiago

As envisioned in the Miami Summit's Plan of Action, the initial work for the construction of the FTAA was done by a tripartite co-operation committee composed of the Organization of American States (OAS,) the Inter-American Development Bank (IDB) and the Economic Commission for Latin America and the Caribbean (ECLAC.) That Committee prepared a compendium on the current state of the subregional integration agreements, focusing on their basic norms, and a comprehensive comparative study on the tariff structure and different rules of origin prevailing in the Americas.

The First Trade Ministerial Meeting took place in Denver, Colorado, in June 1995. The Miami Summit had not actually defined how the FTAA would be negotiated. In Denver, the trade ministers agreed to launch seven intergovernmental hemispheric working groups with precise instructions to ascertain the following key areas for future FTAA negotiations: market access, customs procedures and rules of origin, investment; subsidies, antidumping and countervailing duties, standards and technical barriers to trade; sanitary and phytosanitary measures; and the problems of smaller economies. The trade ministers agreed on certain basic principles for future negotiations:
a) The "integral and balanced" reach of the negotiations.
b) To use "the existing bilateral and subregional agreements" as a basis to widen and deepen hemispheric integration;
c) To reach an "overall compromise" including the mutual rights and obligations of all parties.
d) To guarantee the compatibility between the FTAA process and World Trade Organization (WTO) rules.

The second trade ministerial meeting took place in Cartagena, Colombia, in March 1996. Although it was difficult to arrive at a consensus declaration, several important decisions were made, including a commitment to achieve concrete progress in the FTAA negotiations before the end of the century. The vice-ministers of trade were instructed to formulate recommendations on the approaches, form and opportunity to launch the FTAA negotiations, for consideration at the third trade ministerial meeting. The most controversial aspects of the agenda in the Cartagena meeting were those related to environmental issues, workers' rights, the different approaches for the construction of the FTAA, the deadlines to achieve concrete results, and the relationship between the FTAA and the WTO. The main task of the vice-ministers was to determine when actual negotiations could begin and to make recommendation on this issue at the 1997 trade ministerial meeting.

Between the second and third trade ministerial meetings confidence in the prospects for a successful FTAA diminished due to the failure of the US administration to secure "fast track" negotiating authority from the US Congress. Both in Denver and Cartagena the contact of the private sector with the FTAA process was enhanced with the organisation of business forums that made specific recommendations to the trade ministers and became institutionalised as the *Americas Business Forum*.

The Third trade ministerial meeting in Belo Horizonte, Brazil, May 1997, was a turning point in the FTAA negotiations. The shortcomings of the process were apparent due to the loss of US leadership, Brazil's strategy to delay the FTAA for as long as possible and the predominance of technical work over political commitments. Although the diplomatic machinery to create a hemispheric free trade area was in place, in the absence of political will it would not work. Although the FTAA working groups were gathering the necessary data and creating a "hemispheric community of trade negotiators,"[25] without a political mandate their proposals would never be implemented. The US and the Mercosur countries had divergent goals at the meeting. The US wanted to start negotiations for the FTAA as soon as possible, en bloc, and with a commitment to a quick reduction in tariffs. By contrast, Mercosur advocated a much slower process of market opening, and a three-stage negotiation:
a) First, business facilitation, to be completed by 1999;
b) Second, norms and disciplines, to be ended in 2003;
c) Third, negotiations on tariff schedule, to conclude by 2005.

Continuing domestic opposition to NAFTA in the US and the loss of impetus in efforts to incorporate new members in 1996 had raised some doubts about Washington's commitment to a Western Hemisphere Free Trade Area.[26]

The divergent approaches to the FTAA process between the governments of the US and Brazil were paralleled by their respective national business communities:

> Just as Mercosur businesses, led by Brazil, prefer a gradual pace for negotiations, their Canadian, US, and Mexican counterparts would rather speed up the establishment of the FTAA and concurrent negotiations on all related topics. When the Business Forum failed to reach a consensus on these issues, the report drafted for assessment by the Ministries for Trade at the Belo Horizonte ministerial meeting in May 1997 ended up voicing both positions.[27]

In the end, in their Joint Ministerial Declaration the ministers committed to formally launch the FTAA negotiations at the April 1998 Summit of the Americas in Santiago, Chile, and agreed to so recommend to their respective heads of state. Yet because they could not iron out their differences on how the FTAA would be achieved they agreed to leave the formulation of the FTAA negotiation procedures including such issues as objectives, approaches, structure, and site of the negotiations for their next (fourth) meeting scheduled for March 1998.

Brazil emerged from the Belo Horizonte trade ministerial as the leader of a united South American bloc with a strong bargaining position vis-à-vis the US. The impasse in Belo Horizonte favoured Brazil, because it compelled the US to make important concessions in the subsequent negotiations. By the time of the Santiago Summit, in April 1998, the US found itself sitting down to negotiate an FTAA with a united South American bloc sharing certain interests that do not necessarily coincide with those of NAFTA members. Although the US strategic goal of having the FTAA negotiations launched in Santiago was achieved, it was very difficult to achieve a compromise at the meeting of deputy trade ministers in San Jose, Costa Rica, in February 1998:

1) Mercosur made a proposal to set up a group devoted to seeking the removal of barriers to the region's agricultural exports. The US resisted such a move.
2) There was no agreement on the venue for the FTAA talks, or on the inclusion of study groups about labor and environmental issues, or on the precise number of negotiating groups.

Although most of these issues were ironed out at the fourth PrepCom meeting in San Jose, Costa Rica, March 17, 1998, and the subsequent meeting of hemispheric trade ministers on March 19, 1998, the US had to make significant concessions. First, the FTAA process will be a "single undertaking." Second, the US accepted the creation of a negotiating table for agriculture–a key problem for many Latin American countries seeking to sell in the US market. Third, environmental and labor issues were shunted aside in different ways.[28]

The Santiago Summit: Success or Failure?

The Second Summit of the Americas took place in Santiago, Chile, on April 18 and 19, 1998. There was a parallel "People's Summit" on April 16-19, 1998, involving a large number of non-governmental organisations (NGOs) from throughout the Americas.

In his remarks at the closing of the summit, President Clinton hailed the conference as a success, although warning, "the real work of Santiago begins as we leave." US Trade Representative Charlene Barshefsky was also optimistic: "The leaders have embraced an agenda that genuinely and for the first time, actually connects the FTAA [Free Trade Area of the Americas] with civil society reform and investment in people."

The Santiago Summit approved a Plan of Action and formally launched the FTAA negotiations. The Plan of Action was aimed at improving education, reducing poverty, expanding democracy, strengthening the region's judicial systems, guaranteeing human rights and fighting drug trafficking in the hemisphere. The most important formal item on the summit agenda was education, as an essential instrument in the effort to eradicate poverty. The Plan of Action calls for all governments in the region to "facilitate access of all Americans to pre-school, primary, secondary, and higher education, and ... make learning a lifelong process," as well as place science and technology at the service of education for most students by 2010." The 34 heads of state agreed to provide high school education for 75 percent of the region's youngsters by the same year.

Under the Santiago Plan, the region will have access to $8.3 billion in new loans and grants, mainly from the IDB and World Bank. The money would be used for a variety of programs, including several that would improve teaching, and to buy textbooks and other materials. The US promised only a minuscule $130 million spread out over 1998-2001 for education.

A positive development was the decision to establish the Consultative Committee on Civil Society, thus recognising that non-governmental organisations would be at least heard while implementing the Plan of Action.

The most notable achievement of the Santiago Summit was the launching of the FTAA negotiations with timetables and a work plan. It was agreed that negotiations would conclude "no later than 2005," and that significant progress would be achieved "no later than December 2000." The fact that the Second Summit of the Americas took place, and also the launching of the negotiations, were considered by US Trade Representative Charlene Barshefsky as a diplomatic victory:

> The fact that we do not have fast track is of no particular concern; we launched the Uruguay Round two years before we had fast track authority here. So, there is no question but that the launch will take place, and the US has been very actively working with the countries to insure that they also will launch and join those negotiations.[29]

Other analysts were more cautious. For example, according to Dr. Boris Kozolchyk, director of the National Law Center for Inter-American Free Trade, "neither Brazil nor any of the other major Latin American countries taking part in the Summit will undertake substantive negotiations unless President Clinton obtains full negotiating authority."[30] Or, in the words of a journalist during a press conference at the Santiago Summit, "how will the US manage to create a free trade area in all the Americas in only seven years with 34 participating countries if it has not done so with only one country like Chile in four years, considering the economic differences within these 34 countries?"

The Santiago Summit was marred by the disillusionment created by the absence of fast-track authority for the US president, to the extreme that as the date of the summit approached, non-trade issues were upgraded on the summit agenda, just in case President Clinton arrived without "fast-track" authority.

Optimists argue that the Santiago summit was a success since the important issue was to launch the negotiations, "locking in" a summit process that was in the best interest of the US. For example, Richard Feinberg sees the revival of hemispherism in the 1990s as a positive development, while recognising the difficulties to go "from words to deeds," i.e., to implement the Santiago Plan of Action. For Feinberg, "Santiago confirmed that the region has a broad, shared agenda. Part of that agenda derives from 'spill over' issues such as narcotics, immigration and environment. Other parts of the agenda arise from 'substantive symmetry'–the fact that the globalized economy imposes a common policy agenda on all nations of the hemisphere." Feinberg even talks about the emergence of a "strategic alliance" in the Western Hemisphere.[31]

Optimists argue that the "summitisation" of inter-American relations is good because it marks the beginning of an era of co-operation in US/Latin American relations. For example, US Trade Representative Barshefsky is concerned about what she calls the "split dynamic" that is occurring in the Western Hemisphere: on the one hand, the FTAA process, on the other, the acceleration of subregional integration, i.e., "countries integrating with each other *around* the United States, not *with* the United States."[32] According to Barshefsky, the potential danger of the emergence of independent trading blocs in the Western Hemisphere is neutralised by the structural weight of the United States in inter-American relations. With a $7 trillion economy (75 percent of the Western Hemisphere's GDP) Barshefksy claims that the US "will always be at the centre."[33] From this perspective, the Latin American countries "must" move in the direction of the FTAA because there is no alternative for them. Barshefsky believes that the FTAA process:

> Will bring all of these pacts together. Where the FTAA is in effect, we will see a merging of these pacts, and because they already are beginning to open Latin America, we will see the FTAA capitalise on this movement toward openness. At the end of the day it will make the FTAA, while complex to negotiate, an instrument already well understood.[34]

Along similar lines, Isaac Cohen has suggested that the Latin American countries have something to learn from Canada's "asymmetrical but successful trading experience with the United States."[35] Are US/Latin American relations likely to follow the model of US/Canadian relations? The Latin American countries have had a different historical experience with the United States (see chapter 5). Mexico, Brazil, and Argentina have different interests and perceive their role in the hemispheric hierarchy of power as different from Canada.[36] Mexico has accepted the role of junior partner of the United States (thus learning from Canada's "asymmetrical but successful" trading experience) but Brazil has not and has consistently presented an *alternative* vision of hemispheric regionalism, even challenging US leadership in the FTAA process. As Maria Regina Soares de Lima points out, "A certain measure of autonomy in relation to the United States–something Mexico forfeited by joining NAFTA–is seen as important [by Brazil] insofar as it allows for the maintenance of an independent dialogue with extra-hemispheric powers in Europe and Asia (especially Japan and China)."[37] Argentina's automatic alignment/subordination to US foreign policy under Menem is different from Canada's more independent foreign policy behaviour.[38]

On the other hand, the Latin Americans have a lot to learn from the Canadian experience with the US to avoid making the same mistakes as Canadian negotiators did during the negotiations for the Canada-US Free Trade Agreement (CUSFTA). As Bruce Wilkinson points out, "Latin America would do well to take note of a number of negotiating techniques ("ploys") employed by the United States to protect its own interests..." An example is the tactic of the car dealer:

> Once negotiations commence, delay discussion of concessions that the other party is interested in obtaining until close to the deadline for conclusion of negotiations, pressure is on for a deal to be reached and the hopes of the other party are high that a deal will be reached. Then present unreasonable proposals in the hope that the other party will accept them, simply because it is now emotionally or otherwise committed to reaching an agreement.[39]

The idea that the Latin American nations should follow the model of Canadian "asymmetrical but successful" trading experience with the US is based on the assumption that the Latin American countries have to choose between sliding back into depression and dictatorship or accepting the role of junior partners of the United States, opening up their economies to US competition while trusting that the US will reciprocally open up its market to Latin American products. This interpretation leaves no room for an alternative future: a South American Free Trade Area (SAFTA) dealing with the US from a position of strength, as *real equals*, beyond the rhetoric of hemispheric regionalism.[40]

The US and Brazil: Two Competing Visions of the FTAA Process

The lack of fast-track authority of the US president contributed to Brazilian confidence in obtaining a favourable outcome at the end of the long road of FTAA negotiations. In 1994, Brazil's economic integration and foreign trade undersecretary said that "Brazil would only look for a coming together of the continental trading systems once a South American bloc is in place."[41] Yet at the Fourth Western Hemisphere Trade Ministerial Meeting (San Jose, Costa Rica, March 19, 1998) and at the Second Summit of the Americas (Santiago, April

1998) Brazil agreed to start negotiations on the FTAA even though SAFTA was not in place. Truly, Brazil won two important diplomatic victories at both meetings: (1) the FTAA will constitute a "single undertaking" ("nothing is agreed until everything is agreed,") and (2) countries can negotiate as members of a sub-regional trading bloc (thus legitimising Mercosur's stance in the negotiations). According to the "Ministerial Declaration of San Jose," (Costa Rica, March 1998) "the FTAA can co-exist with bilateral and sub-regional agreements, to the extent that the rights and obligations under these agreements are not covered by or go beyond the rights and obligations of the FTAA."[42]

Despite President Clinton's rhetorical declaration of support for Mercosur during his visit to Argentina and Brazil in October 1997, the US has been reluctant to recognise Mercosur's weight in hemispheric affairs and has never been happy with Mercosur's approach to regional and hemispheric integration. The US State Department has described Mercosur as a threat to hemispheric regionalism.[43] The attacks on Mercosur were subsequently followed up by the US Trade Representative Charlene Barshefsky and the office of Secretary of State Madeleine Albright. Mercosur was also criticised in a famous study by Alexander Yeats, of the World Bank, accusing Mercosur of protectionism and trade diversion (see chapter 3). At a press conference in Washington, DC, before the Santiago Summit, Charlene Barshefsky expressed deep suspicion about Mercosur for political, rather than economic reasons:

> And so you see an acceleration of ties between Mercosur and the Central American countries. An acceleration of the ties between Mercosur and the Andeans, an acceleration between Canada and Chile, between Chile and certain of the Central Americans or between Chile and Mexico. Mexico and Mercosur, the EU and Mercosur, Asia and Mexico. That acceleration has occurred because countries see a potential window of opportunity that they might not have envisioned had the US had fast track right now. That's not from our point of view an overly positive development... We do want to ensure that the United States remains at the centre of a constellation of trading relationships. The FTAA launch helps us reassert that central role, but the acceleration of subregional integration is something I think we have to look at very carefully.[44]

From the US perspective, the real goal at the Second Summit of the Americas was to disarm Mercosur "in stages": once the negotiations were under way Mercosur would *have to* make concessions in controversial issue-areas such as telecommunications, government procurement, intellectual property rights, rules of competition, and financial services.

On the other hand, the "Ministerial Declaration of San José" at the Fourth Trade Ministerial Meeting (Costa Rica, March 1998) contained important US concessions, including the acceptance of a broad definition of the FTAA as comprising (at least rhetorically) more than "free trade":

> We reiterate that the negotiation of the FTAA shall take into account the broad social and economic agenda contained in the Miami Declaration of Principles and Plan of Action with a view to contributing to raising living standards, to improving the working conditions of all people in the Americas and to better protect the environment.[45]

Yet, are these goals achievable within the framework of the neoliberal model underpinning the "Washington Consensus" and the concept of "open regionalism"?

As understood by Richard Feinberg, Jeffrey Stark and other scholars, the Summit of the Americas *process* is not only about free trade but also about preserving and strengthening democracy, combating drug trafficking and terrorism; eradicating poverty, and protecting the environment.[46] The Summit of the Americas process is presented as the "only game in town" for inter-American relations, regardless of whether it is the best of all possible strategic visions for the Hemisphere.

Although both the Miami Plan of Action (December 1994) and the Santiago Declaration (April 1998) leave some room for an active role on the part of non-governmental actors in the Summitry process, business organisations have had a greater opportunity to influence it than environmental and labor organisations; arguably the latter lack any *real power* to change the dominant neoliberal discourse on the "best" economic policy, even though the neoliberal model has produced high rates of unemployment and a recession in some countries. Moreover, the compatibility of free trade with the non-trade items in the Miami and Santiago plans of action such as eradicating poverty, strengthening the role of women in society, or encouraging small businesses, is open to question. For example, the unrestricted opening of the Argentine economy to foreign competition has not only produced deindustrialization but also eliminated many small and medium-sized businesses.[47] The promotion of a more active role for non-governmental organisations (NGOs) during the preparations for the Miami Summit was a revolutionary change in hemispheric relations.[48] Yet if those

NGOs (such as environmental groups) received a voice in summit implementation, they could challenge the "economic adjustment" process on which the vision of hemispheric free trade is based.

Finally, although the Latin American nations are a formidable potential market for US products, whole areas of Latin America are out of reach for US companies not only because violence, drugs, and corruption discourage foreign investment, but also because of lack of economic development. Latin America will have to invest billions of dollars in education to develop its economic potential and the technological skills required by modern industrial plants to invest in the region. The Santiago Summit's decision to introduce education as an essential aspect of hemispheric regionalism and to provide loans for education is a recognition of this problem. The issue of equality is an even more daunting problem. As Margaret Daly Hayes points out, "Latin America cannot develop a domestic and a region-based productive capacity if it does not have a consumer market to buy the products that companies produce."[49] Free trade is not the magic formula to solve these problems. On the contrary, it aggravates the problem of social and economic inequality by generating unemployment instead of a booming domestic market for domestic and foreign investment.

Looking Ahead: A Free Trade Area of the Americas in 2005?

Despite President Clinton's failure to win fast-track trade-negotiating authority from the US Congress, the FTAA negotiations were launched anyway at the Santiago Summit, which laid the ground for the institutionalisation of inter-American summitry. The train is moving ahead even if the destination is uncertain. For the US, to get negotiations started in Santiago was a diplomatic victory, even if it did not get all it wanted regarding the structure and timing of the negotiations. Brazil succeeded in delaying/slowing down the negotiations, but by accepting the FTAA concept implicitly agreed to the possibility of an NAFTA-Mercosur agreement that could dilute the specificity of Mercosur as a separate entity. Brazil probably believes that the leverage acquired during the trade ministerial meetings leading to the Santiago Summit will be enough to save Mercosur as a separate entity after the successful conclusion of the FTAA negotiations.[50] Arguably, without strong US engagement, the movement toward the FTAA will probably slow down, as active initiatives at the subregional level (such as Mercosur or the Andean Community) will seek for alternatives (such as a free trade area with the European Union) and/or successfully negotiate a South American Free Trade Area (SAFTA.)

Even if the nine negotiating groups created in Santiago can work out the nitty-gritty of the negotiations smoothly, a successful completion of the negotiations by 2005 still faces serious obstacles.

First, it is not clear that the United States is "definitely" interested in a successful conclusion of the FTAA negotiations. The US has rather powerful reasons to attempt to slow down the negotiations in order to revive the hub-and-spoke model that prevailed early on in the process, when Chile was the prime candidate to join NAFTA. A rapid implementation of free trade might compel the US "to assume financial and security obligations on behalf of a significant number of states that are not seen as important in terms of US interests."[51]

A selective enlargement of NAFTA would be a better option for the US, but the hub-and-spoke model is now hard to sell in Latin America, because several Latin American countries have lost trust in the seriousness of the US as a partner in the negotiations. As Leonard Schoppa points out, "trust" is essential to successfully conclude negotiations in asymmetric international bargaining.[52] After the Santiago Summit, the FTAA negotiations are taking place between a South American bloc, led by Brazil, and a North American bloc, led by the United States. The Latin American countries, coming hat in hand, one after another, asking permission to join NAFTA are a thing of the past.

A second reason for US reticence regarding a quick implementation of the FTAA is that Washington wants to control the "phasing in" of the free trade zone. A NAFTA-centred FTAA process would have allowed the US to do that: countries had to qualify to the strict criteria of the "Washington Consensus" (neoliberal economic reforms) to become candidates to join NAFTA.[53] As Belanger notes, if the US loses control over the phasing in of the FTAA, it may end up providing the benefits of free access to its market to several states "without having to implement the economic and political reforms that Washington could otherwise require them to adopt if trade negotiations remained on a bilateral basis."[54] Perhaps for that reason, Thomas McLarty, former US special envoy to Latin America during the Clinton administration, has suggested that the US should revive *bilateral* trade talks with Chile, urging the Clinton administration "to stop waiting for fast-track."[55]

On the other hand, the US has a powerful incentive to speed up a successful conclusion of the FTAA negotiations by 2005: an FTAA agreement would help the US to deal with the booming US trade deficit. According to the US

Department of Commerce, the US trade deficit totalled a record $21 billion in May 1999.[56] Latin America is a potential market of 430 million customers that would allow the US to significantly reduce its trade deficit. By 2010, according to US Trade Representative Charlene Barshefsky, Latin America alone will be a bigger market for US exports than the EU and Japan combined. US export increases to the Western Hemisphere accounted for 63 percent of US export growth world-wide in 1997, with Canada and Mexico accounting for much of that growth. In 1997, Mexico surpassed Japan as the US's second largest trading partner. The main argument to sell the FTAA to a skittish US Congress is that it would create millions of new jobs for US workers, since one in five new jobs created in the US depend on exports.

The second reason the US has an interest in successfully concluding the FTAA negotiations by 2005 is that the negotiations taking place in the Americas are more far-reaching than those conducted at the multilateral level, in the World Trade Organization. The FTAA agenda is WTO-plus. Although the negotiations are a single undertaking ("nothing is agreed until everything is agreed") the US managed to include deep integration issues in the FTAA agenda, with several negotiating groups addressing issues such as intellectual property rights, trade in services and government procurement. The Latin American countries may holdout on concessions on these thorny issues until the Millennium Round of global trade negotiations. As Paulo Wrobel points out, "if a new round of talks does begin, it might absorb all the energy of participants in the short term and make regional [hemispheric] negotiations for free trade redundant."[57]

Even if the US and the Latin American countries work hard to conclude the FTAA negotiations by 2005 a number of obstacles remain.

First, although "fast-track" authority on the part of the US government was not needed to launch the negotiations in Santiago, it will be certainly needed once the negotiations are concluded; otherwise, the whole exercise might collapse because the Latin American countries would have no guarantee that the US will fulfil its treaty obligations.[58] The absence of fast-track authority weakens the US negotiating position, and may even cause the failure of the FTAA negotiations. In the words of Uruguayan foreign minister Carlos Perez del Castillo, without fast-track authority, "the negotiating process makes no sense."

Second, Mexico is not particularly interested in the successful conclusion of the FTAA negotiations, because it will lose exclusive access to the US market. Mexico opposes the FTAA for the same reasons it opposes NAFTA extension to other Latin American countries. Mexico has already gained access to the US market, and it can always sign individual free trade agreements with its neighbours to the South, as it has already done with Chile, Venezuela, Colombia, Bolivia, and the Central American countries.

Third, as recognised by enthusiastic supporters of the FTAA, the FTAA negotiations will move slowly. Several factors will work in that direction. The FTAA process is deemed a single undertaking. Therefore, unanimity in decision making can prevent agreement on several controversial issues, such as agriculture, government procurement, intellectual property rights, subsidies, anti-dumping measures, or competition policy. Moreover, disagreements on trade-related environmental or labor matters could derail the negotiations. Or, bad enough from the US perspective, the ultimate FTAA agreement that is presented for signature in 2005 may not contain the type of market liberalisation rules (such as transparency in government procurement) that would benefit the most dynamic sectors of the US economy. Because of this and other obstacles, it has even been argued that "the US government lacks a compelling foreign policy rationale for expanding NAFTA or creating an FTAA."[59]

Fourth, the Santiago Summit adopted the definition of "concrete progress by the Year 2000" prepared at the San José trade ministerial meeting (Costa Rica, March 19, 1998):

> We instruct the TNC [Trade Negotiations Committee, formed by vice-ministers of trade] to agree on specific business facilitation measures to be adopted before the end of the century, taking into account the substantive work that has already emanated from the FTAA process.[60]

In San José, Brazil argued for limiting early concrete results to business facilitation, whereas the US argued for a wide-ranging package of early concrete results (the so-called "early harvest"). Although the Brazilian definition of "concrete results" was finally adopted in San José, after the Santiago Summit the US continued pressing for "early harvest" agreements, arguing that they were not incompatible with the requirements of a "single undertaking."[61] These disagreements on procedural matters will probably further contribute to the slow motion of the negotiations. Moreover, it is unlikely that President Clinton will obtain fast-track authority before the end of its administration. As Stephen Lande notes, in the absence of significant progress in the hemispheric trade negotiations by 2000, "with five years still remaining to negotiate, the public and government leaders will have a hard time maintaining interest in FTAA negotiations."[62] Lande argues that to restore credibility to the US negotiating posture and to prevent negotiations from languishing, "fast track should be passed or a decision made to forgo this authority for the FTAA early in the first term of the next US President." This would eliminate the uncertainties surrounding fast track. Yet would the Latin American countries sign an agreement that could be significantly amended by the US Congress? Would the lure of the US market be sufficient to justify the signing of such an agreement?

Fifth, if for domestic political reasons (strong domestic political opposition to NAFTA, resurgent protectionism) the US Congress grants fast-track negotiating authority for the WTO's "Millennium Round" while denying such authority for the FTAA negotiations, the latter would further languish and probably die because it would further erode Latin American trust in the US. The Millennium Round would be the new "ball game" absorbing all the energy of participants in the FTAA negotiations. Conversely, if the US Congress grants fast-track authority for the FTAA negotiations while denying it for global trade negotiations the US government would be on the horns of a dilemma. Considering the history of US "benign neglect" toward Latin America (see chapter 5) would a US administration be willing to forgo fast-track authority for multilateral trade negotiations simply to be able to successfully conclude the FTAA negotiations by 2005?

Will inter-American relations at the beginning of the millennium resemble the positive-sum relationship that prevails between the US and Canada?[63] This optimistic forecast neglects the fact that there are conflicts in the US/Canada trade relationship.[64] Moreover, this forecast is not warranted by the history of hemispheric trade negotiations in 1995-98, where two different conceptions of free trade in the Americas were exposed: the US model of "open regionalism" or "deep integration," following the NAFTA model, and the Brazil-Mercosur approach, pointing to a "model of equals," based on bloc to bloc negotiations and postponing debate of deep integration issues, such as trade in services, government procurement and labor standards. This model allows for the protection of the domestic industries of the weak parties to the agreement, making room for a fair distribution of costs and benefits and recognising the need to compensate the smaller economies for the benefits to the US (and the larger Latin American economies) resulting from structural asymmetries. Following the San José Declaration, a Consultative Group on Smaller Economies was created in Santiago, with the following functions:

> Follow the FTAA process, keeping under review the concerns and interests of the smaller economies; and bring to the attention of the Trade Negotiations

Committee (TNC) the issues of concern to the smaller economies and make recommendations to address these issues.[65]

This is a positive development. Whether the consultative group will be actually heard during the FTAA negotiations allowing the smaller countries to join the FTAA without unbearable adjustment costs is an open question.

The Lessons of the FTAA Process

What are the lessons of US policy during the FTAA negotiations for the future of US/Latin American relations?

As we have seen, the contradictions of US policy toward Latin America after the Miami Summit strengthened Mercosur and weakened NAFTA as the pole of attraction for a future FTAA. There were two turning points:

1) The failure of NAFTA to incorporate Chile as a new member and the subsequent rapprochement between Chile and Mercosur, culminating with the signing of a free trade agreement between Chile and Mercosur during its Tenth Presidential Summit in Potrero de Funes, San Luis, Argentina, in June 1996.

2) The failure of US President Bill Clinton to obtain from the US Congress "fast-track" authority to negotiate free trade agreements, which was seen by Latin American countries as a "litmus test" of the US commitment to open markets.

The emergence of Brazil/Mercosur/SAFTA as the pole of attraction for a future FTAA (which may compel the US to having to "apply" to join a Latin American-centred FTAA!) would have been unthinkable in 1993, when NAFTA was approved by the US Congress. Most Latin American countries at the Miami Summit, according to Clinton administration officials, would have joined NAFTA in 1994 if the US agreed. The US would decide which countries would join NAFTA and *when* they were "ready." Yet by 1998 the roles of the US and Brazil in the FTAA negotiations had been reversed. The South American countries, led by Brazil, were now assessing the "readiness" of the US to join an FTAA. How does one explain the change?[66] The South American countries have not changed their approach to free trade in the Western Hemisphere just because President Bill Clinton did not obtain "fast track" authority to negotiate free trade agreements. Systemic factors were also at stake including the erosion of US hegemony in the Western Hemisphere (see next chapter).

In the mid-1990s several analysts believed that NAFTA provided "the key element in the determination of the direction of regionalism in the Americas in the 1990s."[67] Yet, the history of the FTAA negotiations reviewed in this chapter adds a paradox to the above-mentioned puzzle. On the one hand, the US is the "indispensable partner" for the South American countries in the FTAA negotiations. There is no FTAA without the US, because of the weight of the US economy in the Western Hemisphere. On the other, the US "has so far failed to provide strong leadership or a clear vision in its policy on hemispheric regionalism."[68] The strengthening of the Brazil/Mercosur position during the FTAA negotiations raises the issue of whether US-South American relations are characterised by what Peter Smith calls "hegemony by default,"[69] or by loss of hegemony, since the US seems to be unable to convince the South American countries that "its" model of FTAA is in their best interest. What kind of hegemony, if any, is the US exercising over South America? This is the subject of the following chapter.

Notes

1 See Soares de Lima, M., 1999, "Brazil's Alternative Vision," pp. 133-151, in Mace, G. & Belanger, L. (eds.), *The Americas in Transition: The Contours of Regionalism*, Boulder (CO), Lynne Rienner.

2 Bush, G., 1990, "Latin America: Debt Reduction." Speech delivered at the White House, Washington, DC, June 27, 1990, in: *Vital Speeches of the Day*, Mount Pleasant, SC, No. 20, August 1, 1990, p. 611.

3 Foweraker, J., 1996, "From NAFTA to WHFTA? Prospects for Hemispheric Free Trade," p. 151, in Nishijima, S. & Smith, P. (eds.), *Cooperation or Rivalry: Regional Integration in the Americas and the Pacific Rim*, Boulder, (CO), Westview Press.

4 Petras, J. & Morley, M, 1992, "U.S. Policy Toward Latin America: Military Intervention, Client Regimes, and Economic Pillage in the 1990s," pp. 47-78, p. 56, In: Petras, J. & Morley, M., *Latin America in the Time of Cholera: Electoral Politics, Market Economics, and Permanent Crisis*, New York, Routledge.

5 Martin, P., 1994, "The Politics of International Structural Change: Aggressive Unilateralism in American Trade Policy," pp. 439-452, p. 439, in Stubbs, R. & Underhill, G. (eds.), *Political Economy and the Changing Global Order*, New York, St. Martin's Press.

6   Clinton, B. & Gore, A., 1992, *Putting People First: How We Can All Change America*, New York Times, Times Books, p. 156.
7   See Pastor, R., 1992, *Whirlpool: U.S. Foreign Policy toward Latin America and the Caribbean*, Princeton, (NJ), Princeton University Press, p. 97. Yet the "Americas Initiative" was criticised at the first meeting of congressmen from the Mercosur countries. Deputy Antonio Salum Flecha, president of Paraguay's Chamber of Deputies Foreign Relations Commission, pointed out the lack of "a relative reciprocity on items to be negotiated and on the application of the results"; adding that "the offer involving the debt and investments is strongly conditioned and way below Latin American and Caribbean needs." "Bush Plan Criticized," *Ultima Hora*, Asunción, trans. in *FBIS/Latin America*, May 19, 1991, p. 1.
8   Odell, J., 1986, "Growing Trade and Growing Conflict Between Latin America and the United States, p. 261, in Middlebrook, K. & Rico, C. (eds.), *The United States and Latin America in the 1980s: Contending Perspectives on a Decade of Crisis*, Pittsburgh, University of Pittsburgh Press, pp. 261-294.
9   The "Four plus One Agreement" commits the Mercosur partners to an institutionalised mechanism of consultations with the US to stimulate trade liberalisation and investment between the parties. Since Mercosur was not yet a "subject" of international law, the Rose Garden Agreement was signed individually by each country, although the reference to the "parties of South America" in the Preamble shows the intention to "bilateralize" the treaty in the future.
10 As Richard Feinberg recalls, after the US House of Representatives passed NAFTA on November 17, 1993, "the tenor was decidedly cautious. It was agreed that the vice president would lay out a general vision of post-NAFTA hemispheric relations and that he would not retreat from the president's repeated public calls for freer hemispheric trade. The idea of a summit was mentioned but was as quickly shelved. As one participant recalled, 'There was no appetite for another summit, in light of the president's existing commitments toward the Asia Pacific Economic Cooperation (APEC) forum and the Group of Seven' (G-7)." Feinberg, R., 1997, *Summitry in the Americas: A Progress Report*, Washington, DC, Institute for International Economics, pp. 56-57. With the possible exception of Mexico and the Caribbean countries, Latin America has never been a high priority in US foreign policy. Despite optimistic claims about a "new era in US-Latin American relations," the area is still secondary in US foreign policy concerns. (See chapter 5).
11 Wiarda, H., 1995, "After Miami: The Summit, the Peso Crisis, and the Future of US-Latin American Relations," p. 46, *Journal of Interamerican Studies and World Affairs*, vol. 37, pp. 43-68.

12 See Haggard, S., 1995, *Developing Nations and the Politics of Global Integration*, Washington, DC, Brookings Institution, pp. 2-3.
13 See Feinberg, 1997, *op. cit.*, p. 65.
14 See Lipsey, R., 1992, "Getting There: The Path to a Western Hemisphere Free Trade Area and Its Structure," in Saborio, S. (ed.), *The Premise and the Promise: Free Trade in the Americas*, New Brunswick (NJ), Transaction Publishers, pp. 95-116.
15 Smith, P., 1996, *Talons of the Eagle: Dynamics of U.S.-Latin American Relations*, New York, Oxford University Press, p. 261.
16 See Feinberg, 1997, *op. cit.*, p. 165.
17 Mace, G. & Bélanger, L., 1999. "The Structural Contexts of Hemispheric Regionalism: Power, Trade, Political Culture, and Economic Development," p. 57, in Mace, G. & Bélanger, L. (eds.), *The Americas in Transition: The Contours of Regionalism*, Boulder, (CO), Lynne Rienner.
18 Hakim, P., 1992, "President Bush's Southern Strategy," *op. cit.*, p. 100, emphasis added. See also Panagariya, A., 1996, "The Free Trade Area of the Americas: Good for Latin America?" *World Economy* (September), pp. 485-515, p. 504.
19 Smith, 1996, *op. cit.*, p. 311.
20 See note 41 below.
21 See Hirschman, A., 1980, *National Power and the Structure of Foreign Trade*, Berkeley (CA), University of California Press. See also Hakim, P., 1993, "Western Hemisphere Free Trade: Why Should Latin America Be Interested?" p. 133, in Weintraub, S. (ed.), "Free Trade in the Western Hemisphere," *The Annals of the American Academy of Political and Social Science*, vol. 526, pp. 121-134.
22 See Petras, J. & Morley, M., 1992, *Latin America in the Time of Cholera*, *op. cit.*, pp. 51-59.
23 Naim, M., 1994, "Toward Free Trade in the Americas: Building Blocks, Stumbling Blocks, and Entry Fees," p. 56, in Weintraub, S. (ed.), *Integrating the Americas: Shaping Future Trade Policy*, New Brunswick (NJ), Transaction Publishers, pp. 45-88.
24 See Lowenthal, A., 1990, *Partners in Conflict: The United States and Latin America in the 1990s*, Baltimore (MD), Johns Hopkins University Press, p. 141.
25 See Feinberg, 1997, *op. cit.*, p. 181.
26 The US failure to fulfil its promise to incorporate Chile to NAFTA changed the dynamics of the FTAA negotiations, strengthening the Brazilian push for an independent South American posture.
27 Soares de Lima, M., 1999, "Brazil's Alternative Vision," p. 142, in Mace, G. & Bélanger, L. (eds.), *The Americas in Transition: The Contours of Regionalism*, Boulder (CO), Lynne Rienner, pp. 133-151.

28 See "Ground Rules for FTAA Agreed: Mercosur Stance Carries the Day as Washington Cedes," *Latin American Weekly Report*, 24/3/98, p. 136.
29 Srodes, J., 1998, "Charlene Barshefksy on Trade," in *World Trade* (August), p. 41.
30 "Santiago Summit Unlikely to Jump-start FTAA Negotiations, Director Says," Press Release, National Law Center for Inter-American Free Trade, http://www.natlaw.com/media/press10.htm. Brazilian President Fernando Henrique Cardoso made the same point when he said, "as long as President Clinton does not have authorization from Congress, the talks are imaginary," quoted by Dyer, G., 1997, "Brazil Urges 'Realism' in All-America Trade Talks," *Financial Times*, 16/5/97, p. 4.
31 Feinberg, R., 1998, "Integrating the Americas," IGCC Policy Brief n.10, University of California Institute on Global Conflict and Cooperation, http//www.igcc.ucsd.edu/igcc2/PolicyBriefs/pb10.htm.
32 See "Summit of the Americas Preview" (Berger, McLarty, Barshefsky briefing,) unofficial transcript, 13/04/98, in http://www.usembassy.cl/lefl17.htm, p. 9 (emphases added).
33 Ibid., p. 10.
34 Srodes, 1998, *op. cit.*, p. 41.
35 Cohen, I., 1991, "Economic Questions," p. 31, in Atkins, G.P. (ed.), *The United States and Latin America: Redefining U.S. Purposes in the Post-Cold War Era*, Austin (TX), The University of Texas at Austin, pp. 19-34.
36 See Bélanger, L. & Mace, G., 1999, "Building Role and Region: Middle States and Regionalism in the Americas," pp. 153-173, in Mace, G. & Bélanger, L (eds.), *The Americas in Transition: The Contours of Regionalism*, Boulder (CO), Lynne Rienner.
37 Soares de Lima, M. R., 1999, "Brazil's Alternative Vision," *op. cit.*, p. 147.
38 Argentina's foreign policy could become more independent from US foreign policy after the victory of the FREPASO/Radical Party Alliance in the October 1999 presidential election, although the basic tenets of the neoliberal model (the currency board or "convertibility" law) will probably remain unchanged.
39 Wilkinson, B.W., 1997, "NAFTA in the World Economy: Lessons and Issues for Latin America," p. 47, in Lipsey, R. G. & Meller, P. (eds.), *Western Hemisphere Trade Integration: A Canadian-Latin American Dialogue*, New York, St. Martin's Press.
40 For example, Wilkinson advises the Latin American nations to develop "detailed countervailing and anti-dumping duties, as well as safeguard laws, to parallel those in the United States, and have them in place *and be actively using them*

prior to concluding any negotiations with the United States to enter NAFTA." See Wilkinson, B., 1997, "NAFTA in the World Economy," *op. cit.*, p. 49.

41 Statement by José Arturo Denot Medeiros, economic integration and foreign trade under-secretary at the Brazilian Foreign Relations Ministry. Quoted in Fischer, K. P., 1999, "Business and Integration in the Americas: Competing points of View," in Mace, G. & Bélanger, L. (eds.), *The Americas in Transition, op. cit.*, p. 217.

42 This raises important practical questions. For example, could the Mercosur countries keep a higher external tariff than the rest of the hemisphere (e.g., for capital goods, or automobiles) after the signing of an FTAA agreement?

43 See Bernier, I. & Roy, M., 1999, "NAFTA and Mercosur: Two Competing Models?" in Mace, G. & Bélanger, L. (eds.), *The Americas in Transition, op. cit.*, p. 69, 89.

44 "Summit of the Americas Preview (Berger, McLarty, Barshefsky briefing)," *op. cit.*, p. 9.

45 "Ministerial Declaration of San José," Fourth Western Hemisphere Trade Ministerial Meeting of the Free Trade Area of the Americas, San José, Costa Rica, March 19, 1998, Department of Foreign Affairs and International Trade, Ottawa, Canada.

46 See Feinberg, 1997, *op. cit.*; Stark, J., 1998, "The Summit of the Americas Process in Perspective: Global Change, Regional Norms, and State Capacity," paper presented at the 39th Annual Meeting of the International Studies Association, March 17-21, Minneapolis, Minnesota.

47 "La Matanza, (one of the largest working class districts in the greater Buenos Aires area, M. C.) over half of whose people officially live in poverty, once formed part of the capital's [Buenos Aires's] industrial belt. But today the main legacy of Mr. Menem's economic 'miracle' is a string of abandoned factories. Many companies have moved to Brazil, which has lower costs and a bigger market. Others were simply unready and unprotected when the Menem government threw open Argentina's market to foreign competition," "Argentina: After Menem," *The Economist*, 17/7/99, p. 32.

48 "Another important inspiration and source of new ideas was the non governmental sector. The democracy and environmental working groups met repeatedly with people and organisations outside the government and digested their publications. For example, the Interamerican Dialogue provided valuable input on ways to strengthen the pro-democracy programs of the Organization of American States. Transparency International brought anti-corruption expertise. A broad coalition of environmental groups was instrumental in designing the three sustainable development partnerships. NGAs were included in some working group meetings and participated in certain official US delegations to consult with other

hemispheric governments on summit initiatives," Feinberg, 1997, *op. cit.*, p. 89. See also Rosenberg, R. & Stein, S. (eds.), 1995, *Advancing the Miami Process: Civil Society and the Summit of the Americas*, Boulder (CO), Lynne Rienner.

49 Daly Hayes, M., 1992, "Commentary," p. 41, in Atkins, G. P. (ed.), *The United States and Latin America, op. cit.*, p. 35-42.

50 In Belo Horizonte (May 1997) the US formally acknowledged that the FTAA should coexist with subregional trade groups such as Mercosur and NAFTA.

51 Bélanger, L., 1999, "U.S. Foreign Policy and the Regionalist Option in the Americas," in Mace, G. & Bélanger L. (eds.), *The Americas in Transition, op. cit.*, p. 104.

52 Schoppa, L., 1999, "The Social Context in Coercive International Bargaining," in *International Organization*, vol. 53 (2): 307-342, Spring 1999, p. 316.

53 See Hufbauer, G. & Schott, J., 1994, *Western Hemisphere Economic Integration*, Washington, DC, Institute for International Economics, chap. 5, "Latin American Reforms and Readiness Indicators," pp. 63-96.

54 Bélanger, 1999, *op. cit.*, p. 104.

55 See McLarty, M., 1999, "Fast Track Isn't Fast Enough," *New York Times*, 20/7/99.

56 Sanger, D., 1999, "Trade Deficit Set a Record during May: Rising Gap with China is Particularly Thorny," *New York Times*, 21/7/99, p. C1, C4.

57 Wrobel, P., 1998, "A Free Trade Area of the Americas in 2005?" in *International Affairs*, vol. 74 (3): 547-561, p. 559.

58 US officials put the best face on the situation created by the absence of fast-track authority arguing that President George Bush did not have it when he began negotiations on NAFTA, and that the US launched the Uruguay Round two years before the US President obtained fast-track authority from Congress. See Srodes, "Charlene Barshefsky on Trade," *op. cit.*, p. 41; Shorrock, T., 1998, "Trade-USA: Meagre U.S. Offerings at Santiago Summit," in *World News* (Inter Press Service,) 12/4/98.

59 See "Expanding NAFTA: What Should Be Done?" Policy in Perspective, The Century Foundation, in: http//www.tcf.org/Publications/Basics/NAFTA/ Expanding Nafta.html.

60 "Ministerial Declaration of San José," *op. cit.*, p. 5.

61 A week after the Santiago Summit, US Commerce Secretary William Daley said to the Buenos Aires newspaper *La Nación* that the US still favoured partial agreements and negotiations between individual countries. "In the negotiating groups, he said, 'we want to promote the countries, not the trading blocs to which they belong.' He added, 'I don't see why we should wait until 2005 to start

implementing agreements that could be positive for the parties'." See "U.S. Insists on Its Own Formula," *Latin American Weekly Report*, 28/4/98, p. 187.

62 Lande, S., 1998, "Free Trade in the Americas: Launching Negotiations and Concrete Progress by the Millennium," in *Free Trade in the Americas: Fulfilling the Promise of Miami*, North-South Center, University of Miami.

63 See Cohen, I., 1991, "Economic Questions," *op. cit.*, p. 29.

64 See e.g., Wilkinson, B. W., "NAFTA in the World Economy," *op. cit.*; Dearden, R., 1997, "Trade Disputes and Settlement Mechanisms under the Canada-US Free Trade Agreement," pp. 207-231, in Lipsey, R. & Meller, P. (eds.), *Western Hemisphere Trade Integration, op. cit.*; Weston, A., 1997, "Social Issues and Labour Adjustment Policies: The Canada-US FTA Experience," pp. 191-206, in the same volume.

65 "Ministerial Declaration of San José," *op. cit.*, p. 4.

66 To what extent the hub-and-spoke model has lost clout among Latin American leaders and how confident they are in their ability to take charge of their future is shown by a "joke" attributed to President Menem of Argentina before a visit to Washington: "If the United States and its NAFTA partners wished to join Mercosur, they would be welcome to do so." Quoted in Rohter, L., "Free Trade Goes South With and Without US," *New York Times*, 6/1/97.

67 See Axline, W., 1996, "Conclusion: External Forces, State Strategies, and Regionalism in the Americas," p. 200, in Mace, G. & Thérien, J. (eds.), *Foreign Policy and Regionalism in the Americas*, Boulder (CO), Lynne Rienner, pp. 199-218.

68 Bélanger, L., 1999, "U.S. Foreign Policy and the Regionalist Option in the Americas," *op. cit.*, p. 95.

69 See Smith, 1996, *op. cit.*, pp. 6-7.

5 United States-South American Relations After the Miami Summit: Hegemony by Default or Lack of Hegemony?

1. Introduction: The Goals and Instruments of US Hegemony in Latin America

The purpose of this chapter is to situate the analysis in the preceding chapters within the broader framework of US-Latin American relations. US policy toward Latin America has consistently pursued two objectives: to exclude extracontinental rivals or hostile powers from the Western Hemisphere (the Monroe Doctrine) and to secure and maintain a dominant politico-economic presence in the region.

The US has combined the use of different instruments to exercise hegemony over Latin America:

1. Military instruments. The US has used force to realise its "manifest destiny" to become a "continental republic." Thus the US went to war with Mexico and deprived it of more than half of its national territory. The Mexican defeat was formalised in the Treaty of Guadalupe Hidalgo, signed on February 2, 1848. After losing approximately one-third of its territory, Mexico still sold a big chunk of land (the present states of Arizona and New Mexico) to the US, the so-called Gadsden purchase of 1853.[1]

The US acquisition of the Panama Canal Zone, after US naval forces ensured the success of the Panamanian revolt against Colombia in 1903, marks the beginning of US imperialism in Latin America.[2] The US sent the marines to Central America and the Caribbean more than twenty times in the first three decades of the twentieth century. The military power of the US has also influenced Latin America through weapons sales and training facilities. During the Cold War, over a half of the Latin American countries concluded mutual defence agreements with the United States and all of them bought military equipment from the "Colossus of the North." After the Cuban Revolution (1959), inter-American military co-operation focused on counter-insurgency and internal security.[3]

2. *Political Instruments*. The US has been a permanent actor in the political systems of several Central American (e.g., Nicaragua) and Caribbean countries for a long period, especially in the period 1898-1933. The US has used its recognition policy as a major form of intervention in the internal affairs of Latin American states. The withholding of recognition has often encouraged the opponents of certain regimes to overthrow them. Moreover, the US has often invoked international law to exercise hegemony, as shown by the quasi-perpetual treaties to maintain bases at Guantanamo in Cuba and the Panama Canal Zone, or the support of claims by US citizens against Latin American governments.

3. *Economic Aid*. The granting or withholding of economic aid has in the past significantly contributed to US hegemony in Latin America. For example, the US response to the Bolivian revolution of 1952 was supportive, whereas the US was the essential player in the "invisible" economic blockade that significantly contributed to the overthrow of Chilean President Salvador Allende in 1973. US aid programs to Latin America have had the effect of increasing US economic influence since most of the aid has taken the form of loans, which have to be spent in the US.

4. *Cultural instruments*. The US promotes the "American way of life" as an instrument of its foreign policy, taking advantage of the information revolution (an essential component of globalization) and the "hegemonic" role of the English language in international exchanges and commercial transactions, both at the governmental and non-governmental levels. The US Information Agency (USIA) promotes the idea of an essential harmony of interests between the United States and Latin America.

2. The Evolution of US-Latin American Relations

a) From the Monroe Doctrine and "Big Stick" Interventionism to Franklin Roosevelt's Good Neighbour Policy

The hegemonic presumption, the US conviction that it has a "natural right" to achieve and exercise hegemony in the Americas,[4] goes back to the Monroe Doctrine (1823) and Theodore Roosevelt's "big stick" policy of military interventions in Central America and the Caribbean that would continue until 1933.

The gist of the Monroe Doctrine was that the United States would consider any attempt on the part of the European powers to impose their political system upon the Western Hemisphere as "endangering our peace and happiness" and could not view any such attempt in any form "with indifference." The US was to be the only great power in the Western Hemisphere, and the Latin American countries would belong to an American system in which the United States would be paramount. The Monroe doctrine was an official declaration fencing in the Western Hemisphere as a US sphere of influence. In 1904, the Roosevelt Corollary to the Monroe Doctrine established the "right" of the US to militarily intervene in Latin America:

> Chronic wrongdoing, or an impotence which results in a general loosening of the ties of civilized society, may in America, as elsewhere, ultimately require intervention by some civilized nation, and in the Western Hemisphere, the adherence of the United States to the Monroe Doctrine may force the United States, however reluctantly, in flagrant cases of such wrongdoing or impotence, to the exercise of an international police power...[5]

As Molineau points out, the Roosevelt Corollary "was an assertion of the United States as both a patron and a policeman."[6] The US tendency to be condescending, patronising, and "superior" to its neighbours to the South is blatantly summarised in a famous statement by US Secretary of State Richard Olney in 1895:

> Today the US is practically sovereign in this continent. Its infinite resources combined with its isolated position render it master of the situation and practically invulnerable as against any or all other powers.[7]

The Good Neighbour policy inaugurated by US President Franklin Roosevelt in 1933 marked a fundamental change in US policy toward Latin America. The Roosevelt administration formally agreed not to intervene "directly or indirectly and for whatever reason, in the internal and external affairs" of the Latin American countries.[8] In sharp contrast with the thirty years prior to Roosevelt's inauguration, the US withdrew its troops from Central America and the Caribbean. The last US marine left Haiti in 1934, and the US abandoned its five Caribbean protectorates—Cuba, Haiti, the Dominican Republic, Nicaragua, and Panama, although it kept the Panama Canal Zone. The US refrained from intervening in Mexico after the expropriation of US oil company properties by the Mexican government. On the other hand, the US embarked on a policy of multilateralism and adherence to the precepts of international law mutually accepted in Latin America and the United States. Franklin Roosevelt's policy has generally been considered as the most successful pursued by the US toward Latin America, establishing the foundation for modern Pan Americanism. Inter-American co-operation during World War II (Brazil even sent troops to Italy) is often cited as demonstrating the success of the Good Neighbour Policy. Optimists consider it an important precedent to the contemporary Summit of the Americas (SOA) process.[9] Other scholars are more cautious. For example, Molineau argues that the Good Neighbour Policy perpetuated "the myth of a neighbourhood of equals, sharing a common view of the world."[10]

The myth of a relationship of equals did not survive the US/Latin American partnership during World War II. As Connell Smith points out, "the US only too clearly was the senior partner, and growing ever stronger relative to Latin America as the war progressed."[11] The deterioration of the wartime partnership began during the war with problems with Bolivia and Argentina, and was much more pronounced after the war, when the "perennial problem of Argentina" compelled the US to delay a critical post-war meeting to establish an inter-American security system.[12]

b) US Policy toward Latin America during the Cold War (1947-1989)

During the Cold War, the United States paid attention to the region only in times of crisis and only when it perceived its security interests to be threatened, such as during the October 1962 Cuban missile crisis or the 1965 US military intervention in Santo Domingo. The rest of the time, the United States ignored the region. As Lars Schoultz forcefully puts it,

> Most policy makers believe that the security of the United States would not be adversely affected if Latin America were, say, to sink to the bottom of the sea. It is not that policy makers want much of anything from Latin America but rather that they do not want the Soviet Union to have it.[13]

"Security to the South" was narrowly defined by the US in terms of national security and "protective imperialism," without taking into consideration Latin American security concerns, which have been historically closely linked to economic development, social progress, and domestic political unity. US rejection of a Marshall Plan for Latin America at the Inter-American Conference for the Maintenance of Continental Peace and Security (August 15 - September 2, 1947) represents a long-standing US attitude of neglect toward Latin American problems.[14]

The idea that Latin America (especially South America) is geopolitically unimportant is deeply imbedded in the American foreign policy-making establishment. It was summarised in a famous statement made in June 1969 by former Secretary of State Henry Kissinger in his reply to a speech by Chilean Foreign Minister Gabriel Valdés:

> Mr. Minister, you made a strange speech. You come here speaking of Latin America, but this is not important. Nothing important can come from the South. History has never been produced in the South. The axis of history starts in Moscow, goes to Bonn, crosses over to Washington, and then goes to Tokyo. What happens in the South is of no importance. You are wasting your time.[15]

During the Cold War, the tendency of US policymakers to adopt a patronising attitude toward Latin America was reinforced by their image of Latin American elites and peoples as essentially "dependent." A show of autonomy by a nationalist (not necessarily pro-Soviet) regime south of the Rio Grande was immediately perceived as a potential switch of allegiance, threatening US hegemony in the hemisphere and US national interests in the Cold War confrontation with the Soviet Union. Moreover, as Martha Cottam has shown, such an attitude prevented US policymakers from even considering the possibility of an even-handed relationship with the Latin American nations:

> Latin American countries are the prototypical example of the US dependent image: weak, childlike, inferior, inept, and led by a small and often corrupt elite. This type of country is viewed with contempt, and its society and polities are seen in very simple terms: they are not treated as equals because they are not seen as equals.[16]

Whether this attitude has significantly changed after the Cold War is a big open question. Optimists believe that the US no longer has hegemonic pretensions over Latin America, and that the 1994 Miami Summit marks the beginning of a new era in US/Latin American relations, in which the Latin American nations are "really" going to be treated as equals, breaking with the traditional US stereotype of Latin America as a group of "backward" republics. The fact that with the exception of Cuba all of Latin America is currently ruled by formally democratic regimes may have contributed to a change of image. Optimists argue President Bush's Enterprise for the Americas Initiative is the turning point in that respect.[17] However, old habits die hard and one can also argue that in the post-Cold War era, the search for uncontested US hegemony in the whole hemisphere, reinforces the Cold War belief that hegemony is desirable and that as the only superpower left the US "must" exercise a dominant influence in the region.[18]

The turning point in US-Latin American relations during the Cold War was the Cuban Revolution of 1959. The Cuban revolution challenged the US self-image as a benevolent paramount and the liberal idea that there is a mutuality of interests between the United States and Latin America. The traditional framework in which US and Latin American foreign policies were shaped was broken in two fundamental ways: (a) because the Cuban revolution gave rise to a socialist model of development for Latin America, (b) because it linked the Cold War to the problem of underdevelopment. The institutionalisation of a revolutionary socialist regime in Cuba allied with the Soviet Union provided the most dramatic daily reminder that US hegemony in Latin America had significantly declined. The very existence of a communist regime in the Western Hemisphere, with close relations with the Soviet Union, challenged the Monroe Doctrine. It is not by chance that in the 1960s and 1970s, the Latin American countries diversified their external links and increasingly identified themselves with the Third World, while attempting to lessen their economic dependence upon the US and forming a common front in negotiating with it. Several Latin American countries (Brazil, Mexico, Argentina, and Venezuela) adopted independent foreign policies. By the late 1970s, both the decline of US hegemony south of the Rio Grande and the march toward the autonomy of the region in international affairs seemed irreversible.

The Kennedy administration's (1961-1963) response to the Cuban revolution was embodied in President Kennedy's famous quote: "Those who make peaceful revolution impossible make violent revolution inevitable." From now on the US would pay more attention to Latin America, and would do anything (including the use of military force, as in the Dominican Republic in 1965) to prevent the emergence of a "second Cuba." As Gil points out, President Kennedy's Alliance for Progress "was unprecedented in the history of hemispheric relations, for in essence the United States was offering to underwrite a social revolution for Latin America."[19] Yet the fundamental purpose of the Alliance for Progress was to maintain hemispheric stability, and the US would actively support counterinsurgency and civic action programs undertaken by Latin American military establishments. The promotion of democracy was subordinated to the Cold War confrontation with the Soviet Union and the US would support military regimes as long as they advanced the American campaign against international communism.

US policy toward Latin America did not fundamentally change during the Johnson (1963-1969) and Nixon (1969-1974) administrations. Johnson's knowledge and interest in Latin America were limited to Mexico and he was unable and unwilling to provide the Alliance for Progress with the intellectual and political leadership that had disappeared with Kennedy's death. The Alliance was not officially abandoned but was left in an ailing state until it finally died during the Nixon years.

During the Nixon administration (1969-1974) the US reverted to the historical pattern of benign neglect of Latin America, with the exception of a continuing attention to the "Cuban problem" and an active policy to destabilise the Allende regime in Chile, considered a threat to US interests because of its Marxist ideology and its possible alignment with the Soviet Union.

"We went to visit neighbours and found brothers." So began the Rockefeller report on United States-Latin American relations in 1969. The quote captures a recurrent theme in the history of US Latin American policy: the rhetorical attempt to create a new spirit of co-operation with its southern neighbours. Nixon talked about a "more mature partnership" with Latin America, and his Secretary of State Kissinger called for a "new dialogue" and claimed that "the policy of the good partner" would be the new US approach to the region. Yet in practice the Nixon administration followed the traditional pattern of paying attention to the region only in times of crisis. US policy to destabilise Chile (to "make the [Chilean] economy scream") was exactly the opposite of "the policy of the good partner."

The Carter administration (1977-1981) adopted a new approach to US-Latin American relations. Carter's policies were the first serious attempt to go beyond Washington's hegemonic presumption and the premise that there is a "special relationship" between the US and Latin America. Carter made an attempt to place US/Latin American relations within the broader framework of North/South relations, while recognising the increasing international significance of the middle powers (Brazil, Mexico, Argentina, Venezuela) emerging in the region. He took the promotion of democracy and human rights in Latin America seriously, and promised to respond to Latin American concerns on North-South economic issues: trade, aid, finance, and technology transfer. Carter managed to get the Panama Canal treaties negotiated and then ratified by a reluctant US Congress and even explored the possibility of gradually renewing US relations with Cuba. Yet in the end, Carter too subordinated the promotion of democracy and human rights to the confrontation with the Soviet Union when he recommended the US Congress to renew US military aid to the military regime in El Salvador, in spite of its flagrant human rights violations.

The Reagan administration (1981-1989) decided to regain a dominant hemispheric role for the United States, reversing what was perceived as the increasing expansion of Soviet influence in strategically important Third World regions, such as Central America and the Caribbean. Under Reagan, the US again became an "eagle defiant." The Reagan administration linked the revolutionary movement in El Salvador and the Sandinista revolution in Nicaragua to Cuban and Soviet intervention, and spent a disproportionate amount of military and political capital in restoring US political, ideological, and security control of the Caribbean basin while neglecting Brazil and the southern cone countries.[20]

In the 1960s and 1970s, Latin American "emergence" in world affairs appeared increasingly possible; the sights of the major Latin American states had moved beyond the hemisphere. Between the mid-1960s and 1982 Brazil and other key South American states attempted to develop independent foreign policies, with relative success in some cases (Brazil, Mexico.) Arguably, by 1979-1980 the US exerted less dominance in the Western Hemisphere than at any time since World War II. Yet, during the debt crisis of the 1980s the US reasserted its hegemony over South America. The refusal of the Reagan administration to undertake government-to-government negotiations with the major debtor countries (see chapter 2) dealt a severe blow to Latin America's "emergence," by compelling the major Latin American debtors (Argentina, Brazil, Mexico) to go to Washington DC for help. High interest rates in the US damaged Latin America in two ways. First, the rates made recovery in the industrialised countries a slow and drawn out process that tended to reduce the demand for Latin American exports. Second, by increasing the cost of servicing the foreign debt for Latin America, the rates greatly increased the deficit on current account and (as we have seen in chapter 2 contributed to a considerable transfer of resources from Latin America to the rest of the world.

c) US Policy toward Latin America after the Cold War: Continuity or Change?

According to Abraham Lowenthal, "the outbreak of revolutions in Central America and the hemispheric debt crisis of the 1980s made it impossible for Washington to continue to ignore the region."[21] Yet one may argue that the Bush administration continued ignoring Latin America. On the one hand, the end of the Cold War, German reunification, and the breakdown of communist regimes in Eastern Europe and the Soviet Union attracted most of its attention. On the other, the lack of resources for debt relief and an effective anti-drug policy were a major obstacle to undertake a comprehensive Latin American policy. In the words of Howard Wiarda,

> As usual, Latin America is a low priority and "benign neglect" is popular; but benign neglect as a basis for policy can be maintained only for a limited time, while the problems of Latin America continue to fester.[22]

The Bush administration finally agreed to a negotiated solution to the civil wars and guerrilla conflicts in Central America, a policy that had been supported by the Contadora Group (Venezuela, Colombia, Mexico and Panama) and the South American countries for many years. Bush supported the Arias Plan, and promised not to seek military aid for the *contras* in Nicaragua before the general elections scheduled for February 26, 1990 that resulted in the electoral defeat of the Sandinistas.[23] Second, Bush took advantage of the weakness of the Soviet Union (which was on the verge of collapse) and the end of the Cold War to get rid of Panamanian President General Antonio Noriega. As Jorge Castañeda points out, during the Cold War, the "rule of world-wide symmetries and action-counteraction was in play," tacitly implying that if the US brazenly intervened in Latin America the Soviet Union would use such a violation against Washington, "perhaps not in Latin America but certainly elsewhere."[24] With the end of the Cold War, the US was free to militarily intervene in Latin America without fearing Soviet retaliation.

Third, the Bush administration launched the Enterprise for the Americas Initiative (see chapter 4) and developed a "free-trade" plan for Latin America, targeting Mexico for the establishment of a US-Mexico free-trade agreement. The North American Free Trade Agreement (NAFTA) was signed in October 1992 by the leaders of the US, Mexico, and Canada in San Antonio, Texas, and entered into force in January 1994. Coupled with the EAI, NAFTA marked a shift in US policy toward Latin America, from an obsession with the dangers of the "Soviet/Cuban threat" in Central America and the Caribbean to an emphasis on economic co-operation with the Latin American republics, which boiled down to opening the lucrative Latin American market to US exports and investment. The trade component, closely associated with NAFTA, was the most ambitious pillar of the EAI.[25] As Petras and Morley point out, the Bush administration's Latin American policy was significantly different from US economic policy toward the region during the Cold War:

> The "trade not aid" formula is peculiarly suited to the pillage of Latin America-the take-over of local markets and enterprises. In the past, US economic policy was based on trade *and* aid: state assistance involved large-scale, low-interest public loans to finance infrastructure, energy projects, and education to provide the "shell" for long-term, large-scale US and local investments; and short term loans for social programs and the growth of small businesses to cushion the adverse impacts of the market. The new formula of trade not aid that informs the Bush initiative scheme is designed for short-term speculative investments without concern for the socially negative consequences.[26]

The Clinton administration came to office in 1993 with a government program focusing on domestic issues, rather than foreign policy. The new international situation created by the end of the Cold War forced the Clinton administration to pay more attention to international events such as the civil war in Bosnia (1993-1995). On the other hand, Clinton's appointments of Anthony Lake as National Security Council Adviser and Richard Feinberg as the Council's officer on Latin American affairs raised some expectations that there was a "window of opportunity" for a fundamental change in US policy toward Latin America.[27]

Yet there was a basic continuity with the Bush policy of benign neglect; Clinton was the first US president since World War II not to set foot in Latin America or the Caribbean during his first term. In the end, Clinton's policy was basically a continuation of Bush's "free-trade" plan for Latin America. His major achievement was the Summit of the Americas in Miami (December 1994) the first such gathering since the Punta del Este summit of 1967. Yet as we have seen in chapter 4, the summit of the Americas process has lost momentum, partly because of the inability of the Clinton administration to obtain from the US Congress "fast-track" authority to negotiate trade agreements.[28] Clinton reversed his campaign promise to accept refugees persecuted by Haiti's military regime, declaring that the Bush policies on immigration would remain in place. Although the core of Clinton's Latin American policy has remained similar to Bush's, Clinton has placed more emphasis on the promotion of democracy and human rights in the region, as shown by the restoration of democracy in Haiti in September 1994.

Despite the renewed interest in Latin America shown by the convocation of the Miami Summit, the Clinton administration showed the same benign neglect as its predecessors while implementing the proposal.[29] Although NAFTA, the restoration of democracy in Haiti, and the rescue of the Mexican peso in 1995 were foreign policy successes, in other areas, such as the drug war,

> The Clinton administration was slow to make appointments and erratic in co-ordinating policy, with the result that the rest of the US-Latin American agenda was addressed at midlevels of the government's bureaucracy in a highly compartmentalised way. This evoked complaints from some Latin leaders that their region was being ignored and prompted Senator Christopher Dodd, Chairman of the Subcommittee on Western Hemisphere Affairs, to characterise the administration's performance as the "amateur hour."[30]

3. Defining Hegemony: Does International Hegemony Matter?

Part of the ambiguity surrounding the issue of US hegemony in the post-Cold War era stems from the use of different definitions of international hegemony in the literature.[31] Some authors define hegemony broadly, encompassing all the attributes of state power: economic output (GNP) and productivity, military power, ideological/cultural (or "soft") power. Others focus on only one aspect: military strength, or economic power. Some scholars use Gramsci's definition of hegemony, which combines the concepts of coercion (military force) and consent (ideological leadership) as in the often quoted equation: "State = political society + civil society, in other words hegemony protected by the armour of coercion."[32]

Susan Strange claims that the US is still "an extraordinary power" because it still has an enormous amount of "structural power" in the four areas of production, finance, knowledge, and security.[33] Using a "structural liberal" framework Deudney and Ikenberry write about "the penetrated character of American hegemony...and its reciprocal rather than coercive character."[34] This is a contradiction in terms because as the Latin American experience shows, US hegemony in the region has precisely been characterised by Washington's lack of economic reciprocity.

Several Marxist scholars have resorted to the concept of transnational hegemony, exercised by a transnational capitalist class. There are two schools of thought on the impact of globalization on US hegemony. Some scholars argue that "we are witnessing the decline of US hegemony and the early stages of the creation of a transnational hegemony through supranational structures that are still not capable of providing the economic regulation and political conditions for global capitalism to function smoothly."[35] Others argue that a global capitalist hegemony is emerging as an integrated system of economic, political, and military power with the US at the centre.[36]

Still other scholars claim that after the Cold War we have entered a "post-hegemonic" world in which international hegemony no longer matters. In 1989, Francis Fukuyama argued that with the end of the Cold War, the victory of the Western *idea* and the "total exhaustion" of systematic alternatives to Western liberalism, world history was now coming to an end, with the world-wide establishment of free-market oriented economic policies (the neoliberal model) and democratic regimes.[37]

Koji Taira uses the "end of history" theory to argue that "Japan has become a hegemonic candidate during a time when a major hegemonic function, production of peace, is no longer needed, because the end of history has made peace a sort of free good rather than a costly public good that has to be produced by the hegemon."[38]

The hypothesis that Japan could replace the US as the international hegemon lost appeal in the 1990s when Japan fell into a deep economic slump. Moreover, the optimistic idea that after the Cold War a universal "democratic peace" in a "new world order" was at hand proved wrong in the 1990s, with the proliferation of ethnic and religious conflicts, as in the former Yugoslavia or the resurgence of old ones, as in Kashmir (South Asia.) In the end, a US-led coalition (NATO) has proved necessary to provide the public good of international security, at least in Western Europe, as shown by NATO's military interventions in Bosnia (Summer of 1995) and Kosovo, Serbia (Spring of 1999).

Similarly to Taira, Deborah Haber wrote in 1990 that "no single country today has the capacity to dominate the globe in military, political, economic, or cultural terms" and that the inability of Japan to become the next world hegemon poses problems for the entire notion of hegemony."[39] The latter has been confirmed by Japan's inability to exercise international leadership in the 1990s. Haber claims that hegemony no longer makes sense in a world in which several regional players, such as China, India, or Brazil, have increased their power. This scenario seemed accurate in the late 1980s and early 1990s when the dramatic rise in the relative power of several middle-states seemed unstoppable. Can regional powers *really* become stronger in the era of globalization considering the strong performance of the US economy in the 1990s (and the weaknesses of potential regional challengers, such as China, India, or Brazil)? On the other hand, does globalization only benefit the US?

Donald Crone's article, "Does Hegemony Matter?" provides some elements that may help to answer this question. Crone argues that international hegemony now matters *less* than in the past, at least to achieve regional economic co-operation and development. Along the lines of Deborah Haber's region-oriented approach, Crone shows that the erosion of *extreme* international hegemony (such as the one exercised by the US in the Asia-Pacific region during the Cold War) may facilitate regional economic co-operation. On the one hand, "too much, as well as too little, hegemony may affect co-operation negatively."

> The erosion of extreme hegemony changes the incentives of all states. Subordinate actors may desire to provide a multilateral framework that keeps a large actor in the system but also constrains its exercise of unilateral power; the superordinate actor may wish to use its size to preserve bargaining power that is perceived to be eroding. This line of argument suggests that regimes may form as hegemonic deflation opens political space that was previously closed to dependent actors and preserves some advantage for superordinate ones, but that engagement will be wary and cautious on both sides.[40]

Crone productively applies Duncan Snidal's distinction between "coercive" and "benevolent" hegemony.[41] For example, unless it becomes an openly predatory hegemon (running the risk of being condemned by the international community) the United States cannot use force against Japan to truly open the Japanese market to US products. Similarly, the US would be unable to use force to get its way in the FTAA negotiations discussed in chapter 4. Yet the US can brandish its structural power, e.g., by threatening to withdraw support to credits to South American nations from international financial institutions (IMF and World Bank). Would that coerce Brazil to accept an FTAA that does not really open the US market to Brazilian products? If as Peter Smith argues, US supremacy in the Americas is now "uncontested and complete,"[42] the US does not really need the FTAA to exercise hegemony in the Western Hemisphere; bilateral FTAs will do it, along the lines of the unfulfilled promise to incorporate Chile to NAFTA (see chapter 4). Extreme hegemony, as Crone argues, "may inhibit regime formation by shaping the incentives of both superordinate and subordinate actors *away* from joint solutions. Despite (or because of) hegemony, a fragmented, bilateral system of relations, rather than regimes, will be formed."[43]

4. Is America Declining? Hegemonic Stability Theory and US Hegemony

The "declinist" approach dominated the scholarly debate about US hegemony in the mid-1980s, when US control of the Western capitalist economy seemed to be slipping away in the face of an increasingly unified European Community and a threatening Japanese economy. Some scholars argued that Japan represented a world-wide economic threat.[44] The dominant consensus among experts was that "in the closing decades of the twentieth century the United States has found itself caught between its many commitments and decreased power, the classic position of a declining hegemon."[45]

According to Paul Kennedy, a historian from Yale University, the US is facing "imperial overstretch," a problem faced by previous international hegemons, such as Spain, the Netherlands, or Great Britain:

> Washington must face the awkward and enduring fact that the sum total of the United States' global interests and obligations is nowadays far larger than the country's power to defend them all simultaneously.[46]

The declinist school argues that American power is now less than it was; the policies of the Reagan administration (1981-1989) are often mentioned as the main source of deterioration of the economic position of the United States among the Western powers. During the Reagan administration both the rate of national savings and domestic investment declined dramatically while the twin budget and trade deficits increased exponentially.[47] According to Robert

Gilpin, the budget deficit meant a significant decline in capital accumulation and hence "lower productivity growth, accelerated deindustrialization of the American economy, and a significantly lower standard of living in the future."[48]

The second claim of the "declinist" school was that the absence of an international hegemon would produce disorder in the international political economy and undesirable results for individual states. Starting from this premise, the scholarly debate shifted to the *consequences* of American decline for the stability of the international economic and political system.

According to hegemonic stability theory, "Order in world politics is created by a single dominant power."[49] The US played such a role in the Western-dominated international economic order after World War II. Declining US hegemony in the second half of the 1980s would explain, according to this theory, the instability and aimlessness of the world capitalist economy in those years. The two central propositions of hegemonic stability theory are:

(1) An international hegemon (*primus inter pares*), can (a) largely impose and enforce its rules and its wishes in the international political economy (free trade during the *Pax Britannica* and *Pax Americana*,) and (b) maintain international peace, establishing a security framework that prevents great power wars.

(2) "The presence of a single, strongly dominant actor in international politics leads to collectively desirable outcomes for *all* states in the international system."[50]

Does hegemonic stability theory help to explain US/Latin American relations between the Miami (1994) and Santiago (1998) Summits and during the FTAA negotiations? As Snidal notes, the novelty of the theory,

> Is not the claim that strong actors can impose regimes in international politics (which goes back at least as far as Thucydides) but the claim that smaller states gain even more than the hegemon when the latter provides the "public good" of leadership for the emergence of a stable international regime of free trade.[51]

The latter claim is clearly unwarranted in the US/Latin American context. Several studies have shown that if a Free Trade Area of the Americas comes into existence, the US will obtain greater benefits than its Latin American counterparts. According to two World Bank experts,

Overall, full Free Trade Agreement preferences would raise Latin American exports only 8 or 9 percent... US trade gains, particularly for highly protected transport and machinery products, are likely to be considerably greater than those for Latin America are in the US market.[52]

If this is the case, why did the Latin American countries agree to launch the FTAA negotiations in Santiago (see chapter 4)? Because they knew the negotiations were doomed to failure (due to the lack of fast-track negotiation authority on the part of the US president) and it was impolite to say "no" to the US?

There are two versions of hegemonic stability theory. According to the "strong" version, an international hegemon will produce order and stability in the world political economy when it uses its power to enforce order on others. According to the "weak" version, "hegemonic power is a necessary, but not always a sufficient, condition for order, the presence or absence of a hegemon only partially answers why order and stability have prevailed at some times in the international economic system and disorder and instability at others."[53] Before the Asian financial crisis of the Summer of 1997 the "strong" version held sway. One could argue that with a unique combination of economic, political, military, diplomatic, and even cultural power, the United States would be able to prolong the "unipolar moment" of 1989-1990 for a long period of time, as the uncontested hegemonic power of a new world order in the era of the "end of history" and globalization. After the Asian crisis and the looming world financial crisis of 1998, the "weak" version seems closer to reality, now that the neoliberal model has proved to be lacking in key respects and there are no clear ground rules for the management of the world economy.

Several scholars have argued that the US has reasserted its hegemony in the global capitalist economy of the late 1990s and that the description of US hegemony as having declined is incorrect, especially when one considers the military and cultural, as well as the economic elements, of hegemony.[54] For example, Susan Strange argues that the US is "still an extraordinary power" considering American control of the Western security structure (NATO) "the continued domination by the United States of the world's production structure" and the emergence and consolidation of "an entirely new kind of non territorial empire," the "flourishing economic base" of US power.[55]

5. US-Latin American Relations at the Turn of the Millennium: Hegemony in Decline?

How does the end of the Cold War affect US hegemony in Latin America and US policy toward the region? Table 5.1 summarises the state of the literature on the end of the Cold War and US hegemony in Latin America.

Will US policy toward the region significantly change in the post-Cold War era? Does the US still perceive Latin America with Cold War lenses?[56] If not, is the region more valuable now (for example, as a trading partner)? Is the US prepared to redefine "security to the South" taking into consideration Latin American economic security concerns? What are the prospects for the abandonment of the hegemonic presumption and the establishment of a new hemispheric partnership based on reciprocity between North and South America?

In the early 1990s, there appeared to be three principal scenarios for US-Latin American relations in the post-Cold War era.

a) A New Partnership between the United States and Latin America (Lowenthal, Pastor)

Optimists believe the end of the Cold War creates an opportunity for a US "rediscovery" of Latin America while developing the potential for economic, social, political, and even military co-operation between North and South America. Optimists claim that President Bush's Enterprise for the Americas Initiative marks the beginning of a new era in US-Latin American relations based on mutuality of interests and a revival of the "Western Hemisphere Idea," according to which the US and the Latin American countries share a special relationship, similar to family ties, and quite beyond the typical interstate bond:

> The societies of the [Western] hemisphere share more than a geographic location; they also share the desire to pursue a common world project: the construction of non-tyrannical, republican institutions under which citizens could extend their liberties and prosper free from the vestiges of European feudalism.[57]

Table 5.1 Perspectives on the End of the Cold War and US Hegemony in Latin America

	Post-hegemonic World	Borón [neo-trilateralism] (1993) Crone (1993) Haber (1990) Taira (1990) Jervis (1993)
Reassertion of US hegemony	Hegemony by default	Foweraker (1996) Smith (1996 a)
	Reconsolidation/Recovery of US hegemony	Nef (1994) Petras and Morley (1992) Richards (1997)
Decline of US hegemony and early stages of a transnational (Global) hegemony		Burbach and Robinson (1999)
Benevolent hegemony (North/South co-operation in the Americas)		Feinberg (1997) Feinberg and Corrales (1999) Lowenthal (1990) Pastor (1992)
Benign neglect: "Africanization" scenario		Castañeda (1990)
US is forced to pay greater attention to Latin America		Lowenthal (1992)

Both Lowenthal and Pastor start from the assumption that the US is a declining international hegemon. Rediscovering Latin America and the regionalist option in the Western Hemisphere are the best strategy to deal with US hegemony in decline in a world that is rapidly moving in the direction of economic competition among three mega-blocs led by the US, Western Europe and Japan.

Lowenthal argues that "trends in Latin America today are having a significant impact on the United States, and will have even more in the years to come."[58]

The gist of Lowenthal's argument is that in the post-Cold War era Latin America could become increasingly important for the US if global trends compel the US to pay greater attention to domestic problems such as creating new jobs, protecting the environment, or fighting drug consumption: "All these issues will be influenced by Latin America because the region is so close and large, demonstrably capable of growth and tightly intertwined with the United States."[59] From this perspective, Latin America and the Caribbean nations will matter increasingly to the US because of their economic and political weight, their capacity to affect global problems, their demographic links with the United States (more than 20 million persons of Hispanic-American ancestry now live in the US) and their importance for preserving basic US values, such as democracy and human rights (with the exception of Cuba, all the Latin American countries are currently under formally democratic regimes).

Because of geographic proximity and increasing economic, financial, and cultural interdependence, Mexico, with 85 million people, affects the daily lives of people in the United States. Brazil, a megacountry of 150 million people, is already a major economic actor, with considerable political and economic influence and potential. The Andean countries are important for the United States because of the problem of drug traffic and due to their increasing domestic convulsions are bound to have a big impact upon the United States.

Lowenthal argues that the US must move away from the Cold War conception of strategic denial and boldly address "intermestic" issues (including both international and domestic components and involving both foreign and domestic actors) such as drugs, migration, trade, and environmental protection if it wants to make progress in the construction of an effective partnership with its neighbours in the Americas.[60]

Yet is the US prepared to forge a new Latin American policy, going "from insecurity to confianza"? Lowenthal's new US/Latin American partnership could come into existence if NAFTA is extended to the rest of Latin America, or if the FTAA negotiations are successfully concluded by 2005, under US leadership. Yet he is rather cautious about the prospects for this scenario and considers the obstacles for a "new partnership" between the United States and Latin America in the 1990s: the fragmented process of US policy making and competing domestic demands on US government actions.

> Domestic US choices about fiscal and monetary policy, trade and tax reforms, agricultural subsidies, energy, and immigration have major consequences for Latin America. To the extent that these choices conflict with important Latin American needs, attempts to improve inter-American relations cannot amount to more than damage control. Further, non-governmental forces beyond the scope of any US administration shape much of US-Latin American relations.[61]

Other scholars look at the fragmented nature of US foreign policy-making with a more positive bent. For example, according to Richard Feinberg, the involvement of non-governmental actors in the preparatory works for the Miami Summit of the Americas in 1994 bodes well for an assertive US policy toward Latin America:

> In the post-Cold War world, US leaders must broaden citizen interest in foreign affairs if they are to pursue policies of international engagement. The Miami process opened avenues for the engagement of corporate and financial communities and NGOs in partnership with the government to design and advance US foreign policy objectives.[62]

Yet one may argue that the "privatisation" of US foreign policy making could again frustrate efforts for a US/Latin American partnership. Both US private interests and the permanent bureaucracy in Washington may block the major shift in US policy represented by the FTAA, even though, as Corrales and Feinberg note, "the basic tenets of hemispherism-democratic governance, regional economic integration, and social justice," were reaffirmed at the 1998 Santiago Summit.[63]

Robert Pastor goes beyond Lowenthal's cautious optimism, arguing that the United States and Latin America *can* establish a more even-handed relationship in the twenty-first century, if they can negotiate "new mechanisms that will deal with the causes of the recurring conflicts in the region and will offer practical solutions to the region's current and future problems."[64] The Pastor thesis is that the end of the Cold War does not mark the end of the cycles of neglect and attention that have characterised US-Latin American relations in the past. Pastor describes those cycles using the metaphor of a "whirlpool":

> The centre of the whirlpool is the Caribbean Basin, but the whirlpool's force extends throughout Latin America. Caught in the middle, spinning around and around, Americans become possessed by countries previously unimportant to them. Then, almost as suddenly, the United States is released from the whirlpool's force and the names of these countries are forgotten. In 1992,... after more than a decade of swirling in the vortex, the United States found itself on the edge, where it concentrated on other matters.[65]

Pastor claims that the US will be captured once again by the Latin American "whirlpool" unless it takes advantage of the opportunity created by the end of the Cold War to understand the nature of past relationships with its Latin neighbours and establish a new partnership with them based on reciprocity. He argues that this is in the best US interest, because the US is slipping "into economic decline, lacking an economic strategy and burdened by an obsolete geopolitical vision."[66] According to Pastor, the end of the Cold War diminishes the possibility of US interventions in Latin America because far from being a deterrent, the Soviet Union was a motive for intervention.[67] The end of the Cold War means that an important source of tension between the US and Latin America has disappeared, opening up the possibility of Western Hemisphere co-operation in the areas of democracy, security, development, and the protection of the environment. Pastor's ambitious proposals in these areas resemble Lowenthal's above-mentioned scenario. Pastor is aware of the fact that a significant reduction of the gap that separates the Western Hemisphere's economies is a prerequisite for a balanced and mature relationship between the US and Latin America, but he believes that the democratisation of Latin America and "the growing influence and convergence of public opinion" are a solid basis for the US to successfully exercise the "Latin American option."[68]

Pastor claims that the whirlpool is "irresistible" and that the US cannot avoid being attracted by Latin American crises, as if US policy toward Latin America were totally determined by external (systemic) factors and the US could not freely *adopt* those policies. Yet the US can decide *not* to intervene militarily in Latin America; i.e., it can escape the attraction of Pastor's "whirlpool." For example, the United States decided to intervene in Haiti in September 1994 to restore a democratically elected president (Aristide) but not in Peru when President Fujimori closed Congress in 1992.

The fragmented process of US foreign policy making has always affected US policy toward Latin America, which often has frustrated new approaches to US/Latin American relations. As Lowenthal points out, with rare exceptions (the Alliance for Progress, the Reagan administration) the US has lacked a coherent strategic vision toward Latin America, which confirms (and helps to explain) Pastor's "whirlpool." Yet Pastor overlooks the fact that the essential characteristic of US/Latin American relations is asymmetry, i.e., a great power/small powers relationship. With the possible exception of Franklin Roosevelt's Good Neighbour Policy, the US has always taken advantage of asymmetry to attempt to impose its will on Latin America. This is one of the reasons pessimists argue that US/Latin American co-operation is very difficult, if not impossible. As Connell-Smith points out, there can be no authentic and real co-operation (and far-reaching economic and social changes in Latin America) as long as the region remains so dependent upon the United States, as long as the present imbalance of power persists. The US cannot be a benevolent paramount in that context.[69]

b) *Ignorance or Neglect: The "Africanization" Scenario*

Several scholars have suggested that in the absence of the East West conflict the US could pay even less attention to Latin America than during the Cold War, or completely ignore the region, even if the latter were to "sink to the bottom of the sea," to use Lars Schoultz's metaphor.[70]

According to Jorge Castañeda, Latin America runs the risk of getting the worst of both worlds from the end of the Cold War: more US interventionism coupled with "Africanization."

> Paradoxically, after so many years of worrying about excessive US involvement in the region, Latin America may soon suffer from US indifference, compounded by the rest of the world's traditional, relative lack of interest. As the geopolitical motivation for US policy toward Latin America fades, its economic component could also shrink. The hemisphere could well face the prospect of "Africanization"—condemnation to the margins of world financial and trade flows but also, inevitably, to neglect and irrelevance.[71]

The Latin American fear of being left out, while the US government and US private investors diverted private credit lines and investment flows to the new capitalist economies of Eastern Europe and the former Soviet Union, led a new brand of Latin American leaders to embrace market oriented reforms, trade liberalisation and economic co-operation with the United States. This fear came from the perception that "there are now more countries competing for the same pie, and that there will be less pie to go around."[72]

Castañeda's "Africanization scenario" is often quoted by those who argue that the Free Trade Area of the Americas (FTAA) will *not* come into existence, because with the end of the Cold War the US would lack both a pressing security rationale to become involved in a Western Hemisphere bloc and a strong economic motivation for the FTAA.[73] Pessimists argue that Western Europe and Japan are more important for the US than Latin America and that the US is not really prepared to make the economic sacrifices (income transfers and side payments) that would make the FTAA work.[74]

With some exceptions, such as Franklin Roosevelt's Good Neighbour Policy, the US has historically tended to neglect Latin America, considering the region as "something of a nuisance or potential source of trouble."[75] Yet Castañeda's pessimistic "Africanization scenario" is not warranted by the hemispheric rapprochement reviewed in chapter 4. Indeed, as Atkins points out, the apparent abandonment of the concept of "strategic denial" opens up the possibility of placing US policies toward Latin America on a new foundation.[76]

The disappearance of the Soviet (communist) threat has an ambiguous impact on the prospects for US intervention in Latin America. On the one hand, it deprives the US of the traditional security rationale for interventionism, compelling it to find new justifications for sending US troops to Latin America. The Bay of Pigs invasion (1961), the military intervention in the Dominican Republic (1965), US support for military regimes in the 1960s and 1970s, and the Reagan administration's support of the "contras" in the Nicaraguan civil war in the 1980s were all undertaken to contain the Soviet threat. On the other hand, however, the elimination of the Soviet counterweight and the absence of alternative counterweights open up the possibility of greater US interventionism in the region.[77] The European Union and Japan were the obvious candidates to balance the US, but for a number of reasons (Japan was beset by its own economic problems, the EU was concerned with Eastern Europe) they did not fill the vacuum left by the Soviet

Union. Therefore, the US had now a "free rein" to intervene in Latin America, as dramatically shown by the US military intervention in Panama and its ability to violate with impunity the centuries-old rule of diplomatic asylum.

Finally, Castañeda argues that most of the issues in the "new inter-American agenda" (international trade and investment, drug trafficking, immigration, refugees, human rights) have a potential to exacerbate conflict, rather than co-operation, between the US and Latin America, because these new themes,

> Are more directly linked to domestic US politics, they touch rawer, more emotional nerves than geopolitical, strategic consideration, and they lend themselves to more intrusive forms of co-operation [that might be resisted by individual countries, M.C.]. They bring out the worst in US international behaviour (arrogance, self-righteousness, and omnipotence) and sublimate the best (generosity, multilateralism, and attachment to principles.[78]

This is a serious obstacle for the creation of a "new partnership" in the Western Hemisphere along the lines of the preceding scenario *a*).

c) A Reassertion of US Hegemony in Latin America

Several scholars argue that scenario a) is impossible because the asymmetric nature of the relationship will always tempt the US to exercise hegemony and impose its will over Latin America. They claim that the relative decline of the US position in the international political economy does not necessarily mean that it is a declining hegemon in the Western Hemisphere. On the contrary, they claim that after the Cold War the US will compensate for hegemonic decline in the global economy and respond to the challenge of emerging regional economic blocs in Europe and Asia by *reasserting* hegemony in its traditional, Latin American sphere of influence. Some even argue that the US military intervention in Panama (December 1989) marks the beginning of renewed US interventionism in the region that could result in a sort of "Fortress America" or hemispheric isolationism: "Drugs and immigration would thus not only be justifications for intervention and the curtailment of Latin sovereignty but also an ideological coating for a new, purely economic expression of the Monroe Doctrine."[79]

At first sight, the reassertion of US hegemony thesis seems plausible considering the organisation of the Miami Summit in 1994, the Clinton administration's commitment to the Free Trade Area of the Americas process and the formal launching of the FTAA negotiations at the Santiago Summit of 1998. Yet as Louis Bélanger notes, the US foreign policy on hemispheric regionalism has been to keep a regionalist *option* open rather than following a "clear" regionalist *policy*.[80] On the other hand, non-trade issues, such as drugs or immigration have the potential to confirm the reassertion of US hegemony thesis, for example, if the US decides to cross the "sovereignty divide" and militarily intervenes in Colombia, Mexico, or Peru to fight drug trafficking and domestic insurgencies.

The reassertion of US hegemony thesis appears in two forms in the literature: the "recharged hegemony" thesis and hegemony by default.

The Recharged Hegemony Thesis Some Marxist scholars have argued that the US is the dominant capitalist power in the Western hemisphere and follows in its foreign policy an imperialist tradition that has been applied inexorably over a long period to promote the expansion of American capitalism. This approach, sometimes depicted as "dependency theory," lost influence with the end of the Cold War and the delegitimisation of Marxist analysis. Some conservative analysts even proclaimed the demise of dependency analysis. Yet as Barbara Stallings has noted, dependency theory has been abandoned too quickly by mainstream scholars, considering that economic policy making in Latin America has been increasingly constrained by international economic forces in the last two decades.[81]

Dependency theory argues that the structure of US/Latin American relations is inherently *conflictual* and that a model of imperialism is far more appropriate than one of mutuality or harmony of interests to describe and explain US/Latin American relations.[82]

According to Petras and Morley, the major external constraint on Latin American autonomous economic development is the United States, conceived as an "imperial state."[83] From this perspective, far from a "mature partnership among equals" (scenario a) US policy toward Latin America after the Cold War will be "more of the same": the super-exploitation of Latin America to compensate for "the relative decline in the US global position."[84] Petras and Morley argue that the hegemonic presumption is alive and well and that "the end of the Cold War has if anything *strengthened* the drive in Washington to *consolidate* its informal empire in Latin America."[85] From this perspective, the US is not necessarily and irresistibly drawn (as Pastor would have us believe) into the vortex of the Latin American "whirlpool," for the simple reason that it has always pursued a *conscious* imperialist (exploitative) policy toward the region.

Petras and Morley claim that the US has a complex and coherent strategy toward Latin America that operates on three mutually reinforcing and interrelated levels:

a) The promotion of the doctrine of "free markets" (the "Washington Consensus") to open the Latin American economies to US investments and monopoly profits;

b) A military strategy "that is integrally related to the 'free market' doctrine";

c) "A political strategy which involves the promotion of electoral regimes in the interstices of its economic policy and military framework."[86]

The recharged hegemony thesis leads to the conclusion that US-South American co-operation in the area of trade will only serve to strengthen US hegemony in South America. From this perspective, Mercosur is just an instrument of "US imperialism" in the region.[87]

The problem with the "recharged hegemony" thesis is that, as Petras and Morley recognise, the US is still far from having achieved the goal of consolidating its "informal empire" in Latin America, because of the inherent contradiction between the ideological power of the US (acceptance of the "Washington Consensus" on the part of the Latin American ruling elite) and the decline of US economic strength, as shown by the inability of the US to fund the recovery of the ravaged Central American economies in the post-Cold War era.[88] Despite the initial rhetoric surrounding President Bush's Enterprise for the Americas Initiative, it soon became clear that Western Hemisphere economic regionalism would not include large-scale flows of US economic aid to Latin America, nor significant debt reduction. After a "lost decade" of recession in the 1980s the Latin American countries entered the 1990s in deep economic trouble, whereas the US strategy toward the region "accelerated disinvestment, contracted industrial development, and produced worsening hyperinflation in some countries (Argentina and Brazil,) rising indebtedness, and growing marginalisation and immiseration of the Latin American masses."[89]

On the other hand, the continued financial dependence of South American countries on international financial institutions such as the IMF (substantially controlled by the US) does not necessarily guarantee their subservience to US foreign economic policies, as shown by the difficulties faced by the Clinton administration in getting the Mercosur countries to commit to an FTAA by 2005.[90] The revival of subregional trading blocs, such as the Andean Community, and the creation of new ones, such as Mercosur, can be seen as attempts to achieve subregional autonomy in a "new world order" in which the US is no longer perceived as a reliable partner. Even if the world moves toward three or four supra-regional trading blocs, Mercosur could still survive as an independent trading bloc if it can resist US pressures to form an FTAA under US hegemony. Moreover, despite its current economic troubles, Brazil has strong incentives to strengthen Mercosur in order to create a South American Free Trade Area (SAFTA) to consolidate its own hegemony in South America (see chapter 6).[91]

Hegemony by Default (Smith and Foweraker)   The second variant of the reassertion of US hegemony thesis is Peter Smith's contention that after the Cold War the United States continued to be the regional hegemon in the Western Hemisphere through a process of default:

> To a substantial degree, the resurgence of US hegemony in the Western Hemisphere resulted from a systematic retreat by extra-hemispheric rivals. In this respect, the United States came to reassert hegemony through a process of default. This occurred not so much because the end of the Cold War provoked the United States to do anything particularly bold, innovative, or effective; it happened, instead, because outside powers withdrew from the Americas and directed their attention elsewhere.[92]

The Smith thesis challenges the conventional wisdom among experts that the US was losing hegemony in Latin America throughout the Cold War period. Lowenthal, Pastor, and Petras and Morley belong to the "declinist" school of thought, which was dominant in the 1980s in the US after the publication of Paul Kennedy's *The Rise and Fall of the Great Powers* (see section 4 above).

In the early 1990s, Lowenthal made the case for US hegemonic decline in Latin America, providing several examples of the "diminished capacity of the United States to impose its will" in the region:[93]

1) The inability of the United States to prevent the Sandinistas from coming to power in Nicaragua in 1979. The Carter administration refrained from using force, while his proposal to send an OAS-mission to negotiate a

political settlement in Managua and for a multilateral OAS-sponsored peacekeeping force to restore order in Nicaragua got nowhere.

2) The inability of the United States to prevent the Falklands/Malvinas war between Argentina and Great Britain in 1982.

3) "The share of Latin American exports going to the United States decreased from 45 percent in 1958 to 34 percent by the end of the 1970s."[94]

4) The US share of direct foreign investment in Latin America declined in the 1960s and 1970s: "In 1965, for example, the United States accounted for more than 50 percent of Brazil's foreign direct investment; by 1979, the US share of foreign investment in Brazil had dropped to 30 percent..."[95]

5) The Latin American countries have significantly diversified their weapons sources since the late seventies, with several suppliers, from the Soviet Union to Israel, and even Brazil, outpacing the United States.

6) US dominance in the Western Hemisphere has been "substantially diluted" by increasing Western European and Japanese investments in Latin America as well as by their increasing trade with the region.[96]

By contrast, Peter Smith forcefully argues that "the notion of [US] declining hegemony [in Latin America] rests on dubious assumptions."[97] According to Peter Smith,

> The historical record reveals three basic points: first, the United States exercised a strong and continued degree of hegemony over the Western Hemisphere from the 1950s to the 1990s; second, within this overall pattern, US hegemony suffered a slight decline from the 1960s to the 1980s; and third, still within this pattern US hegemony climbed to an all-time high between the mid-1980s and the mid-1990s. Since World War II, in other words, the general trend has *always* been for the United States to exert a great degree of influence over Latin American countries, but the level of this influence revealed some oscillation (up, down, up) from the mid-1950s to the present time.

This interpretation heavily relies on the asymmetric nature of the relationship between the "colossus of the North" and Latin America. Although asymmetry *is* an essential characteristic of US Latin American relations, Peter Smith's assumption that "the economic productivity of the United States has consistently overwhelmed" South America's regional output is problematic. Smith argues that the overall decline in Latin America's economic importance in the world economy from the 1950s to the 1990s has increased its disparity with the United States: "This growing asymmetry gave

Washington great potential leverage over the countries of the region."[98] While this may be true regarding Mexico and the Caribbean Basin, it is more problematic with respect to the rest of South America, particularly the Southern Cone countries. Following the Smith thesis, Joe Foweraker claims that hegemony by default "is still hegemony," considering that the US GDP is "thirteen times greater than that of Mercosur."[99] Yet as table 3.2 shows, according to World Bank figures, in 1995 the US GDP was only seven times greater than that of Mercosur. While in 1990 the US GDP was 10.6 times as large as Argentine-Brazilian GDP (the bulk of Mercosur's GDP) in 1995 it was only 7.1 times larger than Argentine-Brazilian GDP, still an impressive difference, but hardly proving a historical trend toward increasing structural asymmetry between the US and Argentina-Brazil (see table 5.2).

Considering the dramatic rise in the relative power of Brazil in the 1970s (Brazil has become the tenth largest industrial economy) and the structural problems facing the US economy (e.g. between 1980 and 1992 its national debt more than quadrupled, from $900 billion to more than $4 trillion) one may argue that Mercosur will continue narrowing the gap in GDP with the US in the first decade of the new millennium, especially if Mercosur survives its current crisis and Argentina and Brazil manage to co-ordinate their economic policies to get out of their current recessions.

The second problem with Peter Smith's "hegemony by default" thesis is that he exaggerates the importance of the withdrawal of outside powers from the region. In retrospect, the withdrawal of those powers from the Americas was a temporary phenomenon, as shown by the European Union's renewed interest in the region in the mid-to-late 1990s, culminating with the EU-Latin American Summit of June 1999 in Rio de Janeiro. In other words, the "evaporation of the European counterweight" immediately after the end of the Cold War was not as "tragic" and definite for Latin America as Castañeda's pessimistic assessment would have us believe.[100]

Foweraker claims that President Bush's Enterprise for the Americas Initiative (June 1990) was made possible by the reassertion of US hegemony during the debt crisis in the 1980s. Foweraker makes two interrelated points: (1) "All of the critical decisions in regard to the management of the Latin American debt are made in the United States (by US-based multilateral agencies and US-chaired consortia of commercial banks)"; (2) After the Mexican crisis of 1982, "multilateral agencies [controlled by the US] and foreign governments tended to make debt renegotiating conditional on economic liberalisation."[101] Yet one may argue that the South American countries accepted US policies to deal with the debt crisis ("freeing markets") and the "Washington Consensus" because they had no alternative, rather than because of the failure of import-substitution industrialisation policies (see chapter 2). After all, Brazil and Mexico were described as economic "miracles" and reached the highest rates of regional economic growth in the 1970s while pursuing ISI policies.

Coercive leadership is not the same as hegemony.[102] The ability of the US to exercise hegemony by consent has been damaged by the unfulfilled promises of the Enterprise for the Americas Initiative (1990) and NAFTA extension (1994-1998). The EAI promised both trade (i.e., opening the US market to Latin American products) and long-term talks on the Free Trade Area of the Americas. Yet the US can only show NAFTA as proof of its willingness to implement the EAI, whereas because of domestic political opposition it does not appear to be ready to seriously negotiate the opening of its domestic market to South American manufactures. The US continues using section 301 of the US Trade Act and its super 301 successor to often close its market and impose countervailing duties and quotas to South American exports of manufactured goods, a source of past trade tensions with Brazil.[103] Smith and Foweraker downplay the constraining role of domestic factors (e.g., Congressional opposition to free trade agreements) in the making of American foreign economic policy. Neither the Petras and Morley thesis of a "recharged" US hegemony over Latin America nor Peter Smith and Joe Foweraker's "hegemony by default" thesis tell the whole story of post-Cold War US-Latin American relations. Both Petras and Morley and Smith and Foweraker exaggerate US domination of South America and are unable to explain the autonomous foreign policy behaviour of Brazil and her Mercosur partners. Smith and Foweraker overlook the furious EU-US competition for "emerging markets" in Latin America and Asia, and the loss of momentum of the "hub-and-spoke" model for Western hemisphere regional integration, with Mercosur, rather than NAFTA, becoming the major building block of the FTAA after the meeting of the hemisphere's trade ministers at Belo Horizonte in May 1997 (see chapter 4).

Table 5.2 Gross Domestic Product and Population Size in Latin America and the United States, 1950-1995

	1950		1970		1990		1995	
	GDP (billion US$)	Population (million)	GDP (billion US$)	Population (million)	GDP (billion US$)	Population (million)	GDP (billion US$)	Population (million)
Argentina*	9.5	17.1	20.5	23.8	93.3	32.3	281.1	35
Brazil*	8.8	52.2	35.5	92.5	414.1	150.4	688.1	159
Chile	2.6	6.1	8.2	9.4	27.8	13.2	67.3	14
Colombia	2.0	11.3	7.2	20.5	41.1	33.0	76.1	37
Mexico	7.8	25.8	35.5	50.7	237.8	86.2	250.0	92
Paraguay*	--	--	--	--	--	--	7.7	5
Peru	1.5	8.0	7.2	13.5	36.6	22.3	57.4	24
Uruguay*	--	--	--	--	--	--	17.8	3
Venezuela	4.6	5.0	13.4	10.3	48.3	19.7	75.0	22
Latin America	40.9	155.1	143.9	269.0	1,015.2	435.7	1,688.2	478
United States	287.0	152.3	1,011.5	204.8	5,392.2	250.0	6,952.0	263
Mercosur*	--	--	--	--	--	--	994.7	202

Sources: For 1950, 1970, and 1990: Smith, P., 1996, "The United States, Regional Integration, and the Reshaping of the International Order," from Nishijima, S. and Smith, P. (eds.), *Cooperation or Rivalry? Regional Integration in the Americas and the Pacific Rim*, Boulder (CO) Westview Press, Table 3.2, p. 31. Copyright © 1996 by Westview Press, Inc. Reprinted by permission of Westview Press, a member of Perseus Books, L. L. C. Data for 1995 obtained from World Bank, *World Development Report* (New York: Oxford University Press, 1997), Table 4, pp. 220-221, and Table 12, pp. 236-237.

6. Conclusion: Can the US and Latin America achieve a Mature Partnership at the Turn of the Millennium?

The evolution of the FTAA concept since the 1994 Miami Summit and the emergence of SAFTA as a possible alternative raise interesting theoretical questions. As we saw in the previous chapter, the US seems to be unable to convince the South American countries that "its" model of FTAA is in their best interest. This is confirmed by the slow pace of the pre-FTAA negotiations between the Miami and Santiago Summits and by Mercosur's "tough" strategy for the FTAA. Mercosur and its associates do not directly challenge US leadership in the Western Hemisphere, but are ready to adopt independent trade policies if it does not provide sufficient benefits to them. The lack of fast-track authority has eroded US leadership by raising doubts about its ability to deliver the public good of "free trade" at the end of the FTAA negotiations. The possible rise of Mercosur as the pole of attraction for a future FTAA (see chapter 4) would have been unthinkable in 1993, when NAFTA was signed.[104]

As we saw in the previous chapter, US policy-makers still believe that the US "will always be at the centre" because of the sheer weight of its economy. Asymmetry has often been posited as a major impediment for co-operation between the US and the Latin American republics, among other reasons because it breeds resentment in Latin America. The US hegemonic presumption has led US government officials to regard as unacceptable the emergence of *any* anti-American political group in *any* Latin American country. For example, would the United States refrain from militarily intervening in Mexico if a government led by the Zapatistas came to power by democratic means?

The US hegemonic ambition in the Western Hemisphere is well recognised and often deeply resented in Latin America, especially when it goes hand in hand with the arrogance that still pervades certain sectors of the US political elite and the US policy-making apparatuses (the Pentagon, the State Department, the Presidency, and even Congress) when dealing with the region. Unless the US changes its traditional attitude toward Latin America it will be very difficult to achieve a mature hemispheric partnership.

Unfortunately, as Bélanger points out, institutions and ideas forged in the Cold War period (including the image of Latin American elites as essentially "dependent") have managed to survive and continue to shape post-Cold War inter-American relations and US policy toward the region. This state of ideological inertia helps to explain why such policy has *not* fundamentally changed after the Cold War (see section 2.c above). Although it assumes new forms, benign neglect persists; it is more "benign" but still "neglect" because it still ignores the real demands of the Latin American nations. Moreover, the "dependent" image that US decision makers have of Latin American elites has been reinforced by the attitude of certain Latin American leaders, such as President Carlos Menem of Argentina, of deferentially courting the US with a policy of "automatic alignment" and making concessions to the US government in several issue areas without obtaining in exchange material concessions on the part of the US.[105]

American scholars and the public have been very reluctant to recognise US hegemonic pretensions in the Western Hemisphere. As Walter Lippmann puts it, "All the world thinks of the United States today as an empire, except the people of the United States. We shrink from the word 'empire' and insist that it should not be used to describe the dominion we exercise."

Yet regardless of the term used, there is little doubt that US behaviour in the Western Hemisphere throughout the twenty-first century and the first half of the twentieth century fits the "broad" definition of hegemony as the ability of a great power to impose its will over other great powers and international actors without significant challenge.[106] On the other hand, the Cuban revolution of 1959 marked a fundamental change in US-Latin American relations and in the 1960s and 1970s, the large Latin American countries made strong efforts to develop independent foreign policies. The US continued willing to exercise hegemony in Latin America, but it was less able to do so. During the debt crisis of the 1980s, the US attempted to reassert its hegemony in the region, along the lines of scenario c) (see section 5). Yet the failure of the US to provide strong leadership during the FTAA negotiations (see chapter 4) raises the question: What kind of hegemony, if any, is the US still exercising over South America? In order to answer this question, it is useful to distinguish between Mexico and the Central American and Caribbean countries (with the exception of Cuba), on the one hand, and South America, on the other. As Lowenthal rightly points out,

> As in the 1920s and 1930s, the United States is becoming far more closely engaged with Mexico and the Caribbean Basin than with South America, and other world powers are competing with the United States for influence on the South American continent.[107]

The ongoing negotiations between the European Union and Mercosur to establish a free trade area confirm Lowenthal's statement while challenging Peter Smith's claim that outside powers have withdrawn from the Americas. Arguably, US structural power (based on asymmetry) to impose its will on Brazil and Mercosur in the FTAA negotiations has suffered some erosion in the 1990s.

On the other hand, the Mexican, Central American, and Caribbean economies are becoming increasingly integrated with the US economy. US supremacy in Mexico and the Caribbean is arguably becoming, "uncontested and complete."[108] Accordingly, asymmetry and structural power give Washington greater leverage over Mexico, Central America, and the Caribbean (with the exception of Cuba) than over the Southern Cone and Mercosur. The US does not need "its" version of the FTAA (see chapter 4) to consolidate its hegemony over Mexico, Central America, and the Caribbean. Saxe-Fernandez's "Mexico purchase" metaphor may be exaggerated but it marks a trend.[109] The Mexican economy *is* becoming part of the US economy. By contrast, the US *does* need "its" version of the FTAA to regain hegemony over South America because it would give it enormous advantage vis-à-vis extra-hemispheric actors competing for influence on the South American continent.

An important issue is whether US Latin American policy in the post-Cold War era is more influenced by external factors (including extra-hemispheric actors) or by domestic sources, such as the US Congress and US public opinion.

Most of the literature on American foreign policy after the Cold War has focused on external factors. Truly, how changes in the global system affect the inter-American subsystem is clearly important. Yet one has to look at the interplay of external and internal factors to fully grasp the complexities of US policy toward Latin America in the 1990s. An excessive emphasis on external factors may lead to neglect (or subordinate) the weight of the domestic sources of US policy toward Latin America.[110] As Lowenthal shows in his study of the Alliance for Progress (the centrepiece of US Latin American policy in the 1960s) the domestic sources have always been important. Rather than being the choice of a single, rational actor, US policy toward the region has been "the product of a series of overlapping and interlocking bargaining processes within the North American system, involving both intra-governmental and extra-governmental actors."[111] For example, Michael Kryzanek has shown that despite the Reagan administration's unilateral interventions in Central America and the Caribbean, domestic conditions (such as the budget deficit or the reduction in US personnel representing official US interests) were largely responsible for the relative decline of US influence in Latin America in the 1980s:

> This period also will be known as one in which the US government and the private sector was unwilling and in many cases unable to provide the countries of the hemisphere with the trade, aid, and investment necessary to maintain basic levels of development and foster good relations.[112]

This neglect is partly explained by Ronald Reagan's obsessive focus on Nicaragua and the "Cuban/Soviet threat" to Central America, but the contraction of US economic aid to that region continued during the Bush administration. The Clinton administration's focus on the US economy (propelled by domestic political factors) resulted in little or no financial assistance for the reconstruction of the devastated economies of Nicaragua and El Salvador, directly caused by the Reagan-Bush strategy of "containing communism" in Central America.

The domestic sources of US foreign policy have arguably become more important after the Cold War, as shown by the emotional debate in the US Congress preceding the approval of NAFTA in 1993 and the refusal of the US Congress to grant fast-track authority to President Clinton in November 1997 (see chapter 4). Domestic politics, involving both intra-government and extra-governmental actors, played an important role in the bureaucratic process leading to the Summit of the Americas in Miami, in December 1994.[113]

While domestic factors often constrain US policy toward Latin America, external factors are arguably "enabling," rather than "constraining." The collapse of the Soviet Union left the world with only one superpower: the United States, and even if its economic clout among the great powers has suffered some erosion it still has a unique combination of military, economic, and political power allowing it to take the lead in international affairs. The problem is that in its desperate effort to preserve its "unipolar moment" the US is following–as a goal in itself–a strategy of absolute international dominance that may prove self-defeating. The US strategy is to limit independent action by *any* regional bloc, not just Western Europe, as Jochen Hippler seems to suggest.[114] As Christopher Layne points out,

American alliances with Japan and Germany are viewed as an integral part of a strategy that seeks: (1) to prevent multipolar rivalries; (2) to discourage the rise of global hegemons; and (3) to preserve a co-operative and healthy world economy.[115]

These efforts are doomed to failure for at least three reasons: (1) First, "as regional powers become stronger, they limit the capacity of any one nation to exercise dominance, forcing international politics further into the realm of bargaining and increasing the number of players."[116] (2) Second, US dreams of indefinite preponderance are limited by the fact that "the world economy is tripolar and has been since the 1970s... In economics, at least, the United States cannot exercise hegemony."[117] Although one should not carry the argument too far, military predominance is arguably less decisive to exercise hegemony than in the past. After the Cold War, economic issues have tended to eclipse security issues in the restructuring of the international agenda. (3) Finally, even if the US intends to exercise absolute preponderance with benign intent, "other states can justifiably infer that Washington's unipolar aspirations will result in the deliberate application of American power to compel them to adhere to the United States' policy preferences."[118] This will inevitably lead the states that feel threatened by US "benign" hegemony to form a coalition (or even an alliance) in order to balance US power.[119]

The relative decline of US hegemony in the "globalized" post-Cold War international economy, coupled with the above mentioned domestic political constraints, point to serious structural limits on the ability of the US to assert its hegemony over South America in economic matters. What has changed in US-Latin American relations? What are the prospects for enduring co-operation based on common interests, overcoming the mutual distrust and misperceptions of the past? Does the Miami Summit of December 1994 mark the beginning of a new era in US-Latin American relations? In the next chapter, we will examine more closely the emerging global structure and how it will affect the prospects for SAFTA and the Free Trade Area of the Americas at the turn of the millennium.

Notes

1 See Kryzanek, M., 1990, *US-Latin American Relations*, New York, Praeger, p. 29. John Saxe-Fernandez has described the US buy-out of Mexican resources and US policy toward Mexico in the late twentieth century as the "Mexico purchase." Quoted in Petras, J., 1997, "Latin America: The Resurgence of the Left," *New Left Review*, vol. 223 (May/June), p. 39.
2 See Molineau, H., 1990, *US Policy toward Latin America: From Regionalism to Globalism*, Boulder, (CO), Westview Press, pp. 44-45.
3 For example, the US and Peru signed in the early 1990s a 35 million dollar military aid package to help Peru fight leftist guerrillas who were said to protect coca growers and drug traffickers.
4 Abraham Lowenthal coined the phrase "hegemonic presumption." See Lowenthal, A., 1976, "Ending the Hegemonic Presumption: The United States and Latin America," *Foreign Affairs*, vol. 55 (Autumn), p. 201. Opinion is divided over whether US policy toward Latin America is still inspired by the hegemonic presumption. In the early 1980s, some scholars argued that the decline in US influence and the redistribution of power in the inter-American system meant that US policy in the region was no longer "imperialist." See Lowenthal, A., 1983, "Change the Agenda," *Foreign Policy*, vol. 52 (Fall), pp. 64-77; Smith, T., 1981, *The Pattern of Imperialism*, Cambridge (UK), Cambridge University Press, pp. 211-214.
5 Quoted in Gil, F., 1971, *Latin American-United States Relations*, New York, Harcourt Brace Jovanovich, p. 70.
6 Molineau, 1990, *op. cit.*, p. 41.
7 Kryzanek, 1990, *op. cit.*, p. 33.
8 See the "Additional Protocol Relative to Non-Intervention," signed by the United States and the Latin American republics at the Inter-American Conference for the Maintenance of Peace, Buenos Aires, 1-23 December 1936. See Connell-Smith, G., 1974, *The United States and Latin America: A Historical Analysis of Inter-American Relations*, New York, John Wiley & Sons, p. 167.
9 See Feinberg, R., *Summitry in the Americas, op. cit.*, pp. 23-24; Corrales, J. & Feinberg, R., 1999, "Regimes of Cooperation in the Western Hemisphere: Power, Interests, and Intellectual Traditions," *International Studies Quarterly*, vol. 43 (1), pp. 1-36.
10 Molineau, 1990, *op. cit.*, p. 23.
11 See Connell-Smith, 1974, *op. cit.*.
12 US-Argentina relations reached their lowest point in 1945-47. US ambassador Braden campaigned against Peron's candidacy for the free

elections of February 1946, when Peron won the presidency. Argentina did not attend the Inter-American Conference on the Problems of War and Peace in Mexico City (the Chapultepec Conference) in March 1945. The US eventually succeeded in sealing Argentina's adherence to an inter-American security arrangement at the Rio Conference in August 1947. See Child, J., 1980, *Unequal Alliance: The Inter-American Military System, 1938-1978*, Boulder (CO), Westview Press, pp. 85-90; Perruci, G., 1993, "Southern Cone Politics in US-Latin American Relations, 1945-1950," *SouthEastern Latin Americanist* (Spring), pp. 33-50.

13 Schoultz, L., 1987, *National Security and United States Policy Toward Latin America*, Princeton (NJ), Princeton University Press, p. 310.

14 An analysis of US economic aid to Latin America between 1962 and 1987 shows the low priority accorded to Latin America compared to other regions of the world. The area, despite its poverty, its proximity, and its 413 million people, received only 12.9 percent of US economic assistance over that period. See Molineau, 1990, *op. cit.*, p. 102 and p. 103, table 4.7. By comparison to Israel or Turkey, Latin America was considered less critical to the "strategic interests" of the United States.

15 Quoted in Francis. M., 1988, "United States Policy toward Latin America during the Kissinger Years," p. 30, in Martz, J., (ed.), *United States Policy in Latin America: A Quarter Century of Crisis and Challenge, 1961-1986*, Lincoln (NE), University of Nebraska Press.

16 Cottam, M., 1994, *Images and Intervention: US Policies in Latin America*, Pittsburgh, University of Pittsburgh Press, p. 25. Quoted in Bélanger, L., 1999, "US Foreign Policy and the Regionalist Option in the Americas," pp. 101-102, in Mace, G. & Bélanger, L. (eds.), *The Americas in Transition: The Contours of Regionalism*, Boulder (CO), Lynne Rienner.

17 See e.g., Pastor, R., 1992, *Whirlpool: US Foreign Policy toward Latin America and the Caribbean*, Princeton (NJ), Princeton University Press.

18 See Smith, P., 1996, *Talons of the Eagle: Dynamics of US-Latin American Relations*, New York: Oxford University Press, p. 334. As Lars Schoultz points out "There is a difference between the maintenance of a sphere of influence and the maintenance of hegemony, or *dominant* influence" (emphasis added). Despite the power asymmetry between the US and Western Europe (especially in military capabilities) the US has always treated with certain respect its European allies. As Schoultz, notes, "Washington exerts much more influence upon Europe than Europe exerts upon the United States, and this alliance based power asymmetry is what we call 'sphere of

influence.' Hegemony, in sharp contrast, implies domination," Schoultz, 1987, *op. cit.*, p. 283.

19 Gil, F., 1988, "The Kennedy-Johnson Years," p. 10, in Martz, J. (ed.), *United States Policy in Latin America*, *op. cit.*, pp. 3-27.

20 Despite opposition from the US Congress, US economic and military aid to El Salvador, Honduras, and Guatemala was enormously increased during the Reagan administration. See Kryzanek, 1990, *op. cit.*, pp. 80-81. Congressional restrictions, via the Boland Amendment of December 1982, prohibited the use of US funds for the overthrow of the Nicaraguan government. Yet Reagan administration officials managed to circumvent those limitations by secretly channelling "unofficial" non-governmental money to the *contras* who were waging a guerrilla war to overthrow the Sandinista government in Nicaragua. On the Iran-Contra affair, see Molineau, 1990, *op. cit.*, pp. 207-208.

21 Lowenthal, A., 1990, *Partners in Conflict: The United States and Latin America in the 1990s*, Baltimore (MD), Johns Hopkins University Press, p. 39.

22 Wiarda, H., 1990, "United States Policy in Latin America," *Current History*, vol. 89 (543), pp. 1-4, p. 2.

23 For details, see Pastor, 1992, *op. cit.*, pp. 86-88; Molineau, 1990, *op. cit.*, pp. 212-213.

24 Castañeda, J., 1990, "Latin America and the End of the Cold War," *World Policy Journal*, vol. 7 (3), pp. 469-492, p. 474.

25 See Feinberg, 1997, *op. cit.*, p. 48.

26 Petras, J. & Morley, J., 1992, *op. cit.*, p. 56.

27 Both Lake and Feinberg had opposed hard-line interventionist policies when they worked in the State Department in the 1970s, and they were both critics of the Reagan administration. See Burbach, R., 1993, "Lake and Feinberg: The Best and the Brightest?" *NACLA Report on the Americas*, vol. 26 (5,) pp. 18-19.

28 Robert Pastor argues that Clinton's new policy initiatives toward Latin America became hostage to the whims of a new Republican Congress after the mid-term elections of November 1994. "Not only did the new Republican Congress constrain the president's trade policy, but it also goaded his Cuban and Central American policies into an obsolete, Cold War direction and forced a more belligerent approach to drugs and immigration." Pastor, R., 1997, "The Clinton Administration and the Americas: The Postwar Rhythm and Blues," *Journal of Interamerican Studies and World Affairs*, pp. 99-128, p. 123.

29 "During a visit to Mexico, vice-president Albert Gore proposed that a summit meeting, attended by all the "democratically -elected heads of state" of the Americas, be convened. Though it was a bold idea and well received, the administration was slow to follow up with details and a plan. It took four months and a heavy lobbying campaign on the part of the state of Florida before the site and date of the proposed summit meeting was announced: Miami (FL) in December 1994. Meanwhile, the administration had still not decided on its goals for the meeting, which made it difficult to tie together the other issues to be placed on the Hemispheric agenda." Pastor, 1997, *op. cit.*, p. 108.
30 Ibid.
31 "The concept of hegemony is loose and ambiguous regarding both its attributes and its application." Strange, S., 1987, "The Persistent Myth of Lost Hegemony," *International Organization*, vol. 41 (4), pp. 551-574, p. 554.
32 See Gramsci, A., *Prison Notebooks*, edited and translated by Hoare, Q. & Smith, G. New York, International Publishers, p. 263.
33 See Strange, S., 1988, *States and Markets: An Introduction to International Political Economy*, New York, Basil Blackwell, pp. 24-27. Strange claims that structural power, "the power to shape frameworks within which states relate to each other," has become more important than relational power as traditionally defined by realist theory.
34 Deudney, D. & Ikenberry, J., 1999, "The Nature and Sources of Liberal International Order," *Review of International Studies*, vol. 25 (2), pp. 179-196, p. 181.
35 Burbach, R. & Robinson, W., 1999, "The Fin De Siecle Debate: Globalization as Epochal Shift," *Science and Society*, vol. 63 (1), pp. 10-39, p. 37.
36 See Cox, R., 1999, "Civil Society at the Turn of the Millennium: Prospects for an Alternative World Order," *Review of International Studies*, vol. 25 (3), pp. 3-28, pp. 11-12.
37 See Fukuyama, F., 1989, "The End of History?" *The National Interest* (Summer), pp. 3-18.
38 Taira, K., 1994, "Japan, An Imminent Hegemon?" p. 153, in Rourke, J. (ed.,) *Taking Sides: Clashing Views on Controversial Issues in World Politics*, Guilford (CT), Dushkin Publishing Group.
39 Haber, D., 1990, "The Death of Hegemony: Why 'Pax Nipponica' Is Impossible?" *Asian Survey*, vol. 30 (9), pp. 892-907, p. 906.
40 Crone, D., 1993, "Does Hegemony Matter? The Reorganization of the Pacific Political Economy," *World Politics*, vol. 45 (4), pp. 501-525, p. 505.

41 See Snidal, D., 1985, "The Limits of Hegemonic Stability Theory," *International Organization*, vol. 39 (4), pp. 579-614, p. 582.
42 See Smith, P., 1996, *Talons of the Eagle*, op. cit., p. 225.
43 Crone, D., 1993, "Does Hegemony Matter?" *op. cit.*, p. 504.
44 See Pikcunas, D., 1990, "Japan's Economic 'Pearl Harbor' Threatens the United States," *Conservative Review*, vol. 1 (7).
45 Gilpin, R., 1987, *The Political Economy of International Relations*, Princeton (NJ), Princeton University Press, p. 347.
46 Kennedy, P., 1987, *The Rise and Fall of the Great Powers: Economic Change and Military Conflict from 1500 to 2000*, New York, Random House, p. 515. For a critique, see Nye, J., 1990, *Bound to Lead: the Changing Nature of American Power*, New York, Basic Books, p. 9. Nye claims that "even after President Reagan's military build-up, the current [1990] US defence outlay is only about 6 percent of GNP; in the Eisenhower and Kennedy administration, it was near 10 percent." Yet as Gholz, Press, and Sapolsky point out, by 1997 the US was far ahead of other nations in terms of its current and potential military power: "Its defence budget, measuring more than a quarter of a trillion dollars, accounts for about 35 percent of the world's total annual military expenditures... The United States not only leads the pack but out-distances its closest rival [Russia] by more than a factor of three." Gholz, E., Press, D. & Sapolsky, H., 1997, "Come Home, America: The Strategy of Restraint in the Face of Temptation," *International Security*, vol. 21 (4), pp. 5-48, p. 8. Kennedy argues that the US will be increasingly unable to keep such a high level of military expenditures because they impose an unbearable burden on the US economy.
47 The Clinton administration managed to balance the US budget deficit in 1998, but the US trade deficit with Japan has grown from $43.4 billion in 1991 (of which about 40 percent is due to automobile imports) to about $120 billion in 1998. As Clyde V. Prestowitz points out, "We now have as big of a [trade] deficit in one month as we once had in an entire year." See Petersen, M., 1999, "Imports Push Trade Deficit to a New High: More Worry that US Lives Beyond its Means," *New York Times*, 20/8/99, pp. C1-C2.
48 Gilpin, 1987, *op. cit.*, p. 346.
49 Keohane, R., 1984, *After Hegemony: Co-operation and Discord in the World Political Economy*, Princeton (NJ), Princeton University Press, p. 31.
50 Snidal, 1985, *op. cit.*, p. 579.
51 Ibid. p. 581.
52 Erzan R. & Yeats, A., 1992, "Free Trade Agreements with the United States: What's in It for Latin America." Quoted by Castañeda, J., 1993, *Utopia*

Unarmed: The Latin American Left After the Cold War, New York, Vintage Books, p. 316.
53 Strange, 1987, *op. cit.*, pp. 554-555.
54 See e.g., Strange, 1987, *op. cit.*; Strange, S., 1988, "The Future of the American Empire," *Journal of International Affairs*, vol. 42 (1), pp. 1-17; Strange, S., 1982, "Still an Extraordinary Power: America's Role in a Global Monetary System," in Lombra, R. & Witte, W. (eds.), *Political Economy of International and Domestic Monetary Relations*, Ames (IA), Iowa State University Press, pp. 73-103; Russett, B., 1985, "The Mysterious Case of Vanishing Hegemony; or, Is Mark Twain Really Dead," *International Organization*, vol. 39 (2), pp. 207-231; Nye, 1990, *Bound to Lead*, *op. cit.*; Bartley, R., 1992, "Is America on the Way Down? No," *Commentary* (March).
55 Strange, 1988, "*The Future of the American Empire*," *op. cit.*, pp. 6-7; Strange, 1987, *op. cit.*, pp. 565-571. Strange quotes Robert Keohane's *After Hegemony* to show the inconsistencies of the declinist school's framework.
56 See Lars Schoultz's quote in note 13, above.
57 Feinberg, 1997, *op. cit.*, p. 13.
58 Lowenthal, A., 1990, "Rediscovering Latin America," *Foreign Affairs*, vol. 69 (4), pp. 27-41, p. 33.
59 Ibid., p. 34.
60 See Lowenthal, A., 1990, *Partners in Conflict*, *op. cit.*, "Latin America and the United States in the 1990s: An Afterword," pp. 221-222.
61 Lowenthal, 1990. "From Insecurity to Confianza: Forging a New US Policy for the 1990s," in Lowenthal, A., *Partners in Conflict*, *op. cit.*, chapter 7, p. 209.
62 Feinberg, 1997, *op. cit.*, p. 188.
63 See Corrales & Feinberg, 1999, *op. cit.*, pp. 1-36, p. 30.
64 Pastor, 1992, *Whirlpool*, *op. cit.*, p. 272.
65 Ibid., p. 18. Pastor refers to the resolution of the Central American crisis with the electoral defeat of the Sandinistas in the February 1990 presidential elections.
66 Pastor, R., 1992, "The Latin American Option," *Foreign Policy*, vol. 88 (Fall), pp. 107-125, p. 107.
67 Ibid., p. 230. Absent the fear of Soviet involvement, the US would have fewer reasons to militarily intervene in Latin America. The US invasion of Panama challenges Pastor's excessive optimism, showing that the elimination of the Soviet deterrent makes it easier for the US to intervene than in the past.
68 See Pastor, 1992, "The Latin American Option," *op. cit.* Castañeda and Tulchin emphasise the impact of the end of the Cold War on US-Latin

American relations. On the other hand, Pastor argues that developments *within* the region, such as the turn to democracy and free market economic policies, are more important than the end of US-Soviet competition for the future of inter-American relations. See Pastor, 1992, *Whirlpool, op. cit.*, p. 35. In *Partners in Conflict* (1990), Lowenthal also focuses on developments within the region, such as the economic crisis of the 1980s, although his more recent work pays more attention to the impact of global changes on US policy toward Latin America. See Lowenthal, A., 1992, "Changing US Interests and Policies in a New World," in Hartlyn, J., Schoultz, L. & Varas, A. (eds.), *The United States and Latin America in the 1990s: Beyond the Cold War*, Chapel Hill (NC), University of North Carolina Press, pp. 64-85.

69 See Connell-Smith, 1974, *op. cit.*

70 See Lars Schoultz's quote in note 13 above. "Several conservative writers worried that the end of the Cold War meant that the United States would pay even less attention to Latin America than it had in the recent past, although some noted casually that such disinterest was only right and natural since Latin America was not likely to present a threat to US interests." Tulchin, J., 1995, "The United States and Latin America in the World," pp. 321-322, in Martz, J. (ed.), *United States Policy in Latin America: A Decade of Crisis and Challenge*, Lincoln (NE), University of Nebraska Press, pp. 320-356. Tulchin quotes an article by Mark Falcoff in *The Washington Post*, and Kim R. Holmes, "The New World Disorder," in *The Heritage Lectures*.

71 Castañeda, 1990, "Latin America and the End of the Cold War," *op. cit.*, p. 477.

72 Ibid., p. 475.

73 See Foweraker, J., 1996, "From NAFTA to WHFTA? Prospects for Hemispheric Free Trade," in Nishijima, S. & Smith, P. (eds.), *Cooperation or Rivalry? Regional Integration in the Americas and the Pacific Rim*. Boulder (CO), Westview Press, pp. 162-164. As we have seen in chapter 4, other scholars believe that the US *does* have strong motivations to sign an FTAA on schedule.

74 See Foweraker, 1996, *op. cit.*, p. 161.

75 Tulchin, 1995, "The United States and Latin America in the World," *op. cit.*, p. 323.

76 See e.g., Atkins, G. P., 1992, "Reorienting US Policies in the New Era," p. 1, in Atkins, G. (ed.), *The United States & Latin America: Redefining US Purposes in the Post-Cold War Era*, Austin, The University of Texas at Austin.

77 As Castañeda notes, during the Cold War, "The United States could not do anything it wanted in Latin America because, among other things, the rule of

world-wide symmetries and action-counteraction was in play in spite of tacit Soviet acceptance of the US sphere of influence," Castañeda, 1990, *op. cit.*, p. 474.
78 Ibid., p. 473.
79 Ibid.
80 See Bélanger, L., 1999, "US Foreign Policy and the Regionalist Option in the Americas," *op. cit.*, pp. 96-97.
81 See Stallings, B., 1992, "International Influence on Economic Policy: Debt, Stabilization, and Structural Reform," p. 43, in Haggard, S. & Kaufman, R. (eds.), *The Politics of Economic Adjustment: International Constraints, Distributive Conflicts, and the State*, Princeton (NJ), Princeton University Press, pp. 41-88.
82 See e.g., Ianni, O., 1974, "Imperialism and Diplomacy in Inter-American Relations," in Cotler, J. & Fagen, R. (eds.), *Latin America and the United States: the Changing Political Realities*, Stanford (CA), Stanford University Press. On dependency theory see among others, Frank, A., 1967, *Capitalism and Underdevelopment in Latin America*, New York, Monthly Review Press; Cardoso, F. & Faletto, E., 1979, *Dependency and Development in Latin America*, Berkeley (CA), University of California Press.
83 Petras & Morley, 1992, *op. cit.*, p. 2.
84 Ibid., p. 47.
85 Ibid.
86 Ibid., p. 48.
87 See Richards, D., 1997, "Dependent Development and Regional Integration: A Critical Examination of the Southern Cone Common Market," *Latin American Perspectives*, vol. 24 (6), pp. 133-155, p. 133.
88 Petras and Morley, 1992, *op. cit.*, pp. 71-72.
89 Ibid., p. 59.
90 The "tough" Mercosur strategy for FTAA was summarised by President Carlos Menem of Argentina, in his opening address to the World Economic Forum in Sao Paulo, "I don't want to rule out the Free Trade Area of the Americas, but charity begins at home." Quoted by Diana Schemo, "With or Without the US, Latin Trade Group is Marching Forward," *New York Times*, 18/9/97, p. A10.
91 As Susan Kaufman Purcell notes, if SAFTA comes into existence, Brazil "would have a stronger negotiating position vis-à-vis the United States and be treated more as an equal if a Western Hemisphere free trade area were formed by uniting a North American free trade area, dominated by the United States, and a South American free trade area, dominated by Brazil." Kaufman Purcell, S., 1997, "The New US-Brazil Relationship," p. 94, in Kaufman

Purcell, S. & Roett, R. (eds.), *Brazil under Cardoso*, Boulder (CO), Lynne Rienner, pp. 89-102. See also Soares de Lima, 1999, "Brazil's Alternative Vision," *op. cit.*, p. 147.

92   Smith, P., 1996, "The United States, Regional Integration, and the Reshaping of the International Order," pp. 33-34, in Nishijima, S. & Smith, P. (eds.), *Cooperation or Rivalry?*, *op. cit.*

93   Lowenthal, 1990, *Partners in Conflict*, *op. cit.*, pp. 35-39.

94   Ibid., p. 36.

95   Ibid.

96   Other scholars disagree. For example, Alberto van Klaveren argues that "Europe did not play the leading role in Latin America during the 1970s and 1980s," and that Latin America has never been "particularly high in European priorities." See van Klaveren, A., 1994, "Europe and Latin America in the 1990s," p. 81, 99, in Lowenthal, A. & Treverton, G. (eds.), *Latin America in a New World*, Boulder (CO), Westview Press.

97   Smith, 1996, *Talons of the Eagle*, *op. cit.*, p. 224.

98   Smith, 1996, "The United States, Regional Integration, and the Reshaping of the International Order," *op. cit.*, p. 33.

99   Foweraker, 1996, *op. cit.*, p. 157.

100 "It is one more tragic Latin American paradox that at the same time that the Soviet Union and the 'socialist bloc' disappear as effective counterweights, Western Europe consummates a gradual withdrawal from its scant Latin American involvement..." Castañeda, 1990, *op. cit.*, p. 474.

101 Foweraker, 1996, *op. cit.*, pp. 154, 157.

102 Snidal makes the useful distinction between (1) *fully benevolent hegemony*, that "will benefit all and especially the weaker members of the international system," (2) *partly benevolent hegemony*, i.e., coercive leadership that "provides sufficient benefits to subordinate states that they will accept it as legitimate" and (3) hegemony that is coercive *and* exploitative: "when power is distributed asymmetrically but hegemony is exercised in ways that do not benefit all states subordinate states will chafe under the (coercive) leadership." See Snidal, 1985, *op. cit.*, p. 582.

103 See Lowenthal, 1990, *Partners in Conflict*, *op. cit.*, p. 141.

104 To what extent the US-centred "hub-and-spoke" model has lost clout among Latin American leaders and how confident they are in their ability to take charge of their future is shown by a "joke" attributed to President Menem of Argentina before a visit to Washington: "If the United States and its NAFTA partners wished to join Mercosur, they would be welcome to do so." Quoted

in Rohter, L., 1997, "Free Trade Goes South With and Without US," *New York Times*, 6/1/97.
105 The US decision to grant Argentina "major non-NATO ally" status is only a symbolic reward that has done some damage to Argentine-Brazilian relations.
106 This is a slightly modified version of the definition provided by Peter Smith. See Smith, 1996, *op. cit.*, p. 348. The only possible exception is Argentina's resistance to the formation of an inter-American defence system between the Chapultepec (1945) and Rio de Janeiro (1947) conferences. See section 2.*b* above.
107 Lowenthal, 1992, *op. cit.*, p. 79.
108 See Smith, 1996, "The United States, Regional Integration, and the Reshaping of the International Order," *op. cit.*, p. 34.
109 Quoted by Petras, J., 1997, "Latin America: The Resurgence of the Left," *New Left Review*, vol. 223 (May/June), p. 39.
110 Smith claims that the systemic changes produced by the end of the Cold War (the redistribution of power in the international arena) have "revised the terms and nature of inter-American diplomacy" and that "the fundamental determinants of US-Latin American relations have been the role and activity of extra hemispheric actors, *not the United States or Latin America itself.*" Smith, 1996, *Talons of the Eagle, op. cit.*, p. 7. By excessively focusing on changes in the distribution of power at the global level, Peter Smith unwarrantedly subordinates the role of domestic factors in his framework of analysis.
111 Lowenthal, A., 1974, "Liberal," "Radical," and "Bureaucratic" Perspectives on US Latin American Foreign Policy: The Alliance for Progress in Retrospect," p. 227, in Cotler, J. & Fagen, R. (eds.), *Latin America and the United States, op. cit.*, pp. 212-237.
112 Kryzanek, 1990, *op. cit.*, p. 222.
113 See Feinberg, 1997, *op. cit.*, chap. 5, "Decision Making and Decentralized Functionalism," pp. 79-97.
114 See Hippler, J., 1994, *Pax Americana? Hegemony or Decline*, London, Pluto Press, p. 151.
115 Layne, C., 1993, "The Unipolar Illusion: Why New Great Powers Will Rise," *International Security*, vol. 17 (4), p. 33.
116 Haber, 1990, *op. cit.*, p. 906.
117 Nye, J., 1992, "What New World Order?" *Foreign Affairs*, vol. 71 (2), pp. 87-88.
118 Layne, 1993, *op. cit.*, pp. 34-35.

119 "Structural realism leads to the expectation that hegemony should generate the rise of countervailing power in the form of new great powers." See ibid., pp. 11-12 and p. 34.

6 Beyond Open Regionalism: Mercosur, SAFTA, and the Future of Regional Integration in South America

> The nations of Latin America must act, and act soon or the opportunity may pass, and a new framework will be imposed on them which could reduce their autonomy to less than it is today or than it has been in the past... More than at any time since their independence the nations of Latin America have the opportunity to take their destiny into their own hands.
>
> Joseph Tulchin (1997)

Introduction

The term regionalism has two quite different meanings for the Latin American nations: (1) *intra*-regional co-operation within the framework of the Latin American Integration Association (LAIA) and several subregional groupings (such as Mercosur, the Andean Community, or the Central American Common Market,) and (2) *inter*-American or hemispheric co-operation involving the United States. In the preceding chapters, I have examined the revival of intra-regional co-operation in the 1990s and the prospects for the emergence of a South American Free Trade Area (SAFTA) as an autonomous trading bloc. In this chapter, I will consider different scenarios for South American and hemispheric regionalism at the turn of the millennium.

Is globalization driving the South American countries toward "deep" integration with the United States through a Free Trade Area of the Americas (FTAA)? Alternatively, does it provide an opportunity for the South American countries to define an independent role in the emerging global economy, taking their destiny "in their own hands"? The dominant approach in the literature is that the new regionalism is an aspect of globalization and does not have a dynamics of its own. Globalization, however, does not explain everything. Countries do not have to dance to the tune of globalization if they do not want to. There are alternatives to globalization. Autonomous regional integration leading to regional governance is an alternative worth exploring. Mercosur and a prospective SAFTA are examples.

The end of the Cold War has compelled individual states to re-evaluate their place in the international system by seeking new relationships with the major powers (such as the US) and their immediate neighbours. The rediscovery of regional strategies for economic and social development is part of that process. Globalization (or increasing internationalisation of trade, capital, and financial flows) has eroded the capacity for the management of the national economy of the traditional state. Yet the "retreat of the state,"[1] has opened up the possibility of *regional* management of national economies, and even of regional currencies, as shown by the adoption of the *euro* by the European Union and the debate on the possibility of a South American currency after the Brazilian devaluation of January 1999. The dominant model of "open regionalism" promoted by the "Washington Consensus" in the 1990s might give way in the first decade of the twenty-first century to more closed regional blocs, along the lines of "managed trade."[2]

The dominant approach in the literature is that the South American countries have no alternative but to join the US project of hemispheric regionalism. For example, W. Axline wrote in 1996 that there is a dominant vision of regionalism in the Americas: that of the US. The vision of an autonomous Latin American regionalism, he added, "has succumbed to the vision embodied in the Monroe Doctrine as the dominant organising force in Latin America today."[3] Yet, Bolivar's vision of a united Latin America is still alive. Although the Brazilian government has temporarily shelved the SAFTA proposal, it could be revived if the FTAA negotiations stumble. Considering the tendency toward the northward expansion of Mercosur SAFTA could de facto come into existence. Chile and Bolivia are already associate members, Venezuela has expressed an interest in joining Mercosur; and in spite of the stalled negotiations between Mercosur and the Andean Community, the recent trade agreement between the latter and Brazil could pave the way for SAFTA.[4]

In the first half of the 1990s, the conventional wisdom was that NAFTA was the key to understanding the new regionalism in the Americas. However, as NAFTA failed to incorporate Chile as a new member, the hub-and-spoke model of hemispheric economic integration lost clout and the South American countries managed to redefine the terms of the FTAA negotiations between the Miami and Santiago summits (see chapter 4). Yet the mainstream literature still argues that "the future of Latin America lies in a comprehensive working alliance with its powerful northern neighbour."[5]

As I have shown, an alliance with the US is not necessarily the best option for the South American countries in the era of globalization. US policy makers perceive that the survival of Mercosur as an autonomous trading bloc is *not* in the best interest of the US.[6] Mercosur and a potential SAFTA matter because there has been a transformation in the distribution of power in world politics. As Joseph Nye points out, "today different issues in world politics have different distributions of power; that is, different power structures...in trade, where the European Community acts as a unit, power is multipolar."[7] If this assessment is correct, in the post-Cold War era Mercosur has strong incentives to become an autonomous trading bloc, following the European model. Moreover, the diffusion of power away from *all* the great powers (including the US) creates room for SAFTA, even if it does not come into existence in the immediate future. Autonomous South American regionalism is an alternative, especially after the failure of the US to extend NAFTA to other Latin American countries and the lack of fast-track authority for the US president to sign an FTAA. Mercosur's troubles after the Brazilian devaluation of January 1999 should not obscure the fact that it has become a pole of attraction for business and integration efforts throughout the whole Southern Cone.[8]

In the era of globalization, the US may be "bound to lead," but it is also *constrained* by globalization. The US may have power over individual states (say, Argentina, or even Brazil) but it does not have power over the system of globalization "as a whole." As Nye points out, "as world politics becomes more complex, the power of *all* major states to achieve their purposes will be diminished."[9] This is an important insight because it shows that although the US is "the only military superpower left" it has far less leverage over the more complex, increasingly globalized international political economy. This is significant because it challenges the conventional wisdom that "there is no alternative" to globalization (see chapter 1). As we have seen in chapter 5, we are arguably in the early stages of the formation of a transnational hegemony led by international financial capital.[10] From this perspective, transnational capital, not the US, is the international hegemon. In that context, "the benefits of greater economic exchange among equals" may "outweigh the disadvantages of restricting flows with unequals."[11] If so, SAFTA, not NAFTA is the key to understand the new regionalism in the Americas in the 1990s. The South American countries are not pawns of US hemispheric designs. Paradoxically, by weakening the US grip over South America, globalization opens up the possibility of South American "strategic regionalism" (see figure 6.1) to negotiate their place in a globalized world economy from a position of strength.

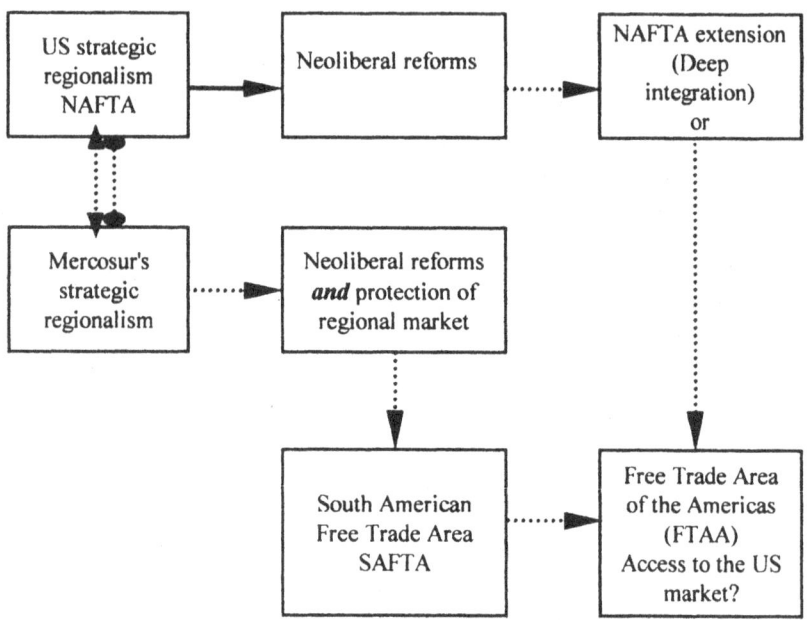

Figure 6.1 Globalization and South American Strategic Regionalism

Note: Dashed lines indicate possible, not firmly. established outcomes or relationships of (•·······•) co-operation, or (◄·······►) conflict.

At present, hemispheric regionalism rests on two models: NAFTA and Mercosur. Whether they come together or move apart will determine the future of economic integration in the Americas. The neoliberal ideology of globalization underlying the concept of "open regionalism" is the common "glue" making possible the current negotiations to achieve a Free Trade Area of the Americas (FTAA.) All the subregional experiments in economic integration share the logic of economic liberalisation with the FTAA proposal. This is an important difference with the state-led, inward-oriented "old regionalism" analysed in chapter 2. Yet how genuine is the South American commitment to neoliberal "open regionalism"?[12] As we have seen, the South American interest in the first half of the 1990s in expanding trade and investment ties with the US by joining NAFTA, grew out of a decade of severe economic crisis (the 1980s). Arguably, the willingness of the Latin American countries to entertain the deep integration agenda can only be understood in light of external economic and political pressures that operated on them during the 1980s.[13] Will the logic of convergence with the "colossus of the North" based on the neoliberal model survive in the new international economic conditions created by the Asian crisis of 1997-1998? Alternatively, will the South American countries form their own trading bloc to protect themselves from the vagaries of international capital flows and future international economic crises?

US strategic regionalism is arguably incompatible with Mercosur's strategic regionalism (see the opposing arrows in figure 6.1).[14] There is, however, a possibility of convergence between them if the neoliberal model of "deep integration" "wins the day" in the FTAA negotiations. Alternatively, in the absence of an FTAA by 2005, Mercosur might survive its present crisis and becomes a full customs union on schedule. Then, the next logical step for the South American countries would be to create SAFTA, leaving the door open for reopening the FTAA negotiations to gain access to the US market while simultaneously negotiating free trade areas with the European Union and Japan.

Abandoning a NAFTA-centred approach to the new regionalism in the Americas has important implications. First, it implies recognition that the South American countries *can* have independent foreign policies.[15] As we have seen in chapter 5, by the late 1970s, US hegemony over South America had steadily declined and the South American countries were successfully defining an independent role in the world stage. The debt crisis of the 1980s dealt a severe blow to such aspirations. Can the momentum toward independent South American foreign policies be revived? Under what conditions? How and why could the South American countries take charge of their future at the dawn of the millennium?

Looking Ahead: US-South American Relations and Free Trade in the Americas after the Santiago Summit

The FTAA negotiations before the Second Summit of the Americas in Santiago, Chile, seem to suggest that the US is unable, rather than unwilling, to exercise leadership in the Americas. From this perspective, regionalism in the Americas is

Table 6.1 US-South American Relations After the Santiago Summit: Three Alternative Scenarios

US-South American relations after the Santiago Summit (April 1998)	A Twenty-first Century international order*		
	(1) Mega-trading blocs and spheres of influence	(2) North/South separation	(3) Global development
(1) Polarisation NAFTA/Mercosur. Deepening of Mercosur and Andean Community. Mercosur becomes the "hard core" of an autonomous South American Free Trade Area (SAFTA)		Lack of concrete progress in FTAA negotiations by 2000 and/or indefinite breakdown of FTAA negotiations. Cooling of ties between the US and South America. Trade disputes and conflict over war against drugs and immigration issues.	
(2) Fast progress toward the FTAA and Reassertion of US hegemony	Signing of FTAA in 2005. Mercosur and Andean Community are absorbed by FTAA		
(3) Emergence of A South American Free Trade Area (SAFTA) as an *alternative* to the deepening of Mercosur			Erosion of US hegemony but continuing US/South American "selective co-operation." FTAA negotiations postponed until 2020. SAFTA/Japan and SAFTA / European Union free trade negotiations.

*On the three alternative scenarios for a twenty-first century international order, see Smith, P., 1996, "The United States, Regional Integration, and the Reshaping of the International Order," *op. cit.*, pp. 43-48.

not being "imposed" unilaterally by the United States. Inter-American cooperation in the 1990s can be seen as a "strategic game" between a northern coalition (NAFTA) dominated by the US and a Southern coalition (Mercosur) dominated by Brazil. Contrary to the reassertion of US hegemony thesis (see chapter 5) the US is *not* free to impose its will throughout the Americas. Instead of an US-dominated "bloc regionalism" in the Western Hemisphere undermining subregional co-operation the tendency seems to go in the opposite direction: subregional co-operation seems to be redefining the parameters of hemispheric regionalism. As we have seen in chapter 4, Mercosur has completely redefined the possibility and limits of a Western Hemisphere Free Trade Area by obtaining significant concessions from the US on the structure, timing, and agenda of the FTAA negotiations.[16]

Is the weakening of the United States position in the FTAA negotiations a temporary phenomenon? Will the current relative decline of US preponderance inevitably be followed by a reassertion of US hegemony and influence over the South American countries?[17]

There are three possible scenarios for US-South American relations after the Santiago Summit. Each scenario corresponds to a possible world order at the turn of the millennium (see table 6.1).

Scenario 1: Polarisation NAFTA/Mercosur. Mercosur becomes the "hard core" of a South American Free Trade Area (SAFTA)

In this scenario, there is a breakdown of the FTAA negotiations by the year 2000. In that case, the South American countries will have strong incentives to formally establish SAFTA both as a fallback option and as a counter-weight to NAFTA; and to be in a better position to negotiate free trade agreements with the European Union and Japan. SAFTA could become an important actor in a new world order organised around several regional and subregional trading blocs.[18]

In the absence of a successful conclusion of the FTAA negotiations in 2005, polarisation between Mercosur in the southern half of the Western Hemisphere and NAFTA in the North is a real possibility. In this scenario, US-South American relations would become increasingly conflictive, not only because of trade disputes, but also regarding the "new security issues"–drugs and immigration. If there is a world economic recession, both regional blocs could become "defensive" trading blocs. Eventually, NAFTA could enlarge itself to comprise Central America and the Caribbean, while Mercosur could become the "hard core" of a South American Free Trade Area (SAFTA).

Trade patterns between the US and its Central American and circum-Caribbean neighbours point in the direction of an increasing integration of these countries, including Venezuela and Colombia, in a North American regional system. Venezuela has not ruled out direct access to NAFTA through relations with the US, but at the same time, it has heavily bet on the regionalist card through the so-called Group of Three (Mexico, Venezuela, and Colombia). Venezuela has strengthened trade relations with Mexico and is seeking greater cooperation with the Central American and Caribbean countries while emphasising the Andean Community. Yet if scenario 1 comes into existence the latter could fall apart if Venezuela and Colombia become part of NAFTA while Bolivia, Peru, and Ecuador join Mercosur.

There are three problems with this scenario:

a) Mercosur has not yet consolidated itself as a trading bloc, and has suffered considerable strains since the Brazilian devaluation of January 1999. Mercosur is paying the price of having followed the policy prescriptions advised by globalization fundamentalists instead of actively promoting the productive integration of the member states' national economies. Had Mercosur followed the independent path of regional industrialisation of the Argentine-Brazilian Economic Co-operation and Integration Program of 1986 (see chapter 3) it would be in a better position to consolidate itself to face up to the challenges of the global economy at the turn of the millennium. Instead, as Aldo Ferrer points out, the adoption of the neoliberal model in 1990 resulted in the progressive specialisation of Argentina in exports of primary products and of Brazil in exports of manufactures, thus generating Argentina's "Brazil-dependency" and severely constraining the future of Mercosur.[19]

In strongly asymmetric integration processes, the perception on the part of the weaker partners of an unequal appropriation of the resulting benefits may endanger regional integration, particularly in times of economic crisis. For example, Argentina claims that several licensing requirements on imports imposed by Brazil to offset the impact of the Asian financial crisis of 1997-1998, together with a series of strict sanitary controls on agricultural goods, are a non-tariff barrier and violate the "spirit" of Mercosur.[20]

b) Mercosur and the Andean Community have made little progress in negotiating a free trade agreement. Without an Andean Community-Mercosur FTA there is no SAFTA, even if Chile becomes a full member of Mercosur. Mercosur insists that all countries should be granted the same status and treatment; most of the preferences should be multilateral in character and benefit the entire bloc. The Andean Community argues that the least developed nations should have more preferences and exceptions, and wants to extend a significant number of preferential tariffs on a strictly bilateral level, as in the negotiations within the framework of the Latin American Integration Association (LAIA).[21] In June 1999 Brazil concluded a separate two-year deal with the Andean Community on mutual trade preferences covering close to 3,000 products.[22] This Brazilian "defection" weakens Mercosur and its ability to become the "hard core" of a South American Free Trade Area (SAFTA).

c) The Asian financial crisis of 1997-1998 was severe and there were certain symptoms of a world recession in the fall of 1998. If there *were* a world recession, the prospects for SAFTA would increase; regionalist responses to a new "great depression" would become attractive. Commodity prices have fallen to their lowest levels in more than twenty years and progress in world trade has slowed down. Yet a prolonged world slump is not a foregone conclusion. Despite the failure of the WTO's conference in Seattle, if a "Round of the Millennium" is finally launched it may revive world trade. The US economy is in good shape; mobile capital is again flowing to "emergent markets" and some analysts are cautiously optimistic on the prospects for a recovery.[23]

Scenario 2: Fast Progress toward the FTAA and Reassertion of US Hegemony

A reassertion of US hegemony over the Southern Cone, facilitated by a continuing world economic and financial crisis, and the strains in Argentine-Brazilian relations provoked by the crisis could lead to this scenario. If Argentine-Brazilian trade wars continue and both countries fail to deal successfully with the "pending assignments" of subregional integration Mercosur might well disappear, absorbed into a hemispheric free trade area resulting from the convergence of several subregional agreements (NAFTA, CACM, AC, Mercosur).

The Asian economic crisis of 1997-1998 showed that trade with Latin America has become more important for the US than in the past. In 1997 US exports to Latin America and the Caribbean grew more than three times as fast as US exports to the rest of the world. During the second half of 1997, the US exported more to the Western Hemisphere than to the entirety of the European Union.

The FTAA is more likely in a world of spheres of influence and mega-trading blocs if the US can re-establish its hegemony over the South American countries, especially the Mercosur partners and Chile.

Will the asymmetric nature of the relationship between the US and South America inevitably lead to a reassertion of US hegemony?[24] There is no doubt that the US has significant structural economic power over Latin America, especially over the more dependent Mexican and Central American and Caribbean economies. Yet the South American countries are *less* affected by US structural power. The Mercosur partners show a diversified pattern of foreign trade and investment and are seeking closer linkages in both areas with the European Union and Japan.

The success or failure of the FTAA negotiations holds the key for the future of regional and subregional integration in the Americas. The FTAA was originally conceived as an instrument to reassert US hegemony over South America. It was an attempt by the US to "normalise" the South American countries by peacefully integrating them in the "global economy" while accepting the fundamental tenets of "deep integration" and fully opening their markets to US firms in the areas of government procurement and trade in services, while relaxing or eliminating domestic restrictions to intellectual property rights and foreign investments. Yet, as we have seen in chapter 4, there were significant disagreements at the trade ministerial meetings between the Miami (1994) and Santiago (1998) Summits of the Americas regarding the structure and pace of the negotiations. In less than four years the dynamics of hemispheric integration dramatically changed, with the strengthening of Mercosur's resolve to keep as much autonomy as possible. Mercosur "won the day" both at the trade ministerial meetings and at the Summit itself. Facing the prospects of an increasing trade deficit due to the Asian crisis, the US agreed to Mercosur's desire for gradual trade liberalisation in three stages, and made significant concessions regarding the ground rules for the FTAA negotiations.[25]

There are serious *structural obstacles* to a successful conclusion of the FTAA by 2005. First, small free trade areas such as Mercosur or NAFTA are easier to negotiate than mega-trading blocs. The FTAA must be negotiated among 34 countries with different national interests and levels of economic development, even if all agree on the basic tenets of the neoliberal model of "free markets." The Western Hemisphere countries are expected to achieve "concrete progress" in the FTAA negotiations by the year 2000.[26] Since the negotiations are considered a single undertaking, significant disagreement in any controversial area (such as trade in services, or intellectual property rights) could derail the whole process.

Second, the United States' demand for reciprocity in the FTAA poses a problem regarding the treatment of asymmetries. The per capita GDP of the United States (US$ 26,890) is 108 times greater than the per capita GDP of Haiti (US$ 250), and there are vast disparities amongst the "middle income developing countries" that make up the rest of the region. For example, in 1995 Bolivia had a GDP per capita of US$ 800, while Argentina's was US$ 8,030. The Trade Ministerial Meeting of San Jose created a Consultative Group to "take into consideration the needs, economic conditions and opportunities of the smaller economies." Without specific compensatory mechanisms, the strict application of a free trade agreement based on neoliberal principles would severely damage the smaller economies of Central America and the Caribbean, and certain South American countries, such as Bolivia, Ecuador, Paraguay, and Peru. If the US insists on its "deep integration" agenda without redistributive mechanisms or some type of special treatment to small countries, the smaller South American countries will have strong incentives to abandon the FTAA negotiations. They may join Mercosur (or a prospective SAFTA) provided that Brazil and Argentina are ready to make concessions to protect their domestic companies. Compensatory mechanisms allowing for slower adjustment for smaller economies are easier to negotiate at the subregional level, as shown by the concessions made by Brazil and Argentina to Paraguay and Uruguay in the Treaty of Asuncion that created Mercosur.

Third, an FTAA treaty would have to solve the problem of fitting together a confusing patchwork of over 50 bilateral and subregional free trade agreements signed by the Western Hemisphere countries.[27] Mercosur and NAFTA are the more important ones and the future of continental integration depends on whether they come together or move apart. Are NAFTA and Mercosur compatible? Thomas O'Keefe argues that despite "the seeming incompatibilities in goals between NAFTA and Mercosur, the tangible results that both economic integration programs will likely achieve by the turn of the century make them more similar than different.[28] By contrast, Bernier and Roy argue that "the two agreements cannot be combined without sacrificing their fundamental objectives."[29]

Arguably, despite their apparent convergence over neoliberal principles, Mercosur and NAFTA are two quite different models of regional integration, and it would be very difficult to make them compatible. Mercosur is an imperfect customs union with a pragmatic and flexible approach to regional integration based on political dynamics allowing for de facto protectionist and compensatory measures. On the other hand, NAFTA represents a mostly legalistic approach based on very detailed contractual obligations and placing rigid controls on the behaviour of members. The Treaty of Asunción has only 24 articles and 3 short annexes, whereas the NAFTA Treaty has more than 2,000 articles covering a broad range of subjects with extreme detail, from rules of origin to dispute settlement. Even O'Keefe recognises some potential stumbling blocs for merging the two agreements, such as the resistance of the Mercosur countries to open up the telecommunications field to the same extent that NAFTA does in North America, or the issue of government procurement that requires an amendment to the Brazilian Constitution.

The different objectives of both treaties are a significant obstacle for a successful conclusion of the FTAA negotiations, unless Mercosur suffers a major crisis and disintegrates, or the Brazilian and Argentine presidents make the political decision to adjust Mercosur to US demands for "deep integration."

The fourth obstacle is increasing domestic political opposition in the US to NAFTA and more free trade areas with the rest of Latin America. Both the Democratic and Republican parties have strong protectionist factions. Two candidates for the 1996 Republican presidential nomination (Robert Dole and Pat Buchanan) questioned the creation of the FTAA.

The US failed to provide strong leadership during the trade ministerial meetings before the Santiago Summit (see chapter 4). The successful conclusion of the FTAA negotiations will depend, to a significant extent, on whether the US president obtains "fast track" authority from Congress to sign an FTAA Treaty. The inability of US President Clinton to obtain such authority in November 1997 significantly diminished the credibility of the US commitment to the FTAA. It was interpreted by South American leaders as showing that the US was not ready for a "mature partnership" with them,[30] thus increasing the prospects for the emergence of SAFTA as an independent trading bloc.

Does the US really want to eliminate non-tariff barriers (such as the use of "Super 301" legislation to protect US firms) and open its market to Latin American exports? Is the US prepared to move from a regionalist *option* to a regionalist *policy* in the Western Hemisphere? An exacerbation of the protectionist sentiment now prevailing in the US Congress could lead to a return to aggressive unilateralism in US trade strategy thus completely derailing the FTAA process.

The US and the Mercosur countries (especially Brazil) have different interpretations of the meaning of "open regionalism." Although a NAFTA-centred FTAA is now out of the question, the US still defines "open regionalism" as a stepping stone before full access to NAFTA, whereas ECLA/Mercosur define "open regionalism" as facilitating the insertion of regional economies in the global economy, *without losing their national and regional identities.* The Brazilian strategy has been to preserve Mercosur's independence and its control of Mercosur while delaying the FTAA for as long as possible. Are both conceptions of "open regionalism" compatible? Brazil has joined the FTAA negotiations and it has not openly challenged the neoliberal ideology underpinning the FTAA proposal. However, Mercosur/SAFTA *is* the strategic regionalist option for South America. Because Mercosur's "pragmatism" and reliance on political interventions are incompatible with NAFTA, eventually it will challenge the US model of "open markets" if the FTAA does not come into existence.

Several factors play in favour of SAFTA, not the FTAA. First, as Moises Naim points out, SAFTA is already "quietly and effectively [providing] profit and growth opportunities for [South American] exporters."[31] Second, it is easier to negotiate a free trade area among nineteen countries than among 34 countries. Third, SAFTA is arguably a geopolitical and geoeconomic necessity for Brazil to reaffirm its independence vis-à-vis the US and as a fallback options if the FTAA does not materialise. With or without the FTAA, SAFTA benefits Brazil because it places the giant of South America in a stronger negotiating position vis-à-vis the US. Fourth, for the reasons mentioned in chapter 5 the distribution of power in the Western Hemisphere may lead to a decoupling of a North American Free Trade Area (embracing Central America and the Caribbean) dominated by the US and a South American Free Trade Area, dominated by Brazil.

Scenario 2 assumes that Mercosur will be eventually engulfed by the FTAA, losing its autonomy and identity as an independent actor in international affairs. However, despite its current troubles, Mercosur is not likely to disappear, for at least two reasons. First, although Mercosur still lacks supranational organs it has achieved a significant amount of "institutional density." The Protocol of Ouro Preto has created permanent decision making bodies and a regional bureaucracy with institutional interests of its own that will fight to "save" Mercosur from its present crisis. Second, Mercosur has achieved significant legitimacy. Despite its "democratic deficit" it has become a "brand name" giving a sense of security to both the four governments and the public. Moreover, in spite of the tremendous social costs of the economic adjustment programs (e.g., 12 percent of unemployment in Argentina) the regional middle classes strongly oppose a return to the hyper-inflationary experiences of the late 1980s (and early 1990s in the case of Brazil). This partly explains the reelection of Fernando H. Cardoso on an austerity platform in the November 1998 presidential elections in Brazil.

Scenario 3: SAFTA as an Alternative to the Deepening of Mercosur

The third scenario is the emergence of a South American Free Trade Area (SAFTA) as an *alternative* to the deepening of Mercosur. SAFTA could even encompass the Central American and Caribbean nations if the Central American Common Market (CACM) and ACS/CARICOM do not reach a satisfactory agreement with NAFTA. This scenario would postpone the resolution of the Argentine/Brazilian differences in Mercosur, which would remain an incomplete customs union in the absence of an agreement on the automobile and sugar sectors. SAFTA would cushion the impact of future world slumps on the Brazilian economy without destroying Mercosur, which is still useful for Brazil as a political entity to negotiate the resolution of the present economic crisis from a position of strength.

Balancing the US by creating SAFTA has become an attractive option for South America because of the failure of the US to deliver the public good of free trade in acceptable terms for its Southern neighbours. If SAFTA comes into existence, the South American countries will have strong incentives to strengthen co-operation with other Southern countries, such as those belonging to the G-15, created in 1989, or even to the formation of a South-South axis. In this scenario, the South American countries will finally have taken charge of their future, breaking their historical economic and political links of dependence on the "colossus of the North" while defining their security and well-being in regional, rather than "national" terms. The South American countries will no longer depend on the willingness of the US and other Northern countries to "share the table" with them. Instead, they will be invited to the table as equal partners. As a trading bloc, SAFTA would be in a position to negotiate on an equal footing with Northern trading blocs. A replay of the Asian crisis of 1997-1998 (this time including China) early in the twenty-first century would create strong incentives for the Northern countries to negotiate with SAFTA on an equal footing.[32] Even in the absence of a world slump, if the FTAA negotiations remain deadlocked SAFTA is also a real possibility, particularly if Argentina and Brazil manage to overcome their ongoing trade disputes and Mercosur survives its present crisis.

The future of US-Latin American relations will be determined by the resolution of the "Mexican dilemma": Will the Mexican economy become fully integrated with the US economy? The Mexican defection from the "Latin American family" had a paradoxical impact on Latin American regional integration. On the one hand, the potential for Latin American co-operation built around Mercosur was undercut by Mexico's defection, because it weakened the collective power of Latin America, while the consolidation of NAFTA threatened the Southern Cone countries, especially Brazil, with significant economic costs.[33] On the other hand, however, Mexico's defection opened up the door for SAFTA by leaving the South American countries "on their own," especially after the failure of NAFTA to incorporate Chile (see chapter 4). Mexico clearly benefits from excluding other Latin American nations from NAFTA membership, because it can get the best of both worlds: exclusive access to the US markets and individual FTAs with South American countries.[34] Although Mexico has become "the obligatory economic bridge between Latin America and the United States" the successful negotiation of the FTAA would deprive it of that role, "because with that success, Mexico would become a player among others."[35]

Will Mexico leave the door open for a free trade agreement with Mercosur while remaining a member of the Latin American Integration Association (LAIA)?[36] Whether Mexico consolidates its "informal" strategic alliance with the US or keeps open the option for a trade agreement or some form of alliance with Mercosur has important implications for the future of regional integration in the Western Hemisphere.[37] A Mexican alliance with Mercosur would revive the Bolivarian idea of Latin American unity; it could even save Mercosur from its current state of disarray while paving the way for SAFTA with Mercosur at its core, embracing Mexico, and the Central American and Caribbean countries.

Looking Ahead: South American Regional Integration in the Twenty-first Century

Despite the above-mentioned problems, scenario (1) is a real possibility: The consolidation of Mercosur, meeting the 2001 and 2006 deadlines for completion of a full customs union and moving toward the formation of a common market, with a complete elimination of non-tariff barriers, a firm commitment not to undertake unilateral trade measures and the establishment of a supranational mechanism for the settlement of trade disputes. In this scenario, Argentina and Brazil would consolidate their "strategic alliance" and a common market that could also take part in a "Free Trade Area of the Americas," but without losing its political, economic (or even military) identity. Both governments insist that they see Mercosur as a permanent geopolitical alliance,[38] not just a trade pact, and there has been increasing military co-operation between the two countries in the 1990s.[39] Both countries have been co-operating in the peaceful uses of nuclear energy after renouncing nuclear weapons and adopting binding non-proliferation commitments in 1991. Mutual confidence building has been reinforced by both the trilateral agreement with the International Atomic Energy Agency (IAEA) and the deepening of trade relations in the 1990s.

SAFTA and the deepening of Mercosur can be seen as a *response* to a failed US attempt to reassert its hegemony over South America, disguised as the false promise to extend NAFTA to the rest of the hemisphere. The failure of the US to impose the NAFTA-centred "hub-and-spoke" model to the FTAA negotiations seems to confirm the hypothesis that US hegemony in the Western Hemisphere is declining. The revival of old subregional integration schemes in South America, such as the Andean Community, and the creation of new ones, such as Mercosur, can be seen as attempts to achieve subregional autonomy in a new world order in which the US was not a reliable partner. The balance of forces in the world political economy seems to be shifting away from "multilateralism" underpinned by a global American hegemony, towards a system based upon competing regional blocs. Yet instead of a world of three macro-regions or blocs which are largely self-sufficient,[40] the South American experience points to a more decentralised world of *many* trading blocs or subregional arrangements that may, or may not, converge at the regional level into a "single" trading bloc.

Although the prospects for SAFTA are greater than when the FTAA negotiations began in 1995, its emergence as *the* South American trading bloc is not a foregone conclusion.[41] An alternative scenario is the consolidation of *several* subregional groupings in the subcontinent. Mercosur and the Andean Community are already customs unions and could become independent common markets in the absence of SAFTA.

Is "open regionalism" in danger in the Americas? The failure of supra-regional trade agreements (FTAA, Asia Pacific Economic Co-operation, APEC) could compel subregional and regional groupings such as Mercosur or the Andean Community to become more closed, out of necessity. A "fortress Mercosur" or SAFTA would undermine globalization and become an obstacle for a reassertion of US hegemony in the Western Hemisphere. Fears of a "fortress Mercosur" may be overdone, but Argentina and Brazil have agreed to raise by 3 percent Mercosur's average common external tariff of 11 percent while both intra-Mercosur trade and intra-South American trade have dramatically increased in the last few years (see figure 6.2).[42] Sub-regional groupings in Latin America want to keep their options open to protect themselves against the uncertainties of the international political economy in the era of globalization. In that context, the creation of SAFTA and the deepening of Mercosur (including the establishment of some supranational institutions) become attractive. By absorbing all prior sub-regional agreements SAFTA would solve the conflicts created by the proliferation of integration initiatives (memberships and commitments to certain groupings are at times contradictory and tend to overlap) while establishing a single mechanism for the resolution of intra-regional trade disputes.

Although a SAFTA Treaty has not yet been signed, SAFTA is already quietly happening. As Moises Naim points out, "economic integration between neighbouring countries [in South America] is taking place less in the speeches of politicians and more in the private transactions of firms located in different countries."[43]

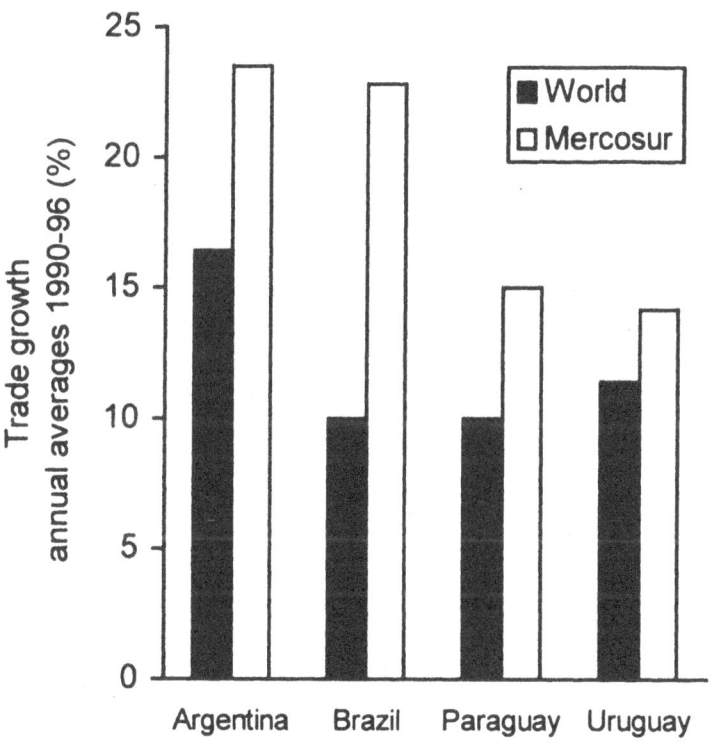

Figure 6.2 Intra-Mercosur Trade Growth, 1990-1996
Source: Latin America Weekly Report, WR-97-43, 28 October 1997, p. 510. Reproduced by permission of Latin American Newsletters, London, England.

Whether SAFTA will formally come into existence is an open question. On the one hand, the lack of progress in the negotiations between the Andean Community and Mercosur does not bode well for SAFTA. Brazil clearly has a strong interest in saving Mercosur from its present crisis, because as Mace and Belanger point out, "its smooth operation will keep the Brazil-Argentina axis healthy and attract neighbours such as Chile, Bolivia, and Peru."[44] Yet, even if Mercosur disintegrates because Argentina and Brazil are unable to manage their trade differences, SAFTA could still come into existence. Brazil, rather than Mercosur, would be the pole of attraction if Mercosur dwindles. In the absence of an FTAA by 2005, the other South American countries, including Argentina, would have strong incentives to join SAFTA (see scenario 3, above). On the other hand, Mercosur's troubles are not insurmountable; Argentina and Brazil have overcome their trade disputes in the past and have strong political incentives to save Mercosur and move forward toward a South American Free Trade Area. If the FTAA does not come into existence, Mercosur could well strengthen links with Europe, while consolidating itself as an independent trading bloc, rather than passively accepting US hegemony as in the past.

A full-fledged world slump in the first decade of the twenty-first century would create strong incentives for regional trading blocs such as Mercosur to cling together. In case of a prompt recovery for the world economy, a multipolar arrangement in which Mercosur celebrates free trade agreements with other trading blocs such as NAFTA is a real possibility because the world financial crisis has challenged the legitimacy of the concept of "open regionalism" and the assumption that there is no alternative to the unlimited globalization of trade and capital flows.

Whether an EU-Mercosur free trade area comes into existence will significantly affect the prospects for the FTAA. A free trade agreement between Mercosur and the EU prior to the conclusion of the FTAA negotiations would mark the "death knell" for the FTAA particularly if there is a SAFTA and Brazil abandons the project of hemispheric integration. The meagre results of the June 1999 EU-Latin American summit in Rio de Janeiro (tariff-cutting rounds will not begin until July 2001) create incentives for Mercosur to play one external trading partner (the EU) against the other (the US) using the threat of an EU-Mercosur FTA as a bargaining chip in the FTAA negotiations.[45] Since the calendar for the EU-Mercosur trade talks is now virtually identical to that of the FTAA, Mercosur can play this game for a while, but sooner or later it will have to choose between the EU and the US as its "privileged" extra-regional bloc partner.[46]

On the other hand, the US could take advantage of a world slump to reassert its hegemony over South America, using its structural power, as during the debt crisis of the 1980s.[47] US President Clinton commended the "openness" of Mercosur during his trip to Argentina and Brazil in 1997. Yet, one may argue that Mercosur threatens US hegemony in the Western Hemisphere, because it has the potential to become an independent trading bloc.

Whether SAFTA comes into existence (scenarios 1 and 3) and whether it is a stepping stone or a stumbling block toward an FTAA will be determined by the evolution of the world economy, domestic politics in the US, and the ability of the South American countries to adopt an autonomous regional foreign policy taking advantage of the inconsistencies of US policy toward the region in the post-Cold War era.

A major theme of this book is that Simón Bolívar's dream of Latin American unity is still possible. As I have shown in chapter 5, the mainstream literature on US-Latin American relations treats the Latin American countries as non-creative actors unable to have independent foreign policies and autonomous regional organisations because of "uncontested" US hegemony. US foreign policy makers and many US scholars have an image of Latin American elites and people as essentially incapable of making independent decisions. On the other hand, several Latin American foreign policy analysts (particularly Brazilian scholars) consider both feasible and desirable an independent foreign policy for their countries. For example, Celso Lafer argues that Brazil should put in place a policy of "multilateralism with differentiated niches of opportunity" to confront the post-Cold War world.[48]

It is certainly true that in the past Latin American countries (and more generally, Third World countries) were used to engage in lots of talk at international conferences and little concrete action.[49] Yet the end of the Cold War opens a window of opportunity for the Latin American countries to have a pro-active foreign policy.[50] The Rio Group and the subregional integration efforts of the 1990s (of which Mercosur is the most dramatic example) show that the South American countries are capable of taking charge of their future through independent collective action.

Whether US-South American relations in the twenty-first century will be characterised by a "model of equals" in which both sides have the same rights of access to each other's market will depend on a variety of factors, including whether the US definitely abandons the "hegemonic presumption" in US-Latin American relations and on the changing meaning of "hegemony" in the post-Cold War world. If the US decides to treat its southern neighbours as equal partners, there is an enormous potential for co-operation based on perceptions of convergent interests that would benefit both the people of the US and Latin America. Free trade alone is not enough. The real test for a future South American Free Trade Area (SAFTA) is to promote economic growth *and* sustainable economic and social development for the tens of millions of South Americans still living in absolute poverty.

Notes

1. See e.g. Strange, S., 1996, *The Retreat of the State*, Cambridge, UK, Cambridge University Press.
2. See Sandholtz, W. *et al.*, 1992, *The Highest Stakes: The Economic Foundations of the Next Security System*, New York, Oxford University Press, pp. 174-175.
3. Axline, W., 1996, "Conclusion: External Forces, State Strategies, and Regionalism in the Americas," in Mace, G. & Therien, J. (eds.), *Foreign Policy and Regionalism in the Americas*, Boulder (CO), Lynne Rienner, 1996, p. 199.
4. Whether the Andean Community (AC) leans toward Mercosur or NAFTA is critical for the prospects for SAFTA. The Brazilian trade deal has "kept" the Andean Community on the South American side for the moment, although at the risk of fracturing Mercosur. Even if the Andean Community disintegrates (Bolivia already trades more with Mercosur than with its Andean partners) the prospects for incorporating its member states to Mercosur are reasonably good, considering Venezuela's close trade ties with Brazil. See Kaufman Purcell, S., 1997, "The New US-Brazil Relationship," in Kaufman Purcell, S. & Roett, R. (eds.), *Brazil under Cardoso*, Boulder (CO), Lynne Rienner, p. 95.
5. Feinberg, 1997, *op. cit.*, p. 199.
6. US officials have depicted Mercosur as "a threat to hemispheric regionalism." According to Bernier and Roy, "implicit to the US offensive (against Mercosur) was the belief that progress by Mercosur was harmful to the FTAA," Bernier & Roy, 1999, *op. cit.*, p. 69, 89.
7. Nye, Jr., J., 1990, *Bound to Lead: The Changing Nature of American Power*, New York, Basic Books, p. 181.
8. See Fischer, K., 1999, "Business and Integration in the Americas: Competing Points of View," in Mace & Belanger (eds.), *The Americas in Transition, op. cit.*, pp. 195-196. See also Sánchez Bajo, C., 1999, "Mercosur's Open Regionalism and Regulation: The Role of Business Actors, Focusing on the Petrochemicals and Steel Sectors." Paper presented at the 40th Annual Meeting of the International Studies Association (ISA), Washington, DC, February 16-20, 1999.
9. Nye, 1990, *op. cit.*, p. 175.

10   See Burbach, R. & Robinson, W., 1999, *op. cit., p. 37*.
11   See Castañeda, J., 1994, *Utopia Unarmed: the Latin American left After the Cold War*, New York, Vintage Books, p. 314.
12   As Barbara Jenkins notes, "Despite the free trade rhetoric surrounding Mercosur, it has much more affinity with the old integration than participants admit, partly because the largest Mercosur partner, Brazil, is still far from the textbook definition of neoliberal, even after a recent turn to the right," Jenkins, B., 1999, "Assessing the 'New' Integration: The Mercosur Trade Agreement," in Thomas, K. & Tetrault, M. (eds.), *Racing to Regionalize: Democracy, Capitalism, and Regional Political Economy*, Boulder (CO), Lynne Rienner, p. 35.
13   See Haggard, S., 1995, *Developing Nations and the Politics of Global Integration*, Washington, DC, Brookings Institution, p. 7; Felix, D., 1998, "Is The Drive toward Free-Market Globalization Stalling?" *Latin American Research Review*, vol. 33 (3), pp. 191-216, p. 197.
14   See Bernier & Roy, 1999, *op. cit.*, pp. 87-89.
15   See Hey, J., 1998, "Is There a Latin American Foreign Policy?" *Mershon International Studies Review*, vol. 42 (1), pp. 106-116, p. 109.
16   See "Ground Rules for FTAA Agreed: Mercosur Stance Carries the Day as Washington Cedes," *Latin American Weekly Report*, 24/3/98, p. 136.
17   Peter H. Smith claims that "since World War II...the general trend has *always* been for the United States to exert a great degree of influence over Latin American countries, but the level of this influence revealed some oscillation (up, down, up) from the mid-1950s to the present time," Smith, P., 1996, "The United States, Regional Integration, and the Reshaping of the International Order," *op. cit.,* p. 30.
18   This is a variant of Abraham Lowenthal's "worst-case scenario" for US-Latin American relations. See Lowenthal, 1990, *Partners in Conflict, op. cit.*, pp. 194-195.
19   See Ferrer, 1997, "Los Dos Modelos de Mercosur," *op. cit.*
20   Brazil has recently imposed restrictions on imports of 400 Argentine products, as a response to Argentina's restrictions on imports of Brazilian footwear. See "Brazil Escalates tit-for-tat Measures," *Latin American Weekly Report*, 21/9/99, p. 434. Mercosur will arguably survive the present trade war between its major partners. See "Mercosur Row May End by December: Rivals Know that Bloc Rules Impose a Strict Deadline," *Latin American Weekly Report*, 28/9/99, p. 452. In the past, political co-operation between presidents Menem and Cardoso allowed Mercosur to survive major Argentine-Brazilian trade disputes (see chapter 3.)
21   See "Southern FTA Talks Hit a Snag: Deadline Passes with Andeans &

Mercosur Far from Deal," *Latin American Weekly Report*, 6/10/98, p. 465.
22 See "Brazil-CAN," *Latin American Weekly Report*, 6/7/99, p. 302.
23 See e.g., Krugman, P., 1999, "The Return of Depression Economics," *Foreign Affairs*, vol. 78 (1), pp. 56-74.
24 Whereas in 1990 the GDP of the US was 58 times that of Argentina and 13 times that of Brazil, in 1995 it was only 25 times that of Argentina and 10 times that of Brazil. See table 5.2 and the discussion of the "hegemony by default" thesis in chapter 5.
25 See chapter 4. See also "Ground Rules for FTAA Agreed," *op. cit.*, and "Building the FTAA: Policy Debate and Prospects," *Latin American Special Reports*, April 1998, pp. 1-12.
26 The negotiation of the FTAA, formally launched at the Santiago Summit, was entrusted to a Trade Negotiations Committee (TNC) formed by deputy trade ministers and nine negotiating groups: (1) market access, (2) investment, (3) services, (4) government procurement, (5) dispute settlement, (6) agriculture, (7) intellectual property rights, (8) subsidies, antidumping and countervailing duties, and (9) competition policy.
27 See the list of bilateral and subregional trade agreements in Hornbeck, J., 1998, "A Free Trade Area of the Americas: Toward Integrating Regional Trade Policies," Congressional Research Service Report, in http://natlaw.com/pubs/spmxcu8.htm.
28 O'Keefe, T., 1995, "The Prospects for Mercosur's Inclusion into the North American Free Trade Agreement (NAFTA)," *International Law Practicum*, vol. 8 (1), pp. 5-13, p. 12.
29 Bernier, I. & Roy, M., 1999, "NAFTA and Mercosur: Two Competing Models?" in Mace, G. & Bélanger, L. (eds.), *The Americas in Transition*, *op. cit.*, p. 88.
30 In the words of Uruguayan Foreign Minister Carlos Perez del Castillo at the close of a meeting of Mercosur in December 1997: without "fast track," "the FTAA negotiating process makes no sense." See "Trade: Preparing for the Santiago Summit," *Latin American Weekly Report*, January 1998, p. 5. On the prospects for a mature partnership between the US and Latin America, see Lowenthal, 1994, *op. cit.*, pp. 245-246.
31 Naim, M., 1992/93, "Instead of NAFTA, Shooting for SAFTA," in *CEO/International Strategies* (December/January), pp. 70-73, p. 73.
32 During the Asian economic crisis of 1997-98 Latin America was considered an important "mini-locomotive" of the world economy. Since the beginning of the 1990s, growth in the countries of the OECD has averaged just 1.9 percent, whereas in Latin America and Asia it has expanded to 5.8 percent.

Nevertheless, because of the Asian financial crisis growth in most Asian countries came to a halt in 1997 while the Latin American economies grew an average 5.3 percent in the same year, spurred by strong growth in Argentina, Chile, and Mexico. See Instituto the Relaciones Europeo-Latinoamericanas (IRELA), 1997, "A Challenge to the Atlantic Triangle? Context and Agenda of an EU-Latin America Summit," IRELA Briefing, in: http://www.irela.es/bf97-2e.htm. See also Bustos, S. & Bamrud, J., 1998, "Weathering the Storm: Economic and Trade Report," *Latin Trade* (April), pp. 33-44, p. 33.

33 See Hurrell, A., 1994, "Regionalism in the Americas," in Lowenthal, A. & Treverton, G. (eds.), *Latin America in a New World*, Boulder (CO), Westview Press, p. 172.

34 Mexico has already signed free trade agreements with Chile, Venezuela, Colombia, and Bolivia.

35 Mace, G. & Bélanger, L., "A Provisional Assessment," in Mace & Bélanger, 1999, *op. cit.*, p. 250.

36 Mexico has been exempted from granting to other LAIA members the preferences that it has granted to imports from Canada and the US under NAFTA. See the *Interpretative Protocol of article 44 of the 1980 Montevideo Treaty*, which was signed in June 1994, six months after NAFTA entered into force.

37 See "Busca Mexico Alianza con Argentina y el Mercosur. Rebolledo: Sería a Mediano Plazo," *La Jornada* (Mexico City), 14/6/97. See also "Feinberg: Si Triunfa Cárdenas, Wall Street No Debería Alarmarse. El TLC Formalizó una Alianza Estratégica, dijo el ex-Director para América Latina del Consejo Nacional de Seguridad de la Casa Blanca," *La Jornada* (Mexico City), 19/6/97.

38 Presidents Menem and Cardoso defined Argentine-Brazilian relations as a "truly strategic alliance" in the Rio de Janeiro Declaration (April 27, 1997) and then signed a "Memorandum of Understanding, Consultation and Co-ordination in Matters of Mutual Interest in the Area of International Defence and Security." See Cimadamore, A., 1997, "La Integración Regional y los Límites de la Cooperación Militar: Reflexiones desde el Mercosur," *Segundas Jornadas Interdisciplinarias del Litoral sobre el Mercosur*, Economics and Statistics Department, National University of Rosario, Argentina.

39 Annual meetings between the Joint Chiefs of Staff of both countries are held for this purpose. Since 1992 Uruguayan and Paraguayan military officers began to participate in these meetings.

40 See Thurow, L., 1992, *Head to Head: The Coming Economic Battle Among*

Japan, Europe, and America, New York, Warner Books.
41 A free trade area between Mercosur and the Andean Community would speed up the formation of SAFTA, but negotiations between the two blocs have been delayed because of the Andean countries' failure to reach a common negotiating position on tariff cuts. See "Mercosur/Andean Community May Delay Tariff Cuts," *Latin American Weekly Report*, 9/6/98, p. 259.
42 See chapters 2 and 3. On the decision to raise Mercosur's common external tariff, see "The Americas: The Free Trade Winds Die Away," *The Economist*, 22/11/97, pp. 35-36.
43 Naim, 1992/93, *op. cit.*, p. 73.
44 Mace & Bélanger, 1999, "A Provisional Assessment," *op. cit.*, p. 250.
45 At the Rio Summit, the Mercosur countries expected a clear commitment from the EU to start talks aimed at reaching an EU-Mercosur free trade agreement by 2005. Yet because of French opposition to include EU agricultural subsidies in the talks, the EU and Mercosur leaders could only agree to a slow timetable of trade negotiations. The final declaration commits them to launch talks aimed at "gradual and reciprocal trade liberalisation." However, talks will be limited to non-tariff issues until July 2001, when tariff-cutting rounds will begin, provided they can reach an agreement on EU agricultural subsidies.
46 Considering the significant differences between NAFTA and the EU (e.g., regarding standards and rules of origin) it may be technically impossible for Mercosur to sign simultaneously free trade agreements with both trading blocs.
47 See chapter 2. On the concept of structural power, see Strange, S., 1988, *States and Markets: An Introduction to International Political Economy*, New York, Basil Blackwell, pp. 24-42.
48 See Lafer, C., 1994, "Brazil in a New World," in Lowenthal, A. & Treverton, G. (eds.), *Latin America in a New World*, *op. cit.*, p. 233.
49 "We haven't had any organisation for action--only for making speeches to one another," claimed Julius Nyerere at a meeting of the G-15, whose participants "agreed they could not rely on the developed world to act as the locomotive of their future," quoted by Smith, P., 1996, "The United States, Regional Integration, and the Reshaping of the International Order," *op. cit.*, p. 46.
50 For example, despite their geographic proximity to the "colossus of the North" the Central American countries have begun talks to transform the Central American Integration System (SICA) into something similar to the European Union. Such a project would have been unthinkable during the

Cold War. See "Central America: Towards a Political Union?" in "SELA Analyses the Trends and Options of Integration," *Integration Bulletin for Latin America and the Caribbean*, No. 8, September, 1997.

Bibliography

Acuña, E. S. (1997), *Mercosur: Entre el Regionalismo y el Continentalismo*, La Plata, Argentina, Centro de Estudios Bonaerenses, La Plata University.
Adler, E. and Barnett, M. (1998), "Security Communities in Theoretical Perspective," in E. Adler and M. Barnett (eds.), *Security Communities*, Cambridge (UK), Cambridge University Press, pp. 29-65.
Agosin, M. R. and Ffrench-Davis, R. (1993), "Trade Liberalization in Latin America," *CEPAL Review*, No. 50, pp. 41-62.
Albrow, M. (1997), *The Global Age: State and Society Beyond Modernity*, Stanford (CA), Stanford University Press.
Alexander, R. (1995), "Import Substitution in Latin America in Retrospect," in J. Dietz (ed.), *Latin America's Economic Development: Confronting Crisis*, Boulder (CO), Lynne Rienner, pp. 159-66.
Anderson, K. and Blackhurst, R. (eds.) (1993), *Regional Integration and the Global Trading System*, New York, Harvester/Wheatsheaf.
Arocena, M. (1997), "Common Market of the Southern Cone (Mercosur)," in A. J. Jatar and S. Weintraub (eds.), *Integrating the Hemisphere: Perspectives from Latin America and the Caribbean*, Washington, DC, Inter-American Dialogue, pp. 152-176.
Atkins, G.P. (1992), "Reorienting US Policies in the New Era," in G. P. Atkins (ed.), *The United States and Latin America: Redefining US Purposes in the Post-Cold War Era*, Austin, The University of Texas at Austin, pp. 1-18.
Atkins, G. (1995), *Latin America in the International Political System*, Boulder (CO), Westview Press.
Axelrod, R. (1984), *The Evolution of Cooperation*, New York, Basic Books.
Axline, W.A. (1996), "Conclusion: External Forces, State Strategies, and Regionalism in the Americas," in G. Mace and J. Thérien (eds.), *Foreign Policy and Regionalism in the Americas*, Boulder (CO), Lynne Rienner, pp. 199-218.
Axline, W. A. (ed.) (1994), *The Political Economy of Regional Cooperation: Comparative Case Studies*, London, Pinter Publishers.

Axline, W.A. (1977), "Underdevelopment, Dependence, and Integration: The Politics of Regionalism in the Third World," *International Organization*, vol. 31, pp. 83-105.

Ayoob, M. (1985), "The Primacy of the Political: South Asian Regional Cooperation (SARC) in Comparative Perspective," *Asian Survey*, vol. 25, pp. 443-57.

Bailey, N. A. (1967), *Latin America in World Politics*, New York, Walker & Company.

Bartley, R. (1992), "Is America on the Way Down? No," *Commentary*, (March).

Bélanger, L. (1999), "US Foreign Policy and the Regionalist Option in the Americas," in G. Mace, L. Bélanger et al. (eds.), *The Americas in Transition: The Contours of Regionalism*, Boulder (CO), Lynne Rienner Publishers, pp. 95-110.

Bélanger, L., Cooper, A., Mace, G. and Monfils, J. (1999),"Middle Powers and Regional Trade Cooperation: Argentina, Brazil, Canada, Mexico and the Setting of the FTAA Negotiation," Paper presented at the Annual Meeting of the International Studies Association, Washington, DC, 16-21 February.

Bello, W. (1996), "Structural Adjustment Programs: 'Success' for Whom?" in J. Mander and E. Goldsmith (eds.), *The Case Against the Global Economy and for a Turn toward the Local*, San Francisco, Sierra Club Books, pp. 285-96.

Benavente, J. M. and West, P. (1992), "Globalization and Convergence: Latin America in a Changing World," *CEPAL Review*, No. 47, pp. 77-94.

Benegas Cristaldo, G. (1994), *A la Búsqueda de Un Mercado Común: Mercosur: Creación de Comercio, Desviación de Comercio, e Implicancias de Politicas Publicas*, Asunción, Paraguay, Universidad Catolica Nuestra Señora de la Asunción.

Bergsten, F. (1992), "The Primacy of Economics," *Foreign Policy*, No. 87, pp. 3-24.

Bernier, I. and Roy, M. (1999), "NAFTA and Mercosur: Two Competing Models?" in G. Mace, L. Bélanger et al. (eds.), *The Americas in Transition: The Contours of Regionalism*, Boulder (CO), Lynne Rienner Publishers, pp. 69-94.

Bhalla, A. S. and Bhalla, P. (1997), *Regional Blocs: Building Blocks or Stumbling Blocks?* New York, St. Martin's Press.

Bienefeld, M. (1996), "Is a Strong National Economy a Utopian Goal at the End of the Twentieth Century?" in R. Boyer and D. Drache (eds.), *States against Markets: The Limits of Globalization*, London, Routledge, pp. 415-40.

Binder, L. (1958), "The Middle East as a Subordinate International System," *World Politics*, vol. 10, pp. 408-29.

Borda, D. and Masi F. (eds.) (1998), *Estabilización y Ajuste de las Economías del Mercosur*, Asunción, Paraguay, Centro de Análisis y Difusión de Economía Paraguaya.

Bouzas, R. (ed.) (1997a), *Regionalización e Integración Económica: Instituciones y Procesos Comparados*, Buenos Aires, Grupo Editor Latinoamericano.

Bouzas, R. (1997b), "Mercosur and Preferential Trade Liberalization in South America: Record, Issues and Prospects," in R. G. Lipsey and P. Meller (eds.), *Western Hemisphere Trade Integration: A Canadian Latin American Dialogue*, New York, St. Martin's Press, pp. 58-89.

Bouzas, R. (1997c), *El Mercosur: Una Evaluación sobre su Desarrollo y Desafíos Actuales*, Buenos Aires, FLACSO, Documento de Investigacion No. 215.

Bouzas, R. (1997d), "El Area de Libre Comercio de las Américas: un Breve Balance Previo a la Cumbre de Santiago," Buenos Aires, Documento de Trabajo No. 22, Instituto del Servicio Exterior de la Nación.

Bouzas, R. (1995a), "Preferential Trade Liberalization in the Western Hemisphere: NAFTA and Beyond," in J. Teunissen (ed.), *Regionalism and the Global Economy: The Case of Latin America and the Caribbean*, The Hague, FONDAD, pp. 132-57.

Bouzas, R. (1995b), "Liberalización Comercial e Integración Regional en el Hemisferio Occidental," Buenos Aires, Documento de Trabajo No. 7, Instituto del Servicio Exterior de la Nación.

Bouzas, R. (1995c), "Integración Económica e Inversion Extranjera: La Experiencia Reciente de Argentina y Brasil," Buenos Aires, Documento de Trabajo No. 9, Instituto del Servicio Exterior de la Nación.

Bouzas, R. and Ros, J. (1994), *Economic Integration in the Western Hemisphere*, Notre Dame (IN), University of Notre Dame Press.

Bouzas, R. and Ros, J. (1993), "The North-South Variety of Economic Integration: Issues and Prospects for Latin America," Documento de Investigación No. 141, Buenos Aires, FLACSO.

Bouzas, R. and Russell, R. (eds.), (1996), *Globalización y Regionalismo en las Relaciones Internacionales de Estados Unidos,* Buenos Aires, Grupo Editor Latinoamericano.

Bulmer-Thomas, V. (1997), "Regional Integration in Latin America Before the Debt Crisis: LAFTA, CACM and the Andean Pact" in A. El-Agraa (ed.), *Economic Integration Worldwide,* New York, St. Martin's Press, pp. 230-52.

Bulmer-Thomas, V. (1997), "Regional Integration in Latin America since 1985: Open Regionalism and Globalization," in A. M. El-Agraa (eds.), *Economic Integration Worldwide,* New York, St. Martin's Press, pp. 253-77.

Burbach, R. (1993), "Lake and Feinberg: The Best and the Brightest?" *NACLA Report on the Americas,* vol. 26 (5), pp. 18-19.

Burbach, R. and Robinson, W. (1999), "The Fin De Siecle Debate: Globalization as Epochal Shift," *Science and Society,* vol. 63, pp. 10-39.

Busch, A. (1998), "The Santiago Summit: Plenty of Talk, Little Action," *Latin Trade* (July), p. 16.

Busch, M. L. and Milner, H. (1994), "The Future of the International Trading System: International Firms, Regionalism, and Domestic Politics," in R. Stubbs and G. Underhill (eds.), *Political Economy and the Changing Global Order,* New York, St. Martin's Press, pp. 259-76.

Bush, G. (1990), "Latin America: Debt Reduction," Speech delivered at the White House, Washington, DC, 27 June, in *Vital Speeches of the Day,* Mount Pleasant (SC), No. 20, p. 611.

Bustos, S. and Bamrud, J. (1998), "Weathering the Storm: Economic and Trade Report," *Latin Trade* (April), pp. 33-44.

Cantori, L. J. and Spiegel, S. (eds.), (1970), *The International Politics of Regions: A Comparative Approach,* Englewood Cliffs (NJ), Prentice-Hall.

Caporaso, J. (1996), "The European Union and Forms of State: Westphalian, Regulatory or Post-Modern?" *Journal of Common Market Studies,* vol. 34, pp. 29-52.

Caporaso, J. and Keeler, J. (1995), "The European Union and Regional Integration Theory," in C. Rhodes and S. Mazey (eds.), *The State of the*

European Union: Building a European Polity?, Boulder (CO), Lynne Rienner, pp. 29-62.

Cardoso, E. and Fishlow, A. (1989), "Latin American Economic Development: 1950-1980," NBER Working Paper No. 3161.

Cardoso, F. (1973), "Associated Dependent Development: Theoretical and Practical Implications: in A. Stepan (ed.), *Authoritarian Brazil*, New Haven (CT), Yale University Press.

Cardoso, F. and Faletto, E. (1979), *Dependency and Development in Latin America*, Berkeley (CA), University of California Press.

Carranza, M. E. (1999a), Review of *Summitry in the Americas: A Progress Report*, by R. E. Feinberg, and *Western Hemisphere Trade Integration: A Canadian-Latin American Dialogue*, R. G. Lipsey and P. Meller (eds.), in *Journal of Interamerican Studies and World Affairs*, vol. 41, pp. 131-36.

Carranza, M. E. (1999b), "Building Block or Stumbling Block? Mercosur and the Future of Economic Integration in the Americas," Paper presented at the 40th Annual Meeting of the International Studies Association, Washington, DC, 16-21 February.

Carranza, M. E. (1998a), "SAFTA or FTAA? Open Regionalism and the Future of Regional Economic Integration in South America," Paper presented at the 39th Annual Meeting of the International Studies Association, Minneapolis (MN), 17-21 March.

Carranza, M. E. (1998b), Review of *The State of the European Union: v. 4: Deepening and Widening*, P. H. Laurent and M. Maresceau, (eds.), *Choice*, vol. 36, No. 1 (September).

Carranza, M. E. (1997), "Transitions to Electoral Regimes and the Future of Civil-Military Relations in Argentina and Brazil," *Latin American Perspectives*, vol. 24, pp. 7-25.

Carranza, M. E. (1995), "Geo-Economic Regionalism in a Post-Sovereign World: The Future of ASEAN and the European Union," Paper presented at the 36th Annual Meeting of the International Studies Association, Chicago (IL), 21-25 February.

Carranza, M. E. (1993a), "Seguranca Regional e Integraçao Economica na America Latina e no Sudeste Asiatico: Um Estudo Comparado," *Contexto Internacional* (Rio de Janeiro), vol. 15, pp. 57-95.

Carranza, M. E. (1993b), "Regional Security and Economic Integration in Latin America and Southeast Asia," Paper presented at the 34th Annual

Meeting of the International Studies Association, Acapulco (Mexico), 23-27 March.

Carranza, M. E. (1993c), "Legal, Political, and Economic Aspects of the Enterprise for the Americas Initiative and Subregional Integration in Latin America," Paper presented at the 34th Annual Meeting of the International Studies Association, Acapulco (Mexico), 23-27 March.

Castañeda, J. (1993), *Utopia Unarmed: The Latin American Left After the Cold War*, New York, Vintage Books.

Castañeda, J. (1990), "Latin America and the End of the Cold War," *World Policy Journal*, vol. 7, pp. 469-92.

Centro de Investigaciones Europeo-Latinoamericanas (EURAL) (1987), *America Latina y Europa en el Debate Estratégico Mundial*, Buenos Aires, Legasa.

Child, J. (1980), *Unequal Alliance: The Inter-American Military System, 1938-1978*, Boulder (CO), Westview Press.

Chudnovsky, D. (1994), "Reviving South-South Co-Operation: Argentina, Brazil and the Mercosur," in L. K. Mytelka (ed.), *South-South Co-Operation in a Global Perspective*, Paris, Organization for Economic Cooperation and Development (OECD).

Cimadamore, A. (1997), "La Integración Regional y los Límites de la Cooperación Militar: Reflexiones desde el Mercosur," II Jornadas Interdisciplinarias del Litoral sobre el Mercosur, Economics and Statistics Department, National University of Rosario, Argentina.

Clark, I. (1998), "Beyond the Great Divide: Globalization and the Theory of International Relations," *Review of International Studies*, vol. 24, pp. 479-98.

Cline, W. (1983), *International Debt and the Stability of the World Economy*, Cambridge (MA), MIT Press.

Clinton, B. and Gore, A. (1992), *Putting People First: How We Can All Change America*, New York Times, Times Books.

Cohen, I. (1996), "Mercosur Under Attack," *Boletim de Integracao Latinoamericana*, Special edition (December), pp. 27-28.

Cohen, I. (1993), "A New Latin American and Caribbean Nationalism," in S. Weintraub (ed.), *Free Trade in the Western Hemisphere*, in *The Annals of the American Academy of Political and Social Science*, No. 526, pp. 36-46.

Cohen, I. (1991), "Economic Questions," in G.P. Atkins (ed.), *The United States and Latin America: Redefining US Purposes in the Post-Cold War Era*, Austin (TX), The University of Texas at Austin, pp. 19-34.

Cohen, S. D. and Blecker, J. R. (eds.) (1996), *Fundamentals of US Foreign Trade Policy: Economics, Politics, Laws, and Issues*, Boulder (CO), Westview Press.

Committee for Development Planning (1990), *Regional Trading Blocs: A Threat to the Multilateral Trading System?*, New York, United Nations.

Conger, L. (1998), "A Fourth Way?, The Latin American Alternative to Neoliberalism," *Current History* (November), pp. 380-84.

Connell-Smith, G. (1974), *The United States and Latin America: A Historical Analysis of Inter-American Relations*, New York, John Wiley & Sons.

Corrales, J. and Feinberg, R. (1999), "Regimes of Cooperation in the Western Hemisphere: Power, Interests, and Intellectual Traditions," *International Studies Quarterly*, vol. 43, pp. 1-36.

Cottam, M. (1994), *Images and Intervention: US Policies in Latin America*, Pittsburgh, University of Pittsburgh Press.

Cox, R. (1999), "Civil Society at the Turn of the Millennium: Prospects for an Alternative World Order," *Review of International Studies*, vol. 25, pp. 3-28.

Cox, R. (1993), "Structural Issues of Global Governance: Implications for Europe," in S. Gill (ed.), *Gramsci, Historical Materialism and International Relations*, Cambridge (UK), Cambridge University Press, pp. 259-89.

Cox, R. (1992), "Global Perestroika," in R. Miliband and L. Panitch (eds.), *Socialist Register 1992*, London, Merlin Press, pp. 26-43.

Crone, D. (1993), "Does Hegemony Matter? The Reorganization of the Pacific Political Economy," *World Politics*, vol. 45, pp. 501-25.

Dauster, J. (1998), "Mercosur and the European Union: Prospects for an Inter-Regional Association," *European Foreign Affairs Review*, vol. 3, pp. 447-49.

Davila Villers, D. (ed.) (1996), *NAFTA, The First Year: A View from Mexico*, Lanham (MD), University Press of America.

Dearden, R. (1997), "Trade Disputes and Settlement Mechanisms under the Canada-US Free Trade Agreement," in R. Lipsey and P. Meller (eds.), *Western Hemisphere Trade Integration: A Canadian-Latin American Dialogue*, New York, St. Martin's Press, pp. 207-31.

Dell, S. (1966), *A Latin American Common Market?*, London, Oxford University Press.
de Melo, J. and Panagariya, A. (eds.), (1993), *New Dimensions in Regional Integration*, Cambridge (UK), Cambridge University Press.
Denham, R. (1969), "The Role of the US as an External Actor in the Integration of Latin America," *Journal of Common Market Studies*, vol. 7, pp. 199-216.
Destler, I. (1999), "Trade Policy at a Crossroads: An Approach for 1999 and Beyond," *Brookings Review*, vol. 17, pp. 27-30.
Deudney, D. and Ikenberry, J. (1999), "The Nature and Sources of Liberal International Order," *Review of International Studies*, vol. 25, pp. 179-96.
Deutsch, K. et al. (1957), *Political Community and the North Atlantic Area*, Princeton (NJ), Princeton University Press.
Devlin, R. (1996), "In Defense of Mercosur," *Boletim de Integracao Latinoamericana*, Special edition (December), pp. 18-19.
Dos Santos, T. (1968), "The Structure of Dependence," *The American Economic Review*, vol. 60, pp. 231-36.
Douglas, I. (1997), "Globalization and the End of the State?," *New Political Economy*, vol. 2, pp. 165-77.
Dunkerley, J. (1994), "Beyond Utopia: The State of the Left in Latin America," *New Left Review*, No. 206, pp. 27-54.
Dyer, G. (1997), "Brazil Urges Realism in All-America Trade Talks," *Financial Times*, 16 May, p. 4.
Economic Commission for Latin America and the Caribbean (1994), *Open Regionalism in Latin America and the Caribbean: Economic Integration as a Contribution to Changing Production Patterns with Social Equity*, Santiago (Chile), United Nations.
(The) Economist (1999), "Argentina: After Menem," 17 July, p. 32.
(The) Economist (1998), "The Americas: The Road from Santiago," 11 April, pp. 25-27.
(The) Economist (1997), "The Americas: The Free-Trade Winds Die Away," 22 November, pp. 35-36.
(The) Economist (1996), "Remapping South America: A Survey of Mercosur," 12 October, pp. 1-30.
Edwards, S. (1995), *Crisis and Reform in Latin America: From Despair to Hope*, New York, Oxford University Press.

Edwards, S. (1993), "Latin American Economic Integration: A New Perspective on an Old Dream," *The World Economy*, vol. 16, pp. 317-338.

Eichengreen, B. (1998), *Does Mercosur Need A Single Currency?*, Working Paper No. 6821, Cambridge (MA), National Bureau of Economic Research.

Einaudi, L. (ed.) (1974), *Beyond Cuba: Latin America Takes Charge of Its Future*, New York, Crane, Russak.

El-Agraa, A. (ed.) (1997), *Economic Integration Worldwide*, New York, St. Martin's Press.

Erzan, R. and Yeats, A. (1992), "Free Trade Agreements with the United. States: What's in It for Latin America," World Bank Policy Research Working Paper No. 827, January, Washington, DC, The World Bank.

Falk, R. (1997), "State of Siege: Will Globalization Win Out?," *International Affairs*, vol. 73, pp. 123-36.

Falk, R. (1995), "Regionalism and World Order After the Cold War," *Australian Journal of International Affairs*, vol. 49, pp. 1-15.

Feinberg, R. (1998), "Integrating the Americas," IGCC Policy Brief No. 10, University of California Institute on Global Conflict and Cooperation.

Feinberg, R. (1997), *Summitry in the Americas: A Progress Report*, Washington, DC, Institute for International Economics.

Feinberg, R. and Boylan, D. (1992), "Modular Multilateralism: North-South Economic Relations in the 1990s," *Washington Quarterly*, vol. 15, pp. 187-99.

Felix, D. (1998), "Is the Drive toward Free Market Globalization Stalling?," *Latin American Research Review*, vol. 33, pp. 191-216.

Felix, D. (1969/70), "The Political Economy of Regional Integration in Latin America," *Studies in Comparative International Development*, vol. 5, pp. 87-102.

Ferguson, Y. (1984), "Cooperation in Latin America: The Politics of Regional Integration," in J. K. Lincoln and E. G. Ferris (eds.), *The Dynamics of Latin American Foreign Policies*, Boulder (CO), Westview Press, pp. 37-55.

Ferrer, A. (1997), "Los Dos Modelos de Mercosur: Integración Sostenible o Consenso de Washington," *Encrucijadas*, University of Buenos Aires (UBA), pp. 9-25.

Ffrench-Davis, R. (1995), "Trends in Regional Cooperation in Latin America: The Crucial Role of Intra-Regional Trade," in J. Teunissen (ed.), *Regionalism and the Global Economy: The Case of Latin America and the Caribbean*, The Hague, FONDAD, pp. 90-118.

Finnemore, M. (1996), "Norms, Culture, and World Politics: Insights from Sociology's Institutionalism," *International Organization*, vol. 50, pp. 325-47.

Fischer, K. (1999), "Business and Integration in the Americas: Competing Points of View," in G. Mace, L. Bélanger et al. (eds.), *The Americas in Transition: The Contours of Regionalism*, Boulder (CO), Lynne Rienner, pp. 195-218.

Fishlow, A. (1994), "From NAFTA to a WHFTA? The Summit May Tell," in S. Weintraub (ed.), *Integrating the Americas: Shaping Future Trade Policy*, Coral Gables (FL), University of Miami North-South Center, pp. 123-36.

Fishlow, A. (1990), "The Latin American State," *Journal of Economic Perspectives*, vol. 4, pp. 61-74.

Fishlow, A. (1985), "Coping with the Creeping Crisis of Debt," in M. Wionczek and L. Tomassini (eds.), *Politics and Economics of External Debt Crisis: The Latin American Experience*, Boulder (CO), Westview Press.

Fishlow, A. and Haggard, S. (1992), *The United States and the Regionalization of the World Economy*, Paris, OECD.

Foweraker, J. (1996), "From NAFTA to WHFTA? Prospects for Hemispheric Free Trade," in S. Nishijima and P. Smith (eds.), *Cooperation or Rivalry? Regional Integration in the Americas and the Pacific Rim*, Boulder (CO), Westview Press, pp. 150-69.

Francis, M. (1988), "United States Policy toward Latin America during the Kissinger Years," in J. Martz (ed.), *United States Policy in Latin America: A Quarter Century of Crisis and Challenge, 1961-1986*, Lincoln (NE) University of Nebraska Press, pp. 28-60.

Frank, A. (1969), *Capitalism and Underdevelopment in Latin America*, New York, Monthly Review Press.

Frankel, J. with Stein E. and Wei, S. (1997), *Regional Trading Blocs in the World Economic System*, Washington, DC, Institute for International Economics.

Frankel, J., Stein, E. and Wei, S. (1995), "Trading Blocs and the Americas: The Natural, the Unnatural, and the Super-natural," *Journal of Development Economics*, vol. 47, pp. 61-95.

Friedman, T. (1999), *The Lexus and the Olive Tree*, New York, Farrar Straus Giroux.

Fukuyama, F. (1989), "The End of History?," *The National Interest* (Summer), pp. 3-18.
Furtado, C. (1999), *El Capitalismo Global*, Mexico City, Fondo de Cultura Económica.
Gamble, A. and Payne, A. (eds.) (1996), *Regionalism and World Order*, London, Macmillan Press.
Garnaut, R. (1994), "Open Regionalism: Its Analytic Basis and Relevance to the International System," *Journal of Asian Economics*, vol. 5, pp. 273-290.
Genberg, H. and De Simone, F.N. (1993), "Regional Integration Agreements and Macroeconomics Discipline," in K. Anderson and R. Blackhurst (eds.), *Regional Integration and the Global Trading System*, New York, Harvester/Wheatsheaf, pp. 167-95.
Gholz, E., Press, D. and Sapolsky, H. (1997), "Come Home, America: The Strategy of Restraint in the Face of Temptation," *International Security*, vol. 21, pp. 5-48.
Gibb, E. and Michalak, W. (eds.), (1994), *Continental Trading Blocs: The Growth of Regionalism in the World Economy*, New York, John Wiley & Sons.
Gil, F. (1988), "The Kennedy-Johnson Years," in J. Martz (ed.), *United States Policy in Latin America: A Quarter Century of Crisis and Challenge, 1961-1986*, Lincoln (NE), University of Nebraska Press, pp. 3-27.
Gil, F. (1971), *Latin American-United States Relations*, New York, Harcourt Brace Jovanovich.
Gills, B. (1997), "Whither Democracy? Globalization and the 'New Hellenism'," in C. Thomas and P. Wilkin (eds.), *Globalization and the South*, New York, St. Martin's Press, pp. 60-75.
Gilpin, R. (1987), *The Political Economy of International Relations*, Princeton (NJ), Princeton University Press.
Goldgeier, J. and McFaul, M. (1992), "A Tale of Two Worlds: Core and Periphery in the Post-Cold War Era," *International Organization*, vol. 46, pp. 467-92.
Goldstein, J. (1999), *International Relations*, New York, Longman.
Goncalves, R. (1992), "Latin America's Trade Issues and Perspectives: A Skeptical View," *The Fletcher Forum of World Affairs*, vol. 16, pp. 1-13.

Grabendorff, W. (1999), "Mercosur and the European Union: From Cooperation to Alliance?," in R. Roett (ed.), *Mercosur: Regional Integration, World Markets*, Boulder (CO), Lynne Rienner, pp. 95-109.

Gramsci, A. (1971), *Prison Notebooks*, edited and translated by Q. Hoare and G. Smith, New York, International Publishers.

Grandi, J. and Bizzozero, L. (1997), "Towards a Mercosur Civil Society: Old and New Actors in the Sub-regional Fabric," *Integration and Trade*, vol. 3, pp. 31-46.

Grugel, J. (1996), "Latin America and the Remaking of the Americas," in A. Gamble and A. Payne (eds.), *Regionalism and World Order*, London, Macmillan Press, pp. 131-67.

Grunwald, J., Wionczek, M. and Carnoy, M. (1972), *Latin American Economic Integration and US Policy*, Washington, DC, The Brookings Institution.

Gupta, S. D. (ed.) (1997), *The Political Economy of Globalization*, Boston, Kluwer Academic Publishers.

Gwynne, R. (1994), "Regional Integration in Latin America: The Revival of a Concept?," in R. Gibb and W. Michalak (eds.), *Continental Trading Blocs: The Growth of Regionalism in the World Economy*, New York, John Wiley & Sons, pp. 189-207.

Haas, E. (1975), *The Obsolescence of Regional Integration Theory*, Institute of International Studies, University of California, Berkeley.

Haas, E. (1968), *The Uniting of Europe: Political, Social, and Economic Forces 1950-1957*, Stanford (CA), Stanford University Press.

Haas, E. (1967), "The Uniting of Europe and the Uniting of Latin America," *Journal of Common Market Studies*, vol. 5, pp. 315-43.

Haas, E. and Schmitter, P. (1966), "Economics and Differential Patterns of Political Integration: Projections about Unity in Latin America," in *International Political Communities: An Anthology*, Garden City (NY), Anchor Books, pp. 259-99.

Haber, D. (1990), "The Death of Hegemony: Why 'Pax Nipponica' Is Impossible?," *Asian Survey*, vol. 30, pp. 892-907.

Haggard, S. (1995), *Developing Nations and the Politics of Global Integration*, Washington, DC, The Brookings Institution.

Haggard, S. and Maxfield, S. (1996), "The Political Economy of Financial Internationalization in the Developing World," in R. Keohane and H.

Milner (eds.), *Internationalization and Domestic Politics*, Cambridge (UK), Cambridge University Press, pp. 209-39.

Haines-Ferrari, M. (1998), "Mercosur: Individual Access and the Dispute Settlement Mechanism," in J. Cameron and K. Campbell (eds.), *Dispute Resolution in the World Trade Organization*, London, Cameron May, pp. 270-84.

Hakim, P. (1993), "Western Hemisphere Free Trade: Why Should Latin America Be Interested?" in S. Weintraub (ed.), *Free Trade in the Western Hemisphere, The Annals of the American Academy of Political and Social Science*, No. 526, pp. 121-34.

Hakim, P. (1992), "President Bush's Southern Strategy: The Enterprise for the Americas Initiative," *Washington Quarterly*, vol. 15, pp. 93-106.

Hart, J. and Prakash, A. (1995), "Globalization and Regionalization: Conceptual Issues and Reflections," paper presented at the Annual Meeting of the International Studies Association (ISA), Chicago, Illinois, 22-26 February.

Hettne, B. (1998), "Regionalism and the New Third World," in N. Poku and L. Pettiford (eds.), *Redefining the Third World*, Basingstoke (UK), Macmillan Press.

Hey, J. (1998), "Is There a Latin American Foreign Policy?," *Mershon International Studies Review*, vol. 42, pp. 106-16.

Hippler, J. (1994), *Pax Americana? Hegemony or Decline*, London, Pluto Press.

Hirschman, A. (1980), *National Power and the Structure of Foreign Trade*, Berkeley (CA), University of California Press.

Hirschman, A. (1979), "The Turn to Authoritarianism in Latin America and the Search for Its Economic Determinants," in D. Collier (ed.), *The New Authoritarianism in Latin America*, Princeton (NJ), Princeton University Press, pp. 61-98.

Hirst, M. (1996), *Democracia, Seguridad e Integración: América Latina en un Mundo en Transición*, Buenos Aires, Grupo Editorial Norma.

Hirst, P. and Thompson, G. (1996), *Globalization in Question: The International Economy and the Possibilities of Governance*, Cambridge (UK), Polity Press.

Hoffmann, S. (1993), "Goodbye to a United Europe?," *New York Review of Books*, 27 May, pp. 27-31.

Hollist, L. and Nielson, D. L. (1998), "Taking Stock of Inter-American Bonds: Approaches to Explaining Cooperation in the Western Hemisphere," *Mershon International Studies Review*, Vol. 42 (2), pp. 257-281.

Hoogvelt, A. (1997), *Globalization and the Postcolonial World: The New Political Economy of Development*, Baltimore (MD), Johns Hopkins University Press.

Hormats, R. (1994), "Making Regionalism Safe," *Foreign Affairs*, vol. 73, pp. 97-108.

Hornbeck, J. (1998), *A Free Trade Area of the Americas: Toward Integrating Regional Trade Policies*, Congressional Research Service Report, National Law Center for Inter-American Free Trade, http://natlaw.Com/pubs/ spmxcu8.htm.

Hout, W. (1997), "Globalization and the Quest for Governance," *Mershon International Studies Review*, vol. 41, pp. 99-106.

Hufbauer, G., and Schott, J. (1994), *Western Hemisphere Economic Integration*, Washington DC, Institute for International Economics.

Hurrell, A. (1998), "An Emerging Security Community in South America?," in E. Adler and M. Barnett (eds.), *Security Communities*, Cambridge (UK), Cambridge University Press, pp. 228-64.

Hurrell, A. (1995a), "Regionalism in Theoretical Perspective," in L. Fawcett and A. Hurrell (eds.), *Regionalism in World Politics: Regional Organization and International Order*, New York, Oxford University Press, pp. 37-73.

Hurrell, A. (1995b), "Explaining the Resurgence of Regionalism in World Politics," *Review of International Studies*, vol. 21, pp. 331-58.

Hurrell, A. (1994), "Regionalism in the Americas," in A. Lowenthal and G. Treverton (eds.), *Latin America in a New World*, Boulder (CO), Westview Press, pp. 167-90.

Hurrell, A. (1992), "Latin America in the New World Order: A Regional Bloc of the Americas?," *International Affairs*, vol. 68, pp. 121-39.

Ianni, O. (1974), "Imperialism and Diplomacy in Inter-American Relations," in J. Cotler and R. Fagen (eds.), *Latin America and the United States: The Changing Political Realities*, Stanford (CA), Stanford University Press.

Iglesias, E. (1993), "The New Latin America and the Inter-American Development Bank," *The Washington Quarterly*, vol. 16, pp. 115-25.

Iglesias, E. (1985), "External Debt Problems of Latin America," in M. Wionczek and L. Tomassini (eds.), *Politics and Economics of External Debt Crisis: The Latin American Experience*, Boulder (CO), Westview Press, pp. 73-96.
Instituto de Relaciones Europeo-Latinoamericanas (IRELA) (1997a), "Constructing the Free Trade Area of the Americas: A European Perspective," IRELA Briefing, in: http://www.irela.es/bf97-2e.htm, 19 June.
Instituto de Relaciones Europeo-Latinoamericanas (IRELA) (1997b), "A Challenge to the Atlantic Triangle? Context and Agenda of an EU-Latin America Summit," IRELA Briefing. In: http://www.irela.es/bf97-2e.htm, 12 May.
Inter-American Dialogue (1997), *The Americas in 1997: Making Cooperation Work*, Washington, DC, Inter-American Dialogue.
International Monetary Fund (IMF) (1997), *Direction of Trade Statistics Yearbook*, Washington, DC, International Monetary Fund.
Jaguaribe, H. (1973), *Political Development: A General Theory and a Latin American Case Study*, New York, Harper and Row.
Jatar, A. J. and Weintraub, S. (eds.) (1997), *Integrating the Hemisphere: Perspectives from Latin America and the Caribbean*, Washington, DC, Inter-American Dialogue.
Jenkins, B. (1999), "Assessing the 'New' Integration: The Mercosur Trade Agreement," in K. Thomas and M. Tetrault (eds.), *Racing to Regionalize: Democracy, Capitalism, and Regional Political Economy*, Boulder (CO), Lynne Rienner, pp. 33-56.
Johnson, H. (1991), *Dispelling the Myth of Globalization: The Case for Regionalization*, New York, Praeger.
Jones, R. J. (1999), "Globalization and Change in the International Political Economy," *International Affairs*, vol. 75, pp. 357-67.
Jones, R. J. (1995), *Globalization and Interdependence in the International Political Economy: Rhetoric and Reality*, London, Pinter Publishers.
Kaiser, K. (1968), "The Interaction of Regional Subsystems: Some Preliminary Notes on Recurrent Patterns and the Role of the Superpowers," *World Politics*, vol. 21, pp. 84-107.
Katzenstein, P. (1996), "Regionalism in Comparative Perspective," *Cooperation and Conflict*, vol. 31, pp. 123-59.

Kaufman Purcell, S. (1997), "The New US-Brazil Relationship," in S. Kaufman Purcell and R. Roett (eds.), *Brazil under Cardoso*, Boulder (CO), Lynne Rienner, pp. 89-102.

Kaufman Purcell, S. and Simon, F. (eds.), (1995), *Europe and Latin America in the World Economy*, Boulder (CO), Lynne Rienner.

Kennedy, P. (1987), *The Rise and Fall of the Great Powers: Economic Change and Military Conflict from 1500 to 2000*, New York, Random House.

Keohane, R. (1984), *After Hegemony: Cooperation and Discord in the World Political Economy*, Princeton (NJ), Princeton University Press.

Keohane, R. and Hoffmann, S. (1994), "Institutional Change in Europe in the 1980s," in B. Nelsen and A. Stubb (eds.), *The European Union: Readings on the Theory and Practice of European Integration*, Boulder (CO), Lynne Rienner, pp. 237-55.

Kotabe, M. (1996), *Mercosur and Beyond: The Imminent Emergence of the South American Markets*, Austin, TX, Center for International Business Education and Research, University of Texas at Austin.

Krasner, S. (1983), "Structural Causes and Regime Consequences: Regimes as Intervening Variables," in S. Krasner (ed.), *International Regimes*, Ithaca (NY), Cornell University Press, pp. 1-21.

Krauss, C. (1999), "Argentines Suffering From Brazil Crisis," *New York Times*, 8 February.

Krugman, P. (1999), "The Return of Depression Economics," *Foreign Affairs*, vol. 78, pp. 56-74.

Krugman, P. (1991), "Regional Blocs: The Good, the Bad and the Ugly," *The International Economy*, vol. 5, pp. 54-56.

Kryzanek, M. (1990), *US-Latin American Relations*, New York, Praeger.

Lafer, C. (1994), "Brazil in a New World," in A. Lowenthal and G. Treverton (eds.), *Latin America in a New World*, Boulder (CO), Westview Press, pp. 222-33.

Lahera, E. (1992), "Integration Today: Bases and Options," *CEPAL Review*, No. 47, pp. 63-76.

La Jornada (1997a), "Feinberg: Si Triunfa Cardenas, Wall Street No Debería Alarmarse. El TLC Formalizó una Alianza Estratégica, dijo el ex-Director para América Latina del Consejo Nacional de Seguridad de la Casa Blanca," Mexico City, 19 June.

La Jornada (1997b), "Busca Mexico Alianza con Argentina y el Mercosur. Rebolledo: Sería a Mediano Plazo," Mexico City, 14 June.

Lake, D. and Morgan, P. (eds.) (1997), *Regional Orders: Building Security in a New World*, University Park (PA), Pennsylvania State University Press.

Lake, D. and Morgan, P. (1997), "The New Regionalism in Security Affairs" in D. Lake and P. Morgan (eds.), *Regional Orders: Building Security in a New World*, University Park (PA), Pennsylvania State University Press, pp. 3-19.

Lande, S. (1998), "Free Trade in the Americas: Launching Negotiations and Concrete Progress by the Millennium," in *Free Trade in the Americas: Fulfilling the Promise of Miami*, North-South Center, University of Miami.

Langhammer, R. (1992), "The Developing Countries and Regionalism," *Journal of Common Market Studies*, vol. 30, pp. 211-31.

Laredo, I. M. (ed.) (1992), *La Integración Latinoamericana en el Actual Escenario Mundial: De la ALALC\ALADI al Mercosur*, Rosario, Argentina, UNR Editora.

Latin American Weekly Report (1999), "Mercosur Row May End by December: Rivals Know that Bloc Rules Impose a Strict Deadline," 28 September, p. 452.

Latin American Weekly Report (1999), "Argentina: Budget Cuts Trigger Dual Response," 11 May, p. 206.

Latin American Special Reports (1998), "Building the FTAA: Policy Debate and Prospects," April (SR-98-02), pp. 1-12.

Latin American Weekly Report (LAWR) (1998a), "Mercosur/Andean Community May Delay Tariff Cuts," 9 June (WR-98-22), p. 259.

Latin American Weekly Report (LAWR) (1998b), "US Insists on its FTAA Formula," 28 April (WR-98-16), p. 187.

Latin American Weekly Report (LAWR) (1998c), "Andeans Agree on Common Market: Deal Struck with Mercosur in Week of Subregional Accords," 7 April (WR-98-14), p. 164.

Latin American Weekly Report (LAWR) (1998d), "Ground Rules for FTAA Agreed: Mercosur Stance Carries the Day as Washington Cedes," 24 March (WR-98-12), p. 136.

Latin American Weekly Report (LAWR) (1998e), "Trade: Preparing for the Santiago Summit," 6 January (WR-98-01), p. 5.

Latin American Weekly Report (LAWR) (1997a), "Three Futures for Mercosur: European Study Presents Scenarios for 2005," 28 October (WR 97-43), pp. 510-11.

Latin American Weekly Report (LAWR) (1997b), "From Mexico to Argentina, the Region's Political 'Geometry' is Shifting," 12 August (WR-97-32), p. 373.

Latin American Weekly Report (LAWR) (1997c), "'Crucial' Meeting on FTAA Postpones Key Debate, but Sets a Launch Date," 20 May, p. 29.

Latin American Weekly Report (LAWR) (1997d), "Should Mercosur Opt for Europe?: Study Says Benefits Are Greater than in the FTAA," 6 May, p. 206.

Lavagna, R. and Giambiagi, F. (1998), "Mercosur: Hacia la Creación de Una Moneda Común," *Archivos del Presente*, (Buenos Aires) (April-June), pp. 45-61.

Lawrence, R. (1996), *Regionalism, Multilateralism, and Deeper Integration*, Washington, DC, The Brookings Institution.

Layne, C. (1993), "The Unipolar Illusion: Why New Great Powers Will Rise," *International Security*, vol. 17, pp. 5-51.

Layne, C. and Schwartz, B. (1993), "American Hegemony without an Enemy," *Foreign Policy*, No. 92, pp. 5-23

Leclair, M. S. (1997), *Regional Integration and Global Free Trade: Addressing the Fundamental Conflicts*, Aldershot (UK), Avebury/ Ashgate Publishing.

Lemann, N. (1999), "A Theory of Everything: Thomas Friedman Goes Global," *The New Yorker*, 10 May, pp. 85-90.

Levinson, J. (1999), "The International Financial System: A Flawed Architecture," *Fletcher Forum of World Affairs*, vol. 23, pp. 10-14.

Lindberg, L. (1963), *The Political Dynamics of Economic Integration*, Stanford (CA), Stanford University Press.

Lindberg, L. and Scheingold, S. (1970), *Europe's Would-Be Polity*, Englewood Cliffs (NJ), Prentice-Hall.

Lipsey, R. (1992), "Getting There: The Path to a Western Hemisphere Free Trade Area and Its Structure," in S. Saborio (ed.), *The Premise and the Promise: Free Trade in the Americas*, New Brunswick (NJ), Transaction Publishers.

Lipson, C. (1981), "The International Organization of Third World Debt," *International Organization*, vol. 35, pp. 603-31.

Lowenthal, A. (1994), "Latin America and the United States in a New World: Prospects for Partnership," in A. Lowenthal and G. Treverton (eds.), *Latin America in a New World*, Boulder (CO), Westview Press, pp. 237-46.

Lowenthal, A. (1992), "Changing US Interests and Policies in a New World," in J. Hartlyn, L. Schoultz and A. Varas (eds.), *The United States and Latin America in the 1990s: Beyond the Cold War*, Chapel Hill (NC), University of North Carolina Press, pp. 64-85.

Lowenthal, A. (1990a), *Partners in Conflict: the United States and Latin America in the 1990s*, Baltimore, Johns Hopkins University Press.

Lowenthal, A. (1990b), "Rediscovering Latin America," *Foreign Affairs*, vol. 69, pp. 27-41.

Lowenthal, A. (1983), "Change the Agenda," *Foreign Policy*, No. 52 (Fall), pp. 64-77.

Lowenthal, A. (1976), "The United States and Latin America: Ending the Hegemonic Presumption," *Foreign Affairs*, vol. 55, pp. 199-213.

Lowenthal, A. (1974), "Liberal, Radical, and Bureaucratic Perspectives on US Latin American Foreign Policy: The Alliance for Progress in Retrospect," in J. Cotler and R. Fagen (eds.), *Latin America and the United States: The Changing Political Realities*, Stanford (CA), Stanford University Press, pp. 212-37.

Lustig, N. and Primo Braga, C.A. (1994), "The Future of Trade Policy in Latin America," in S. Weintraub (ed.), *Integrating the Americas: Shaping Future Trade Policy*, New Brunswick (NJ), Transaction Publishers, pp. 17-43.

Luttwak, E. (1990), "From Geopolitics to Geo-Economics: Logic of Conflict, Grammar of Commerce," *The National Interest* (Summer), pp. 17-23.

Mace, G. (1988), "Regional Integration in Latin America: A Long and Winding Road," *International Journal*, vol. 43, pp. 404-27.

Mace, G. and Bélanger, L. (1999), "The Structural Contexts of Hemispheric Regionalism: Power, Trade, Political Culture, and Economic Development," in G. Mace, L. Bélanger *et al.* (eds.), *The Americas in Transition: The Contours of Regionalism*, Boulder (CO), Lynne Rienner Publishers, pp. 37-68.

Mace, G. and Thérien, J. P. (eds.), (1996), *Foreign Policy and Regionalism in the Americas*, Boulder (CO), Lynne Rienner.

Mace, G., Bélanger, L. et al. (eds.) (1999), *The Americas in Transition: The Contours of Regionalism*, Boulder (CO), Lynne Rienner Publishers.

Machado, J. B. and Motta Veiga, P. (1997), "A ALCA e a Estratégia Negociadora Brasileira," *Revista Brasileira de Comércio Exterior*, No. 51, pp. 33-50.

Mahon, J. (1999), "Economic Crisis in Latin America: Global Contagion, Local Pain," *Current History*, vol. 98, pp. 105-110.

Mahon, J. (1996), *Mobile Capital and Latin American Development*, University Park (PA), Pennsylvania State University Press.

Mander, J. and Goldsmith, E. (eds.) (1996), *The Case Against the Global Economy*, San Francisco (CA), Sierra Club Books.

Mansfield, E. and Milner, H. (1999), "The New Wave of Regionalism," *International Organization*, vol. 53, pp. 589-627.

Mansfield, E. and Milner, H. (eds.) (1997), *The Political Economy of Regionalism*, New York, Columbia University Press.

Manzetti, L. (1993/94), "The Political Economy of Mercosur," *Journal of Interamerican Studies and World Affairs*, vol. 35, pp. 101-141.

Marchand, M. (1994), "The Political Economy of North-South Relations," in R. Stubbs and G. Underhill (eds.), *Political Economy and the Changing Global Order*, New York, St. Martin's Press, pp. 289-301.

Markoff, J. (1997), "Really Existing Democracy: Learning from Latin America in the Late 1990s," *New Left Review*, No. 223, pp. 48-68.

Marshall, D. (1996), "Understanding Late-Twentieth-Century Capitalism: Reassessing the Globalization Theme," *Government and Opposition*, vol. 31, pp. 193-205.

Martin, P. (1994), "The Politics of International Structural Change: Aggressive Unilateralism in American Trade Policy," in R. Stubbs and G. Underhill (eds.), *Political Economy and the Changing Global Order*, New York, St. Martin's Press, pp. 439-52.

McLarty, M. (1999), "Fast Track Isn't Fast Enough," *The New York Times*, 20 July.

Michalak, W. (1994), "The Political Economy of Trading Blocs," in R. Gibb and W. Michalak (eds.), *Continental Trading Blocs: The Growth of Regionalism in the World Economy*, New York, John Wiley & Sons, pp. 37-72.

Milet, P., Gaspar, G. and Rojas, F. (1997), *Chile-Mercosur: Una Alianza Estratégica*, Santiago, Chile, Editorial Los Andes.

Milner, H. (1998), "Rationalizing Politics: The Emerging Synthesis of International, American, and Comparative Politics," *International Organization*, vol. 52, pp. 759-86.

Milner, H. (1991), "The Assumption of Anarchy in International Relations Theory: A Critique," *Review of International Studies*, vol. 17, pp. 67-85.

Milward, A. (1992), *The European Rescue of the Nation-State*, Berkeley (CA), University of California Press.

Minsburg, N., Shilling, P. R., Monte Domecq, R. F. and Couriel, A. (1993), *El Mercosur: Un Problema Complejo*, Buenos Aires, Centro Editor de América Latina.

Mittelman, J. (ed.) (1996), *Globalization: Critical Reflections*, Boulder (CO), Lynne Rienner.

Mittelman, J. (1994), "Rethinking 'the New Regionalism' in the Context of Globalization," Paper presented at the Annual Meeting of the International Studies Association (ISA), Washington, DC, March.

Molineau, H. (1990), *US Policy toward Latin America: From Regionalism to Globalism*, Boulder (CO), Westview Press.

Moller, J. O. (1999), "The Growing Challenge to Internationalism," *The Futurist*, vol. 33, No. 3 (March), pp. 22-27.

Mols, M. (1996), "Regional Integration and the International System," in S. Nishijima and P. H. Smith (eds.), *Cooperation or Rivalry: Regional Integration in the Americas and the Pacific Rim*, Boulder (CO), Westview Press, pp. 9-26.

Mols, M. (1993), "The Integration Agenda: A Framework for Comparison," in P. H. Smith (ed.), *The Challenge of Integration: Europe and the Americas*, Coral Gables (FL), University of Miami North-South Center.

Mondino, G. and Reca, A. (1997), "Toward a Hemispheric Free Trade Area: The Case of Argentina," in A. J. Jatar and S. Weintraub (eds.), *Integrating the Hemisphere: Perspectives from Latin America and the Caribbean*, Washington, DC, Inter-American Dialogue, pp. 177-196.

Morales, I. (1999), "NAFTA and the Governance of Economic Openness. Assessing Trade Regimes as a means for 'Deepening' Integration," Paper presented at the Annual Conference of the International Studies Association (ISA), Washington, DC, February.

Moss, A. H. (1994), "Introduction: The Summit of the Americas, 1994," *Journal of Interamerican Studies and World Affairs*, vol. 36, pp. i-x.

Motta Veiga, P. (1997), "Brazil's Strategy for Trade Liberalization and Economic Integration in the Western Hemisphere," in A. J. Jatar and S. Weintraub (eds.), *Integrating the Hemisphere: Perspectives from Latin America and the Caribbean*, Washington, DC, Inter-American Dialogue, pp. 197-207.

Nader, R. et al. (1993), *The Case Against Free Trade: GATT, NAFTA, and the Globalization of Corporate Power*, San Francisco (CA), Earth Island Press.

Naim, M. (1994), "Toward Free Trade in the Americas: Building Blocks, Stumbling Blocks, and Entry Fees," in S. Weintraub (ed.), *Integrating the Americas: Shaping Future Trade Policy*, Coral Gables (FL), University of Miami North-South Center, pp. 45-88.

Naim, M. (1992/93), "Instead of NAFTA, Shooting for SAFTA," *CEO/International Strategies* (December/January), pp. 70-73.

Nef, J. (1994), "The Political Economy of Inter-American Relations: A Structural and Historical Overview," in R. Stubbs and G. R. D. Underhill (eds.), *Political Economy and the Changing Global Order*, New York, St. Martin's Press, pp. 404-18.

Nofal, M. B. (1994), "Mercosur and Free Trade in the Americas," in S. Weintraub (ed.), *Integrating the Americas: Shaping Future Trade Policy*, New Brunswick (NJ), Transaction Publishers, pp. 137-67.

Nogués, J. and Quintanilla, R. (1993), "Latin America's Integration and the Multilateral Trading System," in J. de Melo and A. Panagariya (eds.), *New Dimensions in Regional Integration*, Cambridge (UK), Cambridge University Press, pp. 278-313.

Nye, Jr. J. (1992), "What New World Order?," *Foreign Affairs*, vol. 71, pp. 83-96.

Nye, Jr. J. (1990), *Bound to Lead: The Changing Nature of American Power*, New York, Basic Books.

Nye, Jr., J. (ed.) (1968), *International Regionalism: Readings*, Boston, Little, Brown and Company.

Ocampo, J. (1985), "Financial Aspects of Intra-regional Trade in Latin America," in A. Gauhar (ed.), *Regional Integration: The Latin American Experience*, Boulder (CO), Westview Press, pp. 112-32.

Odell, J. (1986), "Growing Trade and Growing Conflict Between Latin America and the United States," in K. Middlebrook and C. Rico (eds.), *The United States and Latin America in the 1980s: Contending*

Perspectives on a Decade of Crisis, Pittsburgh, University of Pittsburgh Press.
O'Donnell, G. (1994), "Some Reflections on Redefining the Role of the State," in C. Bradford (ed.), *Redefining the State in Latin America*, Paris, Organization for Economic Cooperation and Development.
O'Donnell, G. (1985), "External Debt: Why Don't Our Governments Do the Obvious?," *CEPAL Review*, No. 27, pp. 27-33.
Ohmae, K. (1995), *The End of the Nation State: The Rise of Regional Economies*, New York, Free Press.
O'Keefe, T. (1995), "The Prospects for Mercosur's Inclusion into the North American Free Trade Agreement (NAFTA)," *International Law Practicum*, vol. 8, pp. 5-13.
Ondarts, G. (1992), "La Nueva Integración," *Integración Latinoamericana*, January-February, p. 175.
Organization for Economic Co-Operation and Development (1995), *Regional Integration and the Multilateral Trading System: Synergy and Divergence*, Paris, OECD.
Palmer, N. (1991), *The New Regionalism in Asia and the Pacific*, Lexington (MA), D. C. Heath and Co.
Panagariya, A. (1996), "The Free Trade Area of the Americas: Good for Latin America?," *World Economy* (September), pp. 485-515.
Panelli, C. and Fernando, L. (1998), *Brasil-Argentina: A Construcao de Uma Alianca Estratégica: Condicionantes, Singularidades e Parámetros para sua Sustentabilidade*, Brasil, Instituto Rio Branco.
Panitch, L. (1994), "Globalization and the State," in R. Miliband and L. Panitch (eds.), *Socialist Register 1994: Between Globalism and Nationalism*, London, Merlin Press, pp. 60-93.
Pastor, R. (1997), "The Clinton Administration and the Americas: The Postwar Rhythm and Blues," *Journal of Interamerican Studies and World Affairs*, pp. 99-128.
Pastor, R. (1992a), *Whirlpool: US Foreign Policy toward Latin America and the Caribbean*, Princeton (NJ), Princeton University Press.
Pastor, R. (1992b), "The Latin American Option," *Foreign Policy*, No. 88, pp. 107-25.
Peña, F. (1996), "Aportes a un Debate sobre Raíces y Sentido del Mercosur," Notes prepared for the conference "O Mercosul e a Integracao Sul Americana: Mais do que Economía," Fortaleza, Brazil, December.

Peña, F. (1995), "New Approaches to Economic Integration in the Southern Cone," *Washington Quarterly*, vol. 18, pp. 113-122.

Pereyra, L.V. (1999), "Toward the Common Market of the South: Mercosur's Origins, Evolution, and Challenges," in R. Roett (ed.), *Mercosur: Regional Integration, World Markets*, Boulder (CO), Lynne Rienner, pp. 7-23.

Perruci, G. (1993), "Southern Cone Politics in US-Latin American Relations, 1945-1950," *SouthEastern Latin Americanist* (Spring), pp. 33-50.

Petersen, M. (1999), "Imports Push Trade Deficit to a New High: More Worry that US Lives Beyond Its Means," *The New York Times*, 20 August, pp. C1-C2.

Petras, J. (1997a), "Latin America: The Resurgence of the Left," *New Left Review*, No. 223, pp. 17-47.

Petras, J. (1997b), "Alternatives to Neoliberalism in Latin America," *Latin American Perspectives*, vol. 24, pp. 80-91.

Petras, J. (1976), "The Reconsolidation of US Hegemony," *New Left Review*, No. 97, pp. 37-53.

Petras, J. and Morley, M. (1992), *Latin America in the Time of Cholera: Electoral Politics, Market Economics, and Permanent Crisis*, New York, Routledge.

Petras, J. and Morley, M. (1990), *US Hegemony under Siege: Class, Politics and Development in Latin America*, London, Verso.

Porta, F. (1992), *Argentina Frente a la Economía Mundial. El Mercosur y las Experiencias de Integración: Perspectivas para los Trabajadores*, Rosario, Argentina, Instituto de Estudios sobre Estado y Participacion.

Poulantzas, N. (1979), *Classes in Contemporary Capitalism*, London, Verso.

Poulantzas, N. (1970), *Political Power and Social Classes*, London, New Left Books.

Prebisch, R. (1964), *Towards a Dynamic Development Policy for Latin America*, New York, UN Sales No. 64.II.G.4.

Preeg, E. H. (1992), "The US Leadership Role in World Trade: Past, Present, and Future," *The Washington Quarterly*, vol. 15, pp. 81-91.

Rapoport, M. (ed.) (1995), *Argentina y Brasil en el Mercosur: Políticas Comunes y Alianzas Regionales*, Buenos Aires, Grupo Editor Latinoamericano.

Regúnaga, C. (1997), "Seguridad Juridica in Mercosur," *Comments on Argentine Trade*, vol. 79, pp. 26-27.
Rey Romay, B. (ed.) (1995), *La Integración Comercial de Mexico a Estados Unidos y Canada: Alternativa o Destino?*, Mexico City, Siglo Veintiuno Editores.
Richards, D. (1997), "Dependent Development and Regional Integration: A Critical Examination of the Southern Cone Common Market," *Latin American Perspectives*, vol. 24, pp. 133-55.
Rodriguez, J. M. (1995), *El Mercosur Después de Buenos Aires: La Ultima Oportunidad*, Montevideo, Fundación de Cultura Universitaria/Centro Uruguay Independiente.
Rodríguez Mendoza, M. (1996), "Which Mercosur Anyway?," *Boletim de Integracao Latino-Americana*, Special edition (December), pp. 20-26.
Rodríguez Mendoza, M., Low, P. and Kotschwar, B. (eds.) (1999), *Trade Rules in the Making: Challenges in Regional and Multilateral Negotiations*, Washington, DC, Brookings Institution Press.
Rodrik, D. (1997), *Has Globalization Gone Too Far?*, Washington DC, Institute for International Economics.
Roett, R. (ed.) (1999), *Mercosur: Regional Integration, World Markets*, Boulder (CO), Lynne Rienner.
Roett, R. (1993), "Why Integration Now? US Interests and Purposes," in P. H. Smith (ed.), *The Challenge of Integration: Europe and the Americas*, New Brunswick (NJ), Transaction Publishers, pp. 93-114.
Rohter, L. (1997), "Free Trade Goes South With and Without US," *New York Times*, 6 January.
Rosenberg, R. and Stein, S. (eds.) (1995), *Advancing the Miami Process: Civil Society and the Summit of the Americas*, Boulder (CO), Lynne Rienner.
Rosenthal, G. (1993), "Regional Integration in the 1990s," *CEPAL Review*, No. 50, pp. 11-19.
Rostow, W. (1990), "The Coming Age of Regionalism," *Encounter*, vol. 74, pp. 3-7.
Ruggie, J. (1993), "Territoriality and Beyond: Problematizing Modernity in International Relations," *International Organization*, vol. 47, pp. 139-74.

Russell, R. (1997), "Democratization and Foreign Policy Collaboration in the Southern Cone: The Case of Argentina," Paper presented at the Annual Meeting of the International Studies Association, Toronto, Canada, 18-22 March.

Russett, B. (1985), "The Mysterious Case of Vanishing Hegemony; or, Is Mark Twain Really Dead?," *International Organization*, vol. 39, pp. 207-231.

Saborio, S. (1992), "The Long and Winding Road from Anchorage to Patagonia," in S. Saborio (ed.), *The Premise and the Promise: Free Trade in the Americas*, New Brunswick (NJ), Transaction Publishers.

Sakamoto, Y. (ed.) (1994), *Global Transformation: Challenges to the State System*, Tokyo, United Nations University Press.

Salazar-Xirinachs, J. (1993), "The Integrationist Revival: A Return to Prebisch's Policy Prescriptions?," *CEPAL Review*, vol. 50, pp. 21-40.

Salgado, G. (1990), "Latin American Integration and External Openness," *CEPAL Review*, No. 42, pp. 135-55.

Sanchez Bajo, C. (1999), "Mercosur's Open Regionalism and Regulation: The Role of Business Actors, Focusing on the Petrochemicals and Steel Sectors," Paper presented at the 40th Annual Meeting of the International Studies Association (ISA), Washington, DC, 16-20 February.

Sandholtz, W. and Zysman, J. (1989), "1992: Recasting the European Bargain," *World Politics*, vol. 42, pp. 95-128.

Sandholtz, W., Borris, M., Zysman, J., Conca, K., Stowsky, J., Vogel, S. and Weber, S. (1992), *The High Stakes: The Economic Foundations of the Next Security System*, New York, Oxford University Press.

Sanger, D. (1999), "Trade Deficit Set a Record during May: Rising Gap with China is Particularly Thorny," *The New York Times*, 21 July, p. C1, C4.

Saxonhouse, G. R. (1997), "Regional Initiatives and US Trade Policy in Asia," *Asian-Pacific Economic Literature*, vol. 11, pp. 1-14.

Schaeffer, R. K. (1997), *Understanding Globalization: The Social Consequences of Political, Economic, and Environmental Change*, Lanham (MD), Rowman & Littlefield.

Schemo, D. (1997), "With or Without the US Latin Trade Group is Marching Forward," *The New York Times*, 18 September, p. A10.

Schmitter, P. (1970), "Central American Integration: Spill-Over, Spill-Around, or Encapsulation?," *Journal of Common Market Studies*, vol. 9, pp. 1-48.

Schoppa, L. (1999), "The Social Context in Coercive International Bargaining," *International Organization*, vol. 53, pp. 307-42.

Schoultz, L. (1987), *National Security and United States Policy Toward Latin America*, Princeton (NJ), Princeton University Press.
Schwartz, G. (1996), "Brazil, Mercosur and SAFTA: Destructive Restructuring or Pan-American Integration?" in P. Smith and S. Nishijima (eds.), *Cooperation or Rivalry? Regional Integration in the Americas and the Pacific Rim*, Boulder (CO), Westview Press, pp. 129-49.
Schwidrowski, A. (1991), "Macroeconomics Policy Coordination and Integration," *CEPAL Review*, No. 45, pp. 83-98.
Scott, A. (ed.) (1997), *The Limits of Globalization: Cases and Arguments*, London, Routledge.
Secretaría de Relaciones Económicas Internacionales (1996), "El Mercosur: Regionalismo Abierto o Un 'Building Block'? Comentarios Acerca del Trabajo de Alexander Yeats," *Boletim de Integracao Latino-Americana*, Special edition (December), pp. 4-17.
Shepherd, M. (1994), "US Domestic Interests and the Latin American Debt Crisis," in R. Stubbs and G. Underhill (eds.), *Political Economy and the Changing Global Order*, New York, St. Martin's Press, pp. 302-12.
Shorrock, T. (1998), "Trade-USA: Meager US Offerings at Santiago Summit," *World News*, Inter Press Service, 12 April.
Simon, F. and Kaufman Purcell, S. (1998), "The Impact of Regional Integration on European-Latin American Relations," Americas Society, Western Hemisphere Affairs, http://www.americas-society.org/europe.html.
Smith, P. (1996a), *Talons of the Eagle: Dynamics of US-Latin American Relations*, New York, Oxford University Press.
Smith, P. (1996b), "The United States, Regional Integration, and the Reshaping of the International Order," in P. Smith and S. Nishijima (eds.), *Cooperation or Rivalry?: Regional Integration in the Americas and the Pacific Rim*, Boulder (CO), Westview Press, pp. 27-51.
Smith, T. (1981), *The Pattern of Imperialism*, Cambridge (UK), Cambridge University Press.
Smith, W., and Korzeniewicz, R. (1997), *Politics, Social Change and Economic Restructuring in Latin America*, Coral Gables (FL), University of Miami North-South Center.
Smith, W. and Messari, N. (1998), "Democracy and Reform in Cardoso's Brazil: Caught Between Clientelism and Global Markets?," North-South

Agenda Paper No. 33, Coral Gables (FL), University of Miami North-South Center.

Smith, W., Acuña, C. and Gamarra E. (eds.) (1994a), *Democracy, Markets, and Structural Reform in Latin America*, New Brunswick (NJ), Transaction Publishers.

Smith, W., Acuña, C. and Gamarra E. (eds.) (1994b), *Latin American Political Economy in the Age of Neoliberal Reform*, New Brunswick (NJ), Transaction Publishers.

Snidal, D. (1993), "Relative Gains and the Pattern of International Cooperation," in D. Baldwin (ed.), *Neorealism and Neoliberalism: The Contemporary Debate*, New York, Columbia University Press.

Snidal, D. (1985), "The Limits of Hegemonic Stability Theory," *International Organization*, vol. 39, pp. 579-614.

Soares de Lima, M. R. (1999), "Brazil's Alternative Vision," in G. Mace and L. Bélanger (eds.), *The Americas in Transition: The Contours of Regionalism*, Boulder (CO), Lynne Rienner, pp. 133-51.

Soares de Lima, M. R. (1996), "Brazil's Response to the 'New Regionalism'," in G. Mace and J. P. Thérien (eds.), *Foreign Policy and Regionalism in the Americas*, Boulder (CO), Lynne Rienner, pp. 137-158.

Solingen, E. (1998), *Regional Orders at Century's Dawn: Global and Domestic Influences on Grand Strategy*, Princeton (NJ), Princeton University Press.

Soros, G. (1999), *The Crisis of Global Capitalism: Open Society Endangered*, New York, Public Affairs.

Sosa, N. E. (1997), "The Effects of a Brazilian Maxi-Devaluation on Argentina," *Comments on Argentine Trade*, vol. 79, pp. 19-21.

Srodes, J. (1998), "Charlene Barshefsky on Trade," *World Trade* (August), p. 41.

Stahringer, O. (ed.) (1998), *El Mercosur en el Siglo XXI*, Buenos Aires, Ediciones Ciudad Argentina.

Stahringer, O. *et al.* (1996), "El Mercosur en Un Mundo en Bloques," in O. Stahringer (ed.), *El Mercosur en el Nuevo Orden Mundial*, Buenos Aires, Ediciones Ciudad Argentina.

Stallings, B. (ed.) (1995), *Global Change, Regional Response: The New International Context of Development*, Cambridge (UK), Cambridge University Press.

Stallings, B. (1992), "International Influence on Economic Policy: Debt, Stabilization, and Structural Reform," in S. Haggard and R. Kaufman (eds.), *The Politics of Economic Adjustment: International Constraints, Distributive Conflicts, and the State*, Princeton (NJ), Princeton University Press, pp. 41-88.

Stallings, B. and Kaufman, R. (eds.) (1989), *Debt and Democracy in Latin America*, Boulder (CO), Westview Press.

Stark, J. (1998), "The Summit of the Americas Process in Perspective: Global Change, Regional Norms, and State Capacity," Paper presented. at the 39th Annual Meeting of the International Studies Association, 17-21 March, Minneapolis, Minnesota.

Stinson, D. (1999), "Building Blocks," in "NAFTA: Five Years Anniversary," *Latin Trade* (January), pp. 40-47.

Strange, S. (1998), "The New World of Debt," *New Left Review*, No. 230, pp. 91-114.

Strange, S. (1996), *The Retreat of the State: The Diffusion of Power in the World Economy*, Cambridge (UK), Cambridge University Press.

Strange, S. (1988a), *States and Markets: An Introduction to International Political Economy*, New York, Basil Blackwell.

Strange, S. (1988b), "The Future of the American Empire," *Journal of International Affairs*, vol. 42, pp. 1-17.

Strange, S. (1987), "The Persistent Myth of Lost Hegemony," *International Organization*, vol. 41, pp. 551-74.

Strange, S. (1982), "Still an Extraordinary Power: America's Role in a Global Monetary System," in R. Lombra and W. Witte (eds.), *Political Economy of International and Domestic Monetary Relations*, Ames (IA), Iowa State University Press, pp. 73-103.

Sunkel, O. (1972), *Capitalismo Transnacional y Desintegración Nacional en America Latina*, Buenos Aires, Ediciones Nueva Vision.

Taira, K. (1994), "Japan, An Imminent Hegemon?," *The Annals of the American Academy of Political and Social Science*, vol. 513 (January 1991).

Taylor, P. (1991), "The European Community and the State: Assumptions, Theories and Propositions," *Review of International Studies*, vol. 17, pp. 109-25.

The New York Times (1997), "With or Without US, Latin Trade Group is Marching Forward," 18 September, p. A10.

Thomas, C. and Wilkin, P. (eds.), (1997), *Globalization and the South*, London, Macmillan Press.

Thomas, K. and Tétrault, M. A. (eds.), (1999), *Racing to Regionalize: Democracy, Capitalism, and Regional Political Economy*, Boulder (CO), Lynne Rienner Publishers.

Thompson, W. (1973), "The Regional Subsystem: A Conceptual Explication and a Propositional Inventory," *International Studies Quarterly* (March), pp. 89-117.

Thurow, L. (1992), *Head to Head: The Coming Economic Battle Among Japan, Europe, and America*, New York, Warner Books.

Tomassini, L. (1991), *La Politica Internacional en un Mundo Postmoderno*, Buenos Aires, Grupo Editor Latinoamericano.

Tulchin, J. (1997), "Hemispheric Relations in the 21st Century," *Journal of Interamerican Studies and World Affairs*, vol. 39, pp. 33-43.

Tulchin, J. (1995), "The United States and Latin America in the World," in J. D. Martz (ed.), *United States Policy in Latin America: A Decade of Crisis and Challenge*, Lincoln (NE), University of Nebraska Press, pp. 320-56.

Tussie, D. (1987), *The Less Developed Countries and the World Trading System*, New York, St. Martin's Press.

Tussie, D. (1982), "Latin American Integration: From LAFTA to LAIA," *Journal of World Trade Law*, vol. 16, pp. 399-413.

Urquidi, V. (1993), "Free Trade Experience in Latin America and the Caribbean," in S. Weintraub (ed.), *Free Trade in the Western Hemisphere*, in *The Annals of the American Academy of Political and Social Science*, No. 526, pp. 58-67.

Van Klaveren, A. (1994), "Europe and Latin America in the 1990s," in A. Lowenthal and G. Treverton (eds.), *Latin America in a New World*, Boulder (CO), Westview Press, pp. 81-104.

Van Klaveren, A. (1993), "Why Integration Now? Options for Latin America," in P. H. Smith (ed.), *The Challenge of Integration: Europe and the Americas*, New Brunswick (NJ), Transaction Publishers, pp. 115-145.

Varas, A. (1995), "Latin America: Toward a New Reliance on the Market," in B. Stallings (ed.), *Global Change, Regional Response: The New International Context of Development*, Cambridge (UK), Cambridge University Press, pp. 272-308.

Viner, J. (1950), *The Customs Union Issue*, New York, Carnegie Endowment for International Peace.
Wade, R. (1998-99), "The Coming Fight Over Capital Flows," *Foreign Policy*, No. 113, pp. 41-54
Wade, R. and Veneroso, F. (1998), "The Gathering World Slump and the Battle Over Capital Controls," *New Left Review*, No. 231, pp. 13-42.
Wallace, W. (1995), "Regionalism in Europe: Model or Exception?," in L. Fawcett and A. Hurrell (eds.), *Regionalism in World Politics: Regional Organization and International Order*, New York, Oxford University Press, pp. 201-27.
Waltz, K. (1979), *Theory of International Politics*, Reading (MA), Addison-Wesley.
Weinert, R. (1983), "Banks and Bankruptcy," *Foreign Policy* (Spring), pp. 138-49.
Weintraub, S. (1997), "US-Latin American Economic Relations," *Journal of Interamerican Studies and World Affairs*, vol. 39, pp. 59-69.
Weintraub, S. (1994a), "The Importance of Trade in the Western Hemisphere," *Journal of Interamerican Studies and World Affairs*, vol. 36, pp. 157-74.
Weintraub, S. (ed.) (1994b), *Integrating the Americas: Shaping Future Trade Policy*, New Brunswick (NJ), Transaction Publishers.
Weintraub, S. (1993), "Western Hemisphere Free Trade: Probability or Pipe Dream?," in S. Weintraub (ed.), *Free Trade in the Western Hemisphere*, in *The Annals of the American Academy of Political and Social Science*, No. 526, pp. 9-24.
Weiss, L. (1998), "Globalization and the Myth of the Powerless State," *New Left Review*, No. 213, pp. 3-27.
Wendt, A. (1999), *Social Theory and International Politics*, New York, Cambridge University Press.
Wendt, A. (1994), "Collective Identity Formation and the International State," *American Political Science Review*, vol. 88, pp. 384-96.
Wendt, A. (1992), "Anarchy is What States Make of It: The Social Construction of Power Politics," *International Organization*, vol. 46, pp. 391-425.
Weston, A. (1997), "Social Issues and Labor Adjustment Policies: The Canada-US FTA Experience," in R. Lipsey and P. Meller (eds.), *Western Hemisphere Trade Integration: A Canadian- Latin American Dialogue*, New York, St. Martin's Press, pp. 191-206.

Whalley, J. (1992), "CUSTA and NAFTA: Can WHFTA Be Far Behind?," *Journal of Common Market Studies*, vol. 30, pp. 125-41.

Whiting Jr., V. R. (ed.) (1996), *Regionalization in the World Economy: NAFTA, the Americas and Asia Pacific*, New Delhi, Macmillan India.

Whiting Jr., V. R. (1993), "The Dynamics of Regionalization: Road Map to an Open Future?," in P. Smith (ed.), *The Challenge of Integration: Europe and the Americas*, New Brunswick (NJ), Transaction Publishers, pp. 17-50.

Wiarda, H. (1995), "After Miami: The Summit, the Peso Crisis, and the Future of US-Latin American Relations," *Journal of Interamerican Studies and World Affairs*, vol. 37, pp. 43-68.

Wiarda, H. (1990), "United States Policy in Latin America," *Current History*, vol. 89, pp. 1-4.

Wilkinson, B. W. (1997), "NAFTA in the World Economy: Lessons and Issues for Latin America," in R. G. Lipsey and P. Meller (eds.), *Western Hemisphere Trade Integration: A Canadian-Latin American Dialogue*, New York, St. Martin's Press, pp. 30-57.

Williamson, J. (ed.) (1990), *Latin American Adjustment: How Much Has Happened?*, Washington, DC, Institute for International Economics.

Wionczek, M. (1970), "The Rise and the Decline of Latin American Economic Integration," *Journal of Common Market Studies*, vol. 9, pp. 49-66.

Wionczek, M. (ed.) (1966a), *Latin American Economic Integration: Experiences and Prospects*, New York, Praeger Publishers.

Wionczek, M. (1966b), "The Latin American Free Trade Association: Toward Economic Cooperation," in *International Political Communities: An Anthology*, Garden City (NY), Anchor Books, pp. 301-49.

Wise, C. (ed.) (1998), *The Post-NAFTA Political Economy: Mexico and the Western Hemisphere*, University Park (PA), The Pennsylvania State University Press.

Wolff, J. R. (1996), "Putting the Cart Before the Horse: Assessing Opportunities for Regional Integration in Latin America and the Caribbean," *The Fletcher Forum*, vol. 20, pp. 103-36.

World Bank (1997), *World Development Report 1997. The State in a Changing World: Selected World Development Indicators*, New York, Oxford University Press.

Wrobel, P. (1998), "A Free Trade Area of the Americas in 2005?," *International Affairs*, vol. 74, pp. 547-61.
Yeats, A. (1997), "Does Mercosur's Trade Performance Raise Concerns about the Effects of Regional Trade Arrangements?," Policy Research Working Paper No. 1729, The World Bank.
Yeats, A. (1996), "Does Mercosur's Trade Performance Justify Concerns About the Global Welfare Reducing Effects of Regional Trading Arrangements? Yes!," Unpublished World Bank Paper.
Young, O. (1969), "Professor Russett: Industrious Tailor to a Naked Emperor," *World Politics*, vol. 21, pp. 486-511.